Vic Lee's
Corona Diary 2020
London

FRANCES
LINCOLN

First published in 2020 by Frances Lincoln,
an imprint of The Quarto Group.
The Old Brewery, 6 Blundell Street
London, N7 9BH,
United Kingdom
T (0)20 7700 6700
www.QuartoKnows.com

A catalogue record for this book is available from
the British Library.

ISBN 978-0-7112-6374-1

10 9 8 7 6 5 4 3

Cover and design by Vic Lee
www.viclee.co.uk
Instagram **vicleelondon**
LinkedIn **Vic Lee**

Printed and bound by CPI Group (UK) Ltd, Croydon, CR0 4YY

Foreword

This diary originally started as a way to deal with the uncertainty, confusion and anxiety I felt shortly after news of the pandemic began.

In January, it didn't seem too worrying, the news was confined to Asia and specifically the city of Wuhan in China. It all seemed so far away from where I was in London. Life was pretty much the same. My partner and I had returned from an amazing three week holiday on 31st December 2019, from Malaysia and Singapore. Our first holiday in 18 months. We were so taken by Malaysia, it's people, lifestyle and food, that we immediately started to plan a three month sabbatical there in January 2021.

As the weeks went by and news came in from other countries and especially Italy, that's when things became more real. Reports of contagion and then fatalities growing daily. The virus, it seemed, was rapidly spreading with ease throughout Europe. This compounded by a government that had little grasp of the situation and acting so slowly to both communicate and control the spread. I found myself lost in thoughts of end of world imaginations and a dystopian future. It probably didn't help that I had just finished a novel based on contagion by bats!

I started this diary in mid-February. I had to piece together the situation the only way I could, by illustration and storytelling. The whole process became incredibly cathartic and helped me gain an understanding through the news and piecing together like a jigsaw, things I had read and heard. I even did a film encouraging children and adults alike to start their own visual diary. Little knowing how this project would escalate, both visually and physically into this printed book.

As the stories came in on the news, it felt like I needed to capture reports both from the UK and internationally too. Not only the numbers of cases and fatalities, but also the good that came out of this whole dark situation. How humanity can pull together, of communities looking after the vulnerable, the incredible sacrifices of those on the frontline. The effect on the planet, the clean air and how humour can lift our spirits in times of uncertainty.

I also felt like I needed to include the decisions made by governments, both here in the UK and abroad. This diary is non political, if any other party was in control, they would equally have been included. I think it's important to remember those we are supposed to trust and guide us, by their comments and actions, or inactions. Most countries responded to the pandemic quickly, working to efficiently control and quarantine and protect their nation. And some did not.

This is a personal journal, containing my daily musings and my day to day living. I have only put in things that affected me, were in my news feed, or raised hope. It is a very spontaneous journal, unplanned, uncut and uncleaned. Exactly as I wrote and illustrated. Some crazy stories, some sad, some funny; some heroic actions and heartbreaking ones. There is no way I could include every moment or situation throughout the world. It's a snapshot of one person's point of view. A diary, a visual reference of an everyday person living through this historical time in their home city of London, UK.

And hopefully, just the once.

Vic

2020 STRANGE TIMES

A Catch up

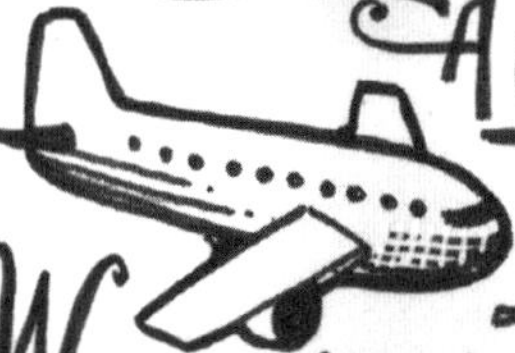

1st JANUARY

We arrive home from an amazing holiday in malaysia settling in to LONDON Life. Good to be home but miss the sun! Planned to go back next year for 3 months! (HMMM) Started 2 MURALS. One in ANDOVER for TWININGS & ONE at UNIVERSITY OF KENT for VIRGINIA WOOLF.

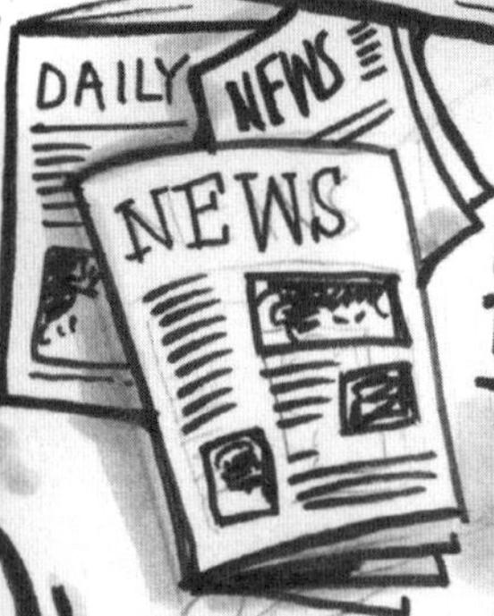

DAILY
NEWS
NEWS

BY MID JANUARY NEWS CAME IN OF THE FIRST FATALATIES

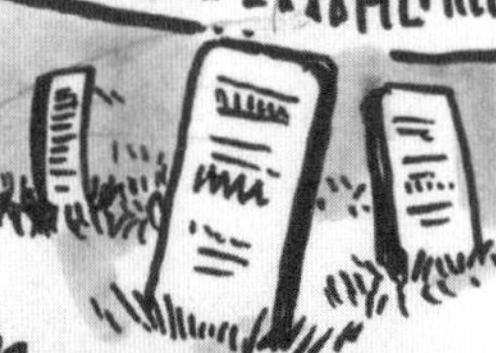

• I was a wee worried!

LIFE WAS NORMAL IN LONDON

JANUARY

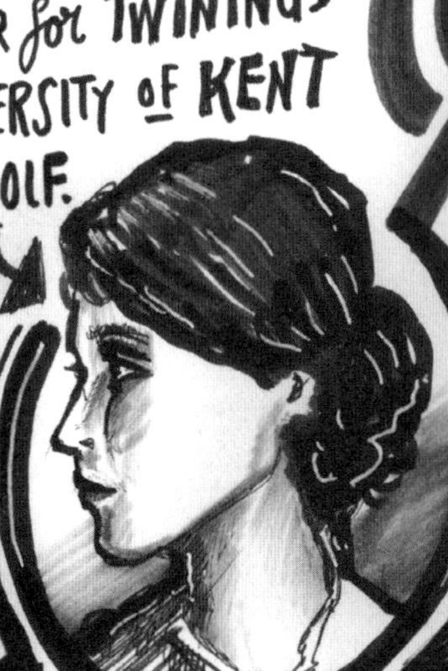

NEWS STARTED COMING IN OF A VIRUS FROM A PLACE CALLED WUHAN

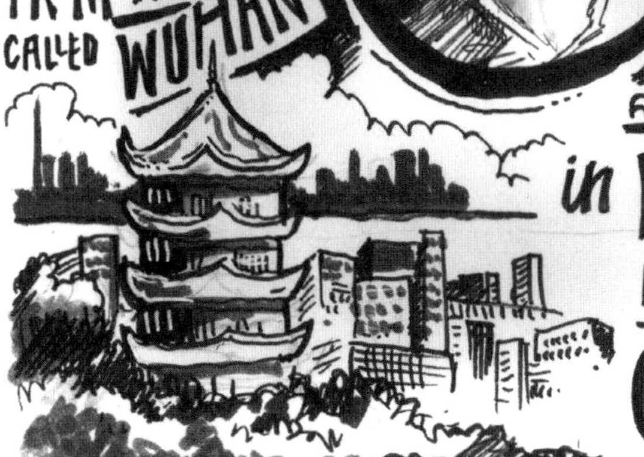

in HUBEI PROVINCE CHINA

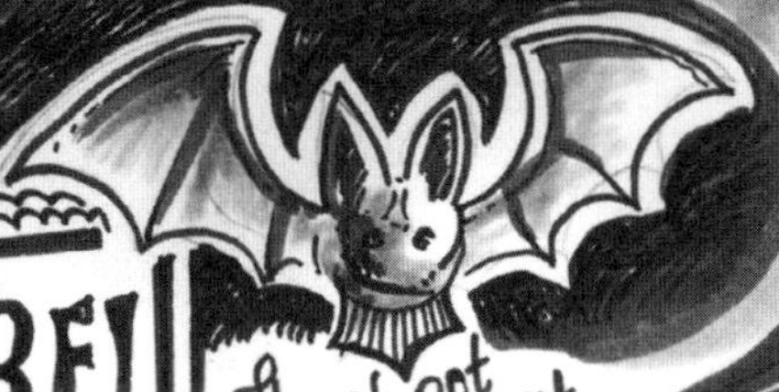

Though not 100% - its thought the virus started in bats affecting other animals in contact with humans.

FLIGHTS ARE GROUNDED TO CHINA

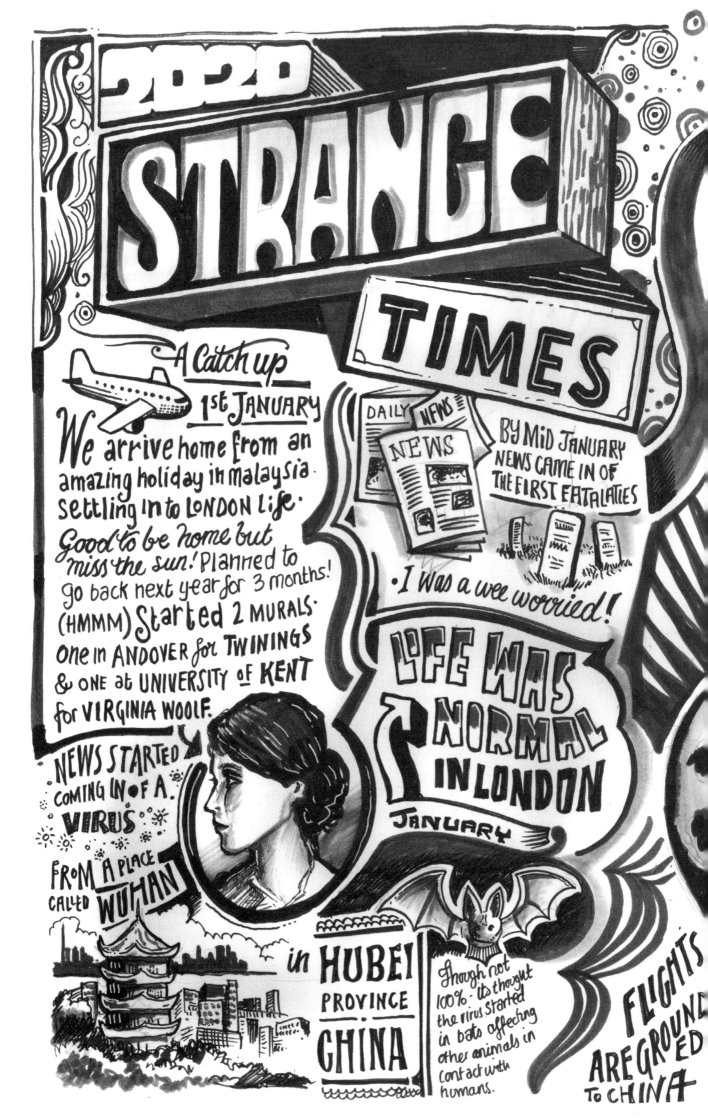

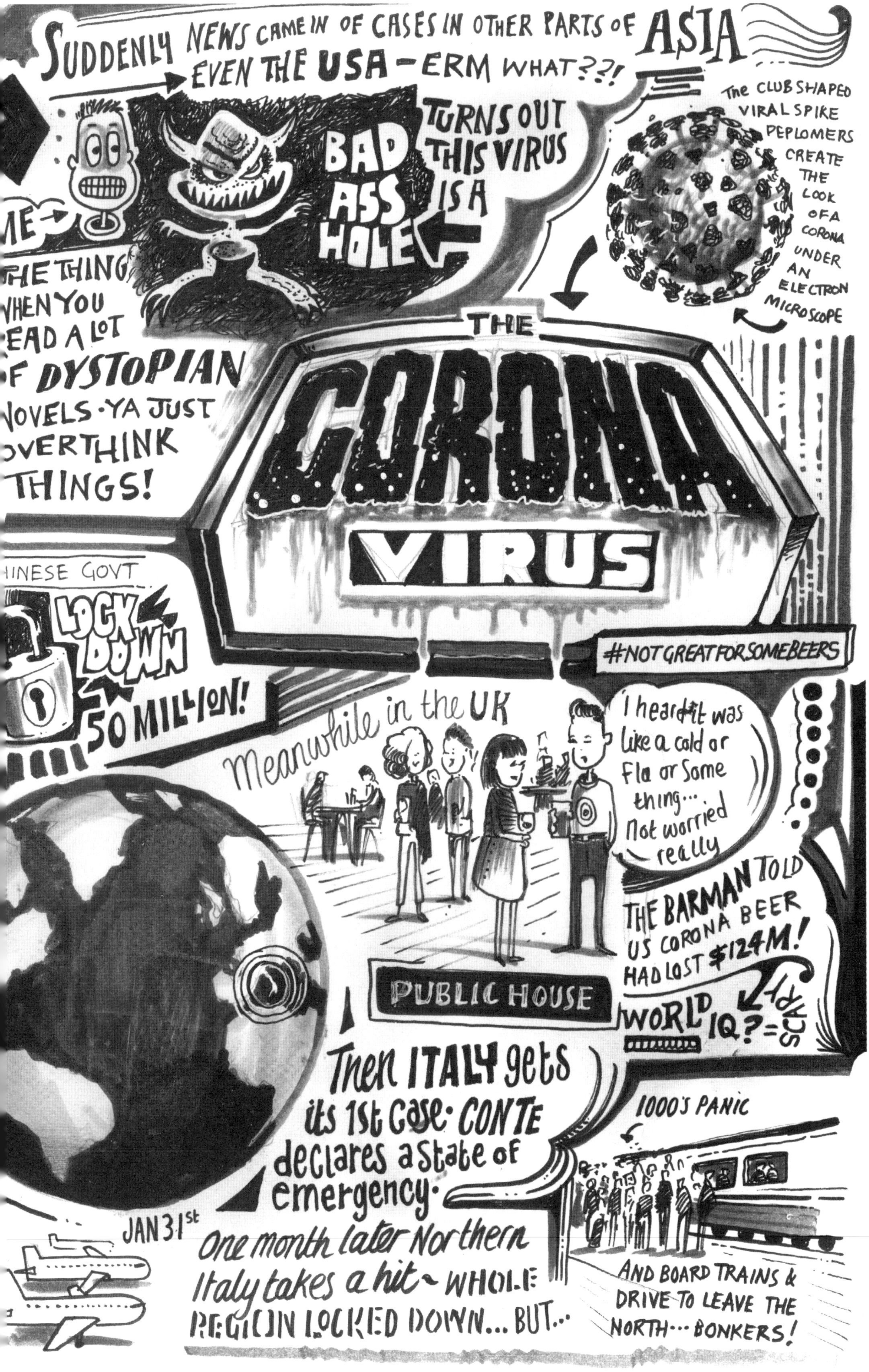

SUDDENLY NEWS CAME IN OF CASES IN OTHER PARTS OF ASIA EVEN THE USA - ERM WHAT??!
ME
TURNS OUT THIS VIRUS IS A BAD ASS HOLE
THE CLUB SHAPED VIRAL SPIKE PEPLOMERS CREATE THE LOOK OF A CORONA UNDER AN ELECTRON MICROSCOPE
THE THING WHEN YOU READ A LOT OF DYSTOPIAN NOVELS - YA JUST OVERTHINK THINGS!
THE CORONA VIRUS
#NOTGREATFORSOMEBEERS
CHINESE GOVT LOCK DOWN 50 MILLION!
Meanwhile in the UK
I heard it was like a cold or Flu or Some thing... Not worried really
THE BARMAN TOLD US CORONA BEER HAD LOST $124M!
WORLD IQ? = SCARY
PUBLIC HOUSE
Then ITALY gets its 1st case: CONTE declares a state of emergency.
JAN 31st
1000'S PANIC
One month later Northern Italy takes a hit - WHOLE REGION LOCKED DOWN... BUT...
AND BOARD TRAINS & DRIVE TO LEAVE THE NORTH... BONKERS!

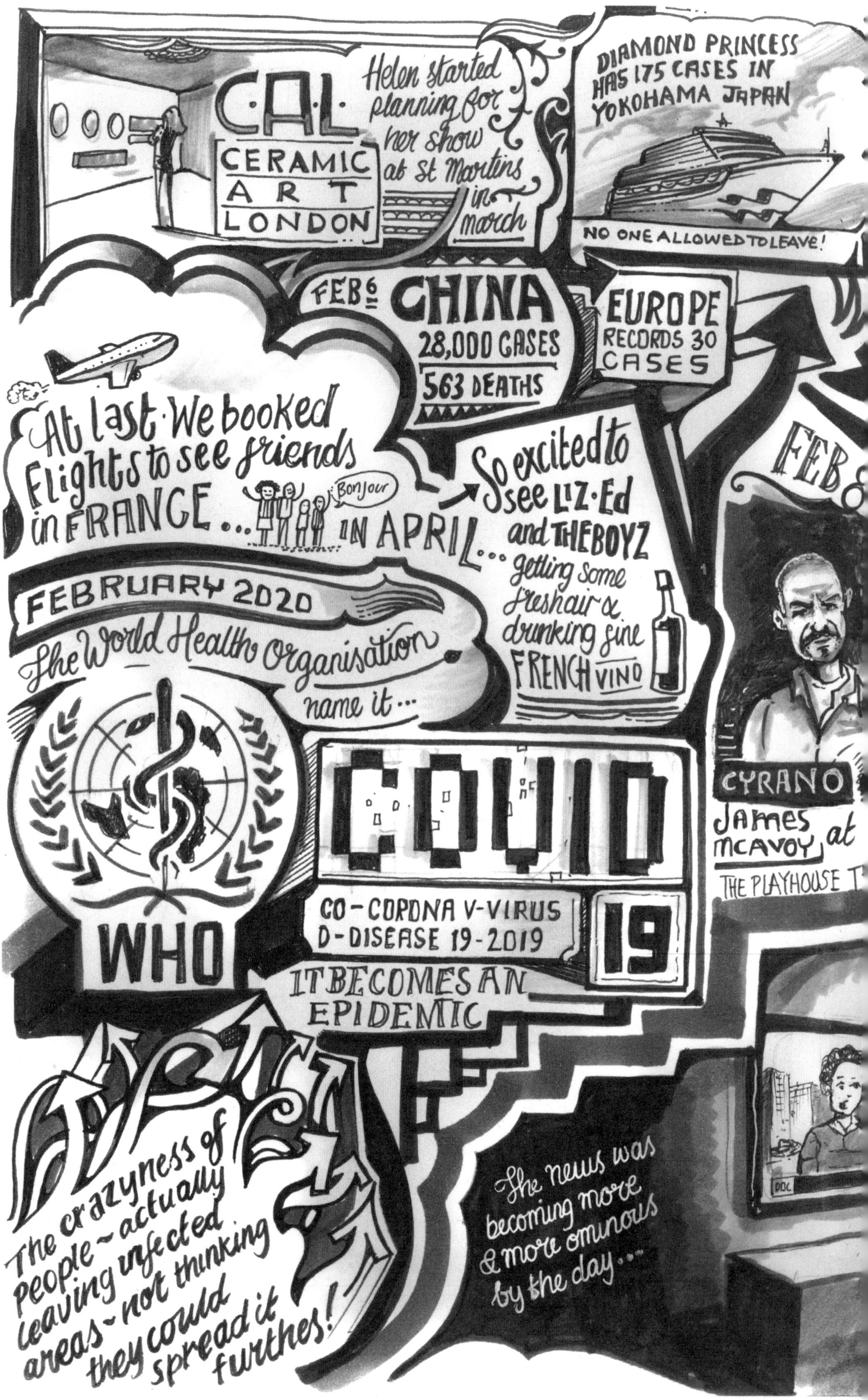

CAL
CERAMIC ART LONDON
Helen started planning for her show at St Martins in march
DIAMOND PRINCESS HAS 175 CASES IN YOKOHAMA JAPAN
NO ONE ALLOWED TO LEAVE!
FEB 6th CHINA
28,000 CASES
563 DEATHS
EUROPE RECORDS 30 CASES
At last. We booked flights to see friends in FRANCE ...
Bonjour
IN APRIL...
So excited to see LIZ · Ed and THE BOYZ getting some fresh air & drinking fine FRENCH VINO
FEB 8
FEBRUARY 2020
The World Health Organisation name it ...
WHO
COVID
CO - CORONA V - VIRUS
D - DISEASE 19 - 2019
19
IT BECOMES AN EPIDEMIC
CYRANO
James McAvoy at
THE PLAYHOUSE T
The crazyness of people ~ actually leaving infected areas ~ not thinking they could spread it furthes!
The news was becoming more & more ominous by the day...

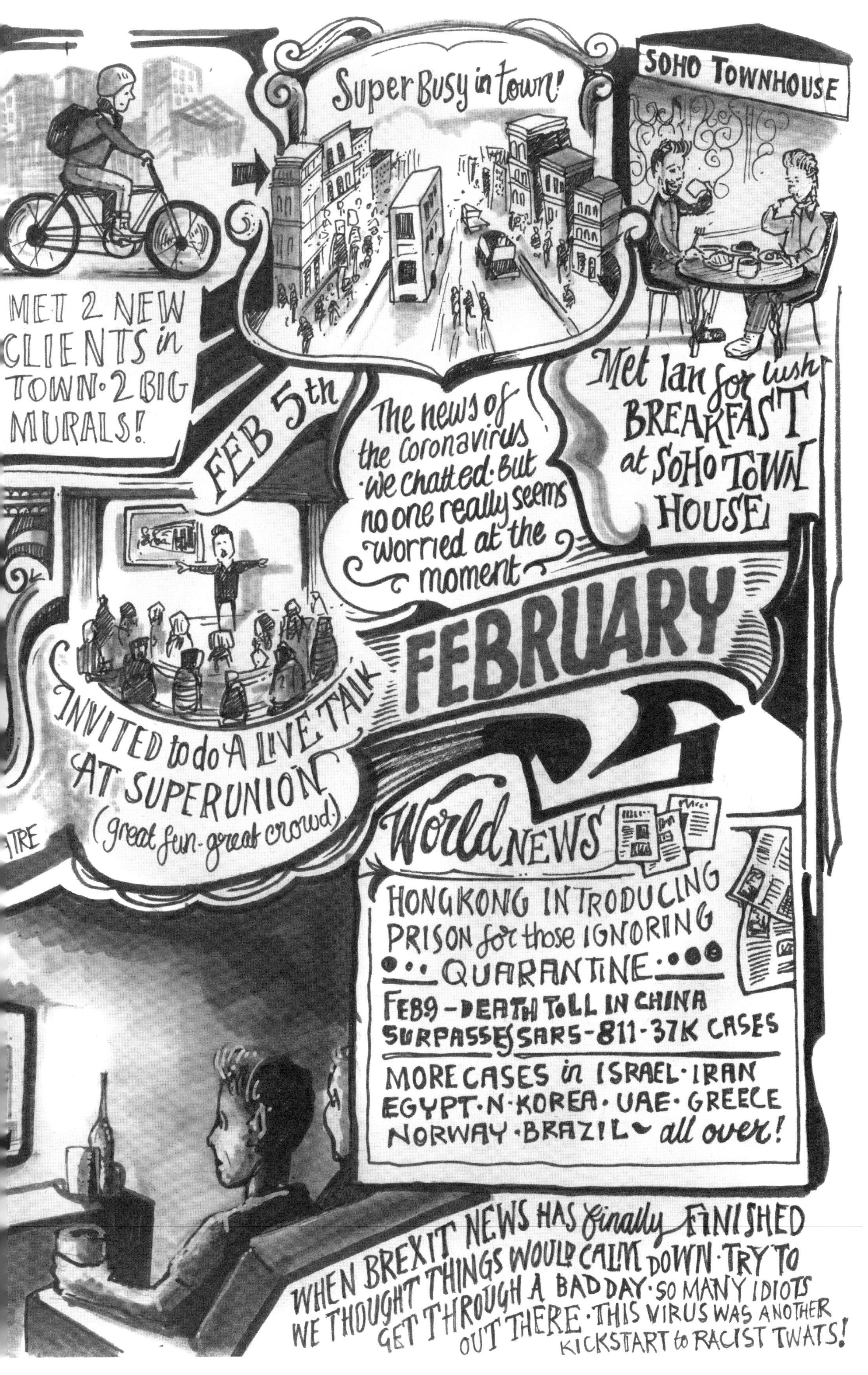

MET 2 NEW CLIENTS in TOWN. 2 BIG MURALS!
Super Busy in town!
SOHO TOWNHOUSE
Met Ian for lush BREAKFAST at SOHO TOWN HOUSE
FEB 5th
The news of the Coronavirus. We chatted. But no one really seems worried at the moment
INVITED to do A LIVE TALK AT SUPERUNION (great fun - great crowd)
TRE
FEBRUARY
2
World NEWS
HONGKONG INTRODUCING PRISON for those IGNORING QUARANTINE
FEB 9 - DEATH TOLL IN CHINA SURPASSES SARS - 811 - 37K CASES
MORE CASES in ISRAEL. IRAN EGYPT. N. KOREA. UAE. GREECE NORWAY. BRAZIL - all over!
WHEN BREXIT NEWS HAS finally FINISHED WE THOUGHT THINGS WOULD CALM DOWN. TRY TO GET THROUGH A BAD DAY. SO MANY IDIOTS OUT THERE. THIS VIRUS WAS ANOTHER KICKSTART to RACIST TWATS!

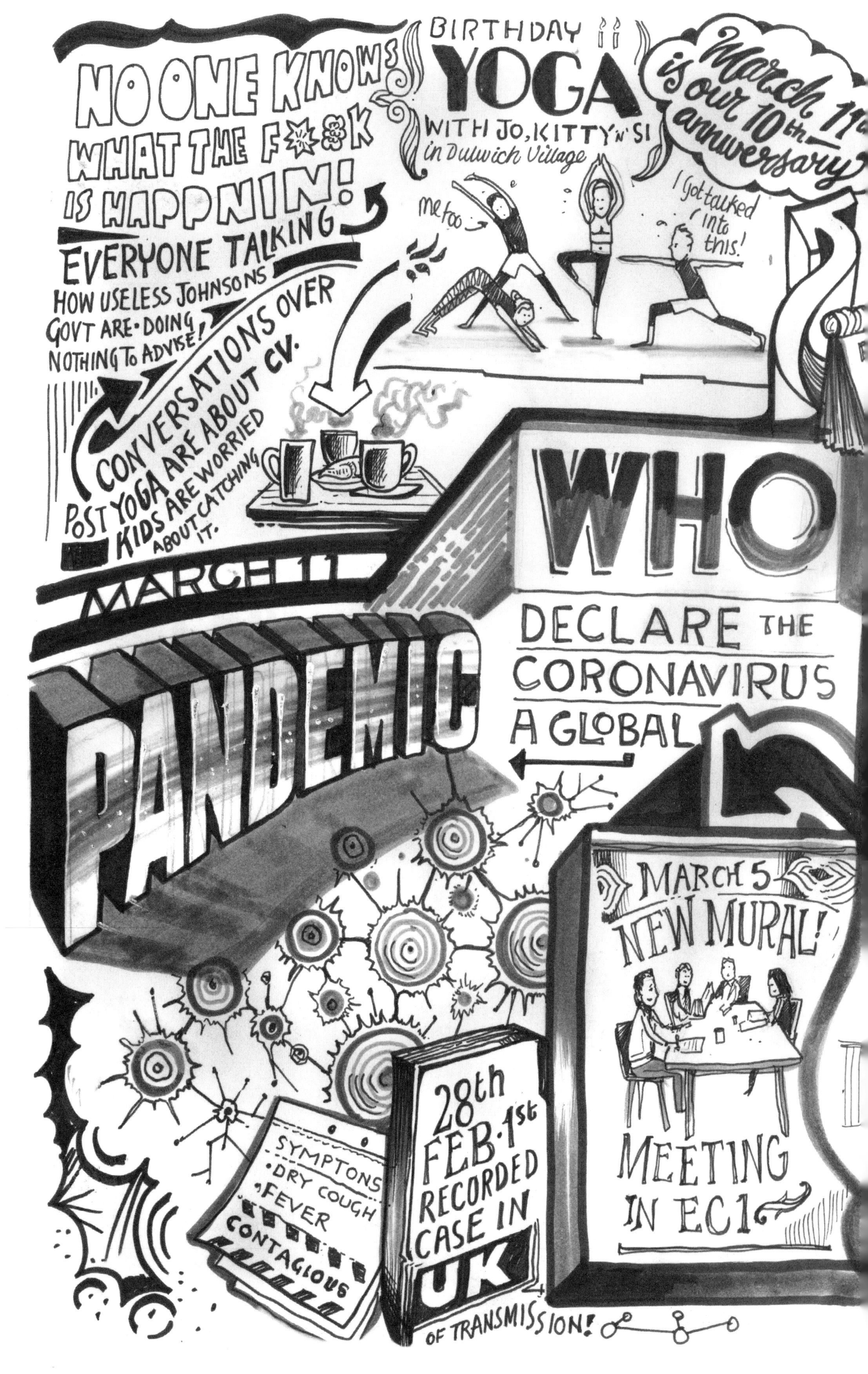
NO ONE KNOWS WHAT THE F*#K IS HAPPNIN!
EVERYONE TALKING
HOW USELESS JOHNSONS GOVT ARE • DOING NOTHING TO ADVISE!
BIRTHDAY YOGA
WITH JO, KITTY 'N' SI
in Dulwich Village
March 11th is our 10th anniversary
me too
I got talked into this!
CONVERSATIONS OVER POST YOGA ARE ABOUT CV. KIDS ARE WORRIED ABOUT CATCHING IT.
MARCH 11
WHO
DECLARE THE CORONAVIRUS A GLOBAL
PANDEMIC
MARCH 5
NEW MURAL!
MEETING IN EC1
SYMPTONS
• DRY COUGH
• FEVER
CONTAGIOUS
28th FEB • 1st RECORDED CASE IN UK
OF TRANSMISSION!

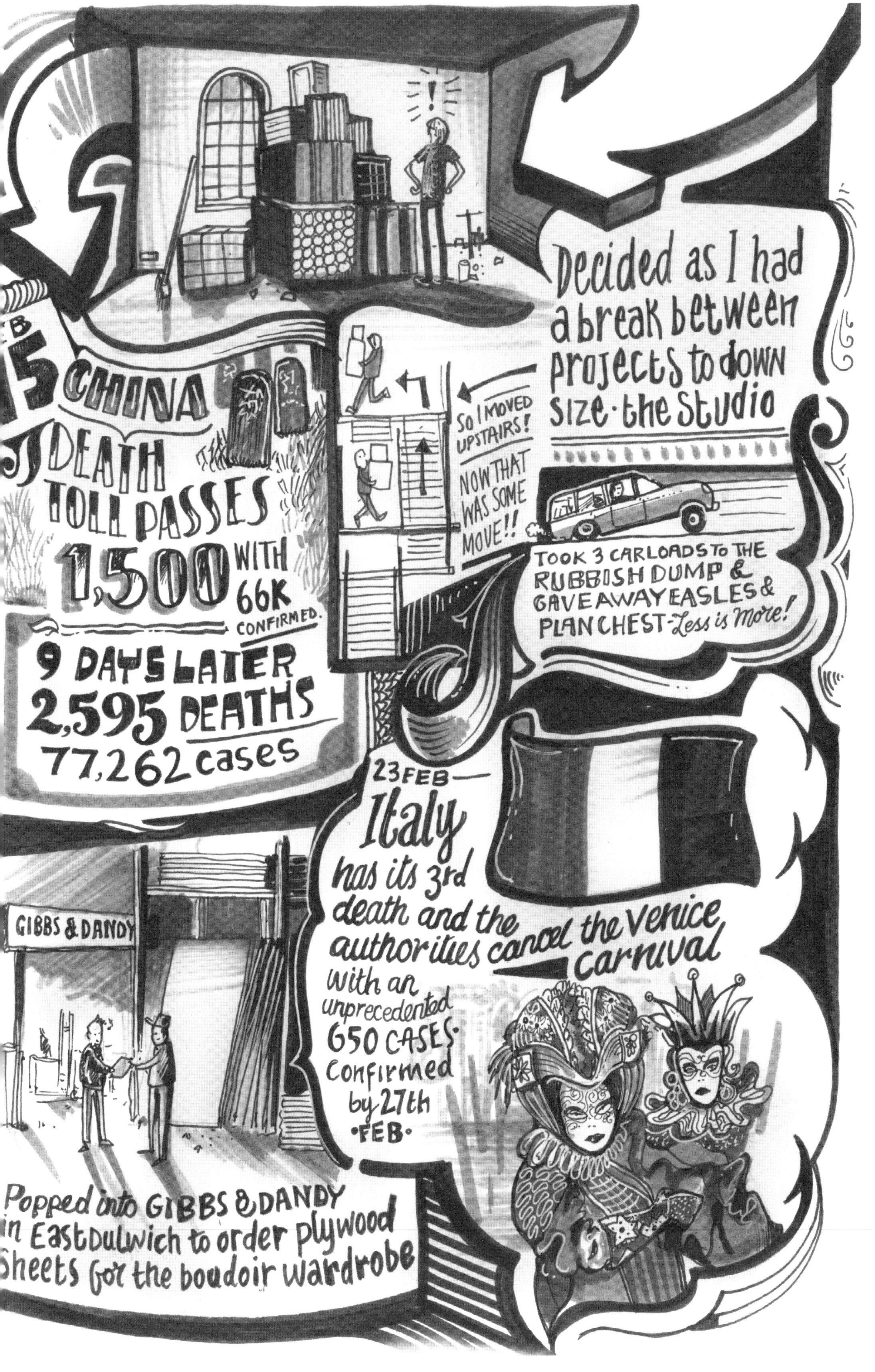

EB
15 CHINA
DEATH TOLL PASSES 1,500 WITH 66K CONFIRMED.
9 DAYS LATER
2,595 DEATHS
77,262 cases
Decided as I had a break between projects to down size · the studio
SO I MOVED UPSTAIRS!
NOW THAT WAS SOME MOVE!!
TOOK 3 CARLOADS TO THE RUBBISH DUMP & GAVE AWAY EASLES & PLAN CHEST - Less is More!
23 FEB —
Italy has its 3rd death and the authorities cancel the Venice carnival
with an unprecedented 650 CASES · Confirmed by 27th · FEB ·
GIBBS & DANDY
Popped into GIBBS & DANDY in East Dulwich to order plywood sheets for the boudoir wardrobe

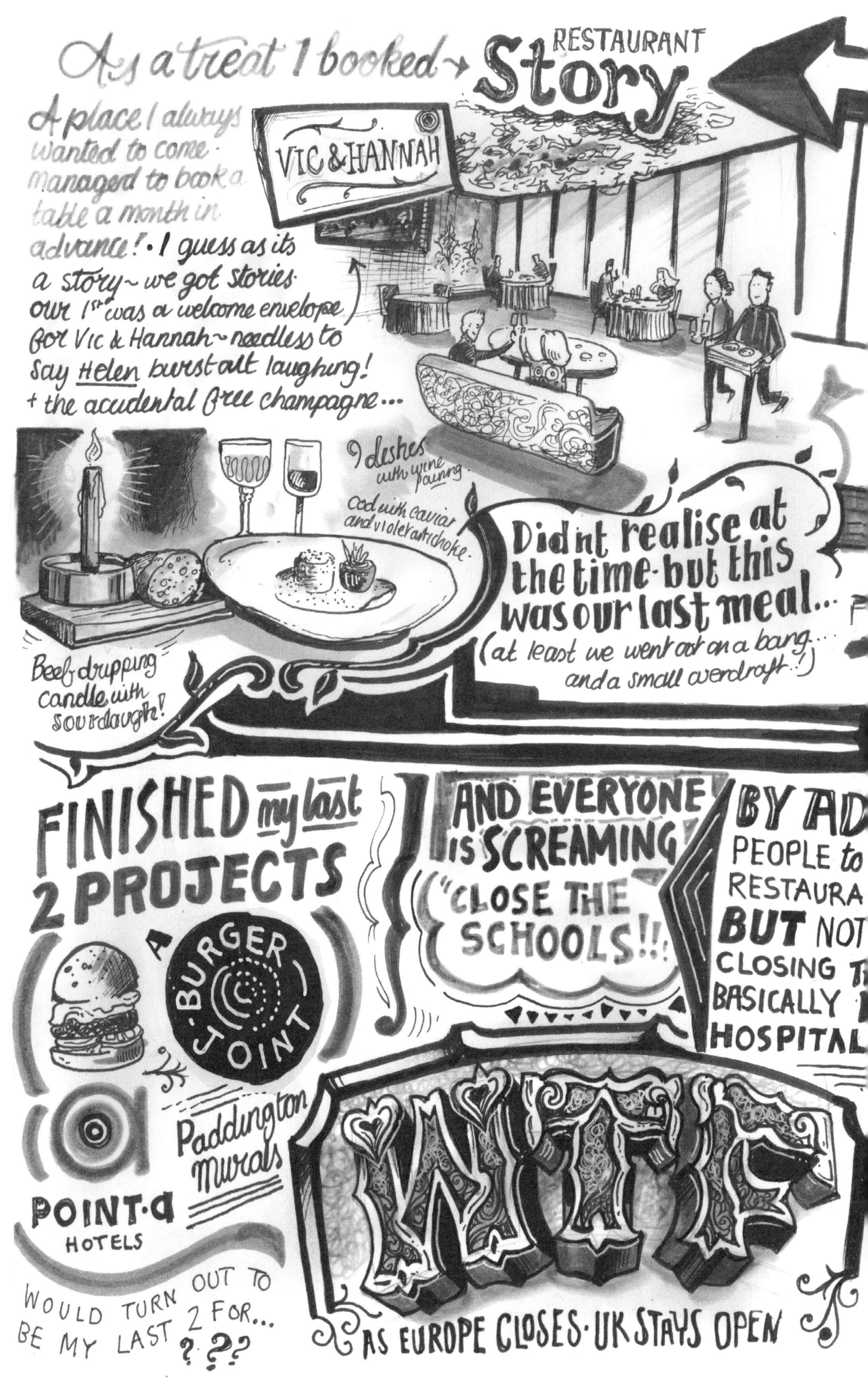

As a treat I booked → RESTAURANT Story
A place I always wanted to come managed to book a table a month in advance! • I guess as its a story ~ we got stories. our 1st was a welcome envelope for Vic & Hannah ~ needless to say Helen burst out laughing! + the accidental free champagne...
VIC & HANNAH
9 dishes with wine pairing
Cod with caviar and violet artichoke.
Didnt realise at the time - but this was our last meal...
(at least we went out on a bang.... and a small overdraft..!)
Beef dripping candle with sourdough!
FINISHED my last 2 PROJECTS
A BURGER JOINT
Paddington murals
POINT·A HOTELS
WOULD TURN OUT TO BE MY LAST 2 FOR... ???
AND EVERYONE IS SCREAMING "CLOSE THE SCHOOLS!!!"
BY AD
PEOPLE to
RESTAURA
BUT NOT
CLOSING T
BASICALLY
HOSPITAL
WTF
AS EUROPE CLOSES · UK STAYS OPEN

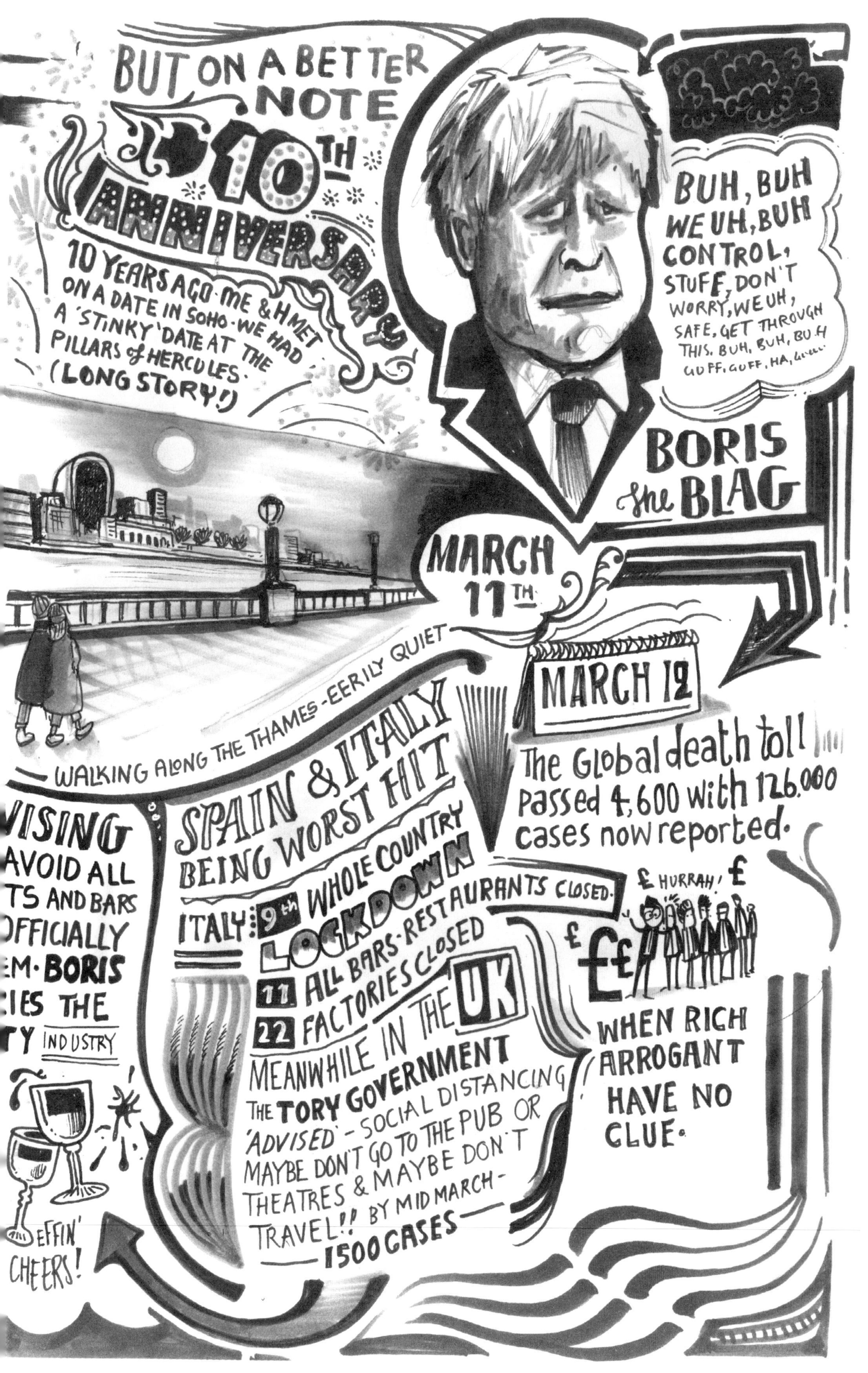

BUT ON A BETTER NOTE
A 10TH ANNIVERSARY
10 YEARS AGO ME & H MET ON A DATE IN SOHO - WE HAD A 'STINKY' DATE AT THE PILLARS of HERCULES (LONG STORY!)
WALKING ALONG THE THAMES - EERILY QUIET
BUH, BUH WE UH, BUH CONTROL, STUFF, DON'T WORRY, WE UH, SAFE, GET THROUGH THIS. BUH, BUH, BUH GUFF, GUFF, HA,
BORIS the BLAG
MARCH 11TH
MARCH 12
The Global death toll passed 4,600 with 126,000 cases now reported.
SPAIN & ITALY BEING WORST HIT
ITALY: 9th WHOLE COUNTRY LOCKDOWN
11 ALL BARS - RESTAURANTS CLOSED
22 FACTORIES CLOSED
MEANWHILE IN THE UK
THE TORY GOVERNMENT 'ADVISED' - SOCIAL DISTANCING MAYBE DON'T GO TO THE PUB OR THEATRES & MAYBE DON'T TRAVEL!! BY MID MARCH - 1500 CASES
VISING
AVOID ALL
TS AND BARS
OFFICIALLY
EM. BORIS
IES THE
TY INDUSTRY
EFFIN' CHEERS!
£ HURRAH! £
£ ££
WHEN RICH ARROGANT HAVE NO CLUE.

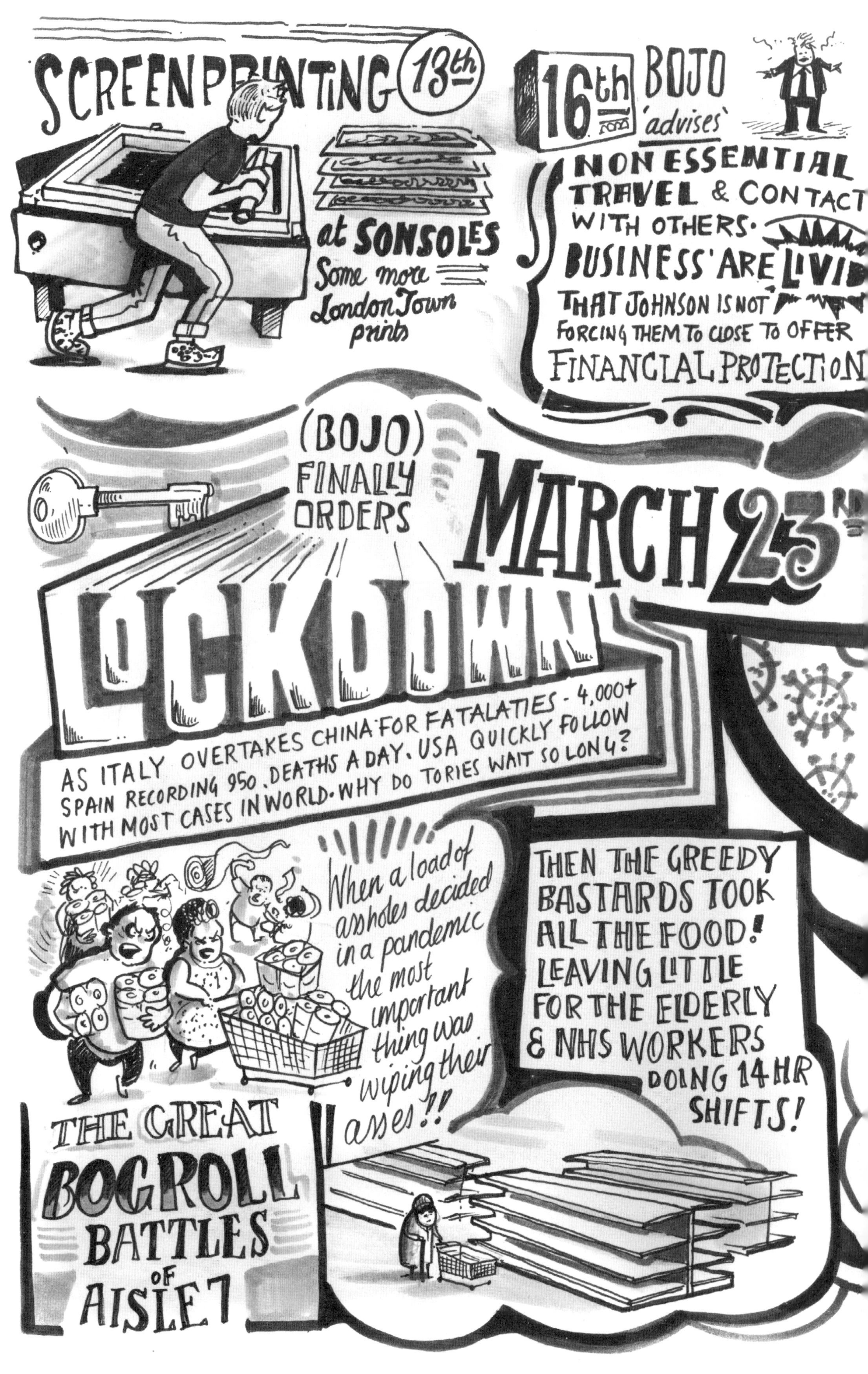
SCREENPRINTING 13th
at SONSOLES
Some more London Town prints
16th
BOJO 'advises'
NON ESSENTIAL TRAVEL & CONTACT WITH OTHERS.
BUSINESS' ARE LIVID THAT JOHNSON IS NOT FORCING THEM TO CLOSE TO OFFER FINANCIAL PROTECTION
(BOJO) FINALLY ORDERS
MARCH 23RD
LOCKDOWN
AS ITALY OVERTAKES CHINA FOR FATALATIES - 4,000+ SPAIN RECORDING 950 DEATHS A DAY. USA QUICKLY FOLLOW WITH MOST CASES IN WORLD. WHY DO TORIES WAIT SO LONG?
When a load of assholes decided in a pandemic the most important thing was wiping their asses?!!
THEN THE GREEDY BASTARDS TOOK ALL THE FOOD! LEAVING LITTLE FOR THE ELDERLY & NHS WORKERS DOING 14 HR SHIFTS!
THE GREAT BOGROLL BATTLES OF AISLE 7

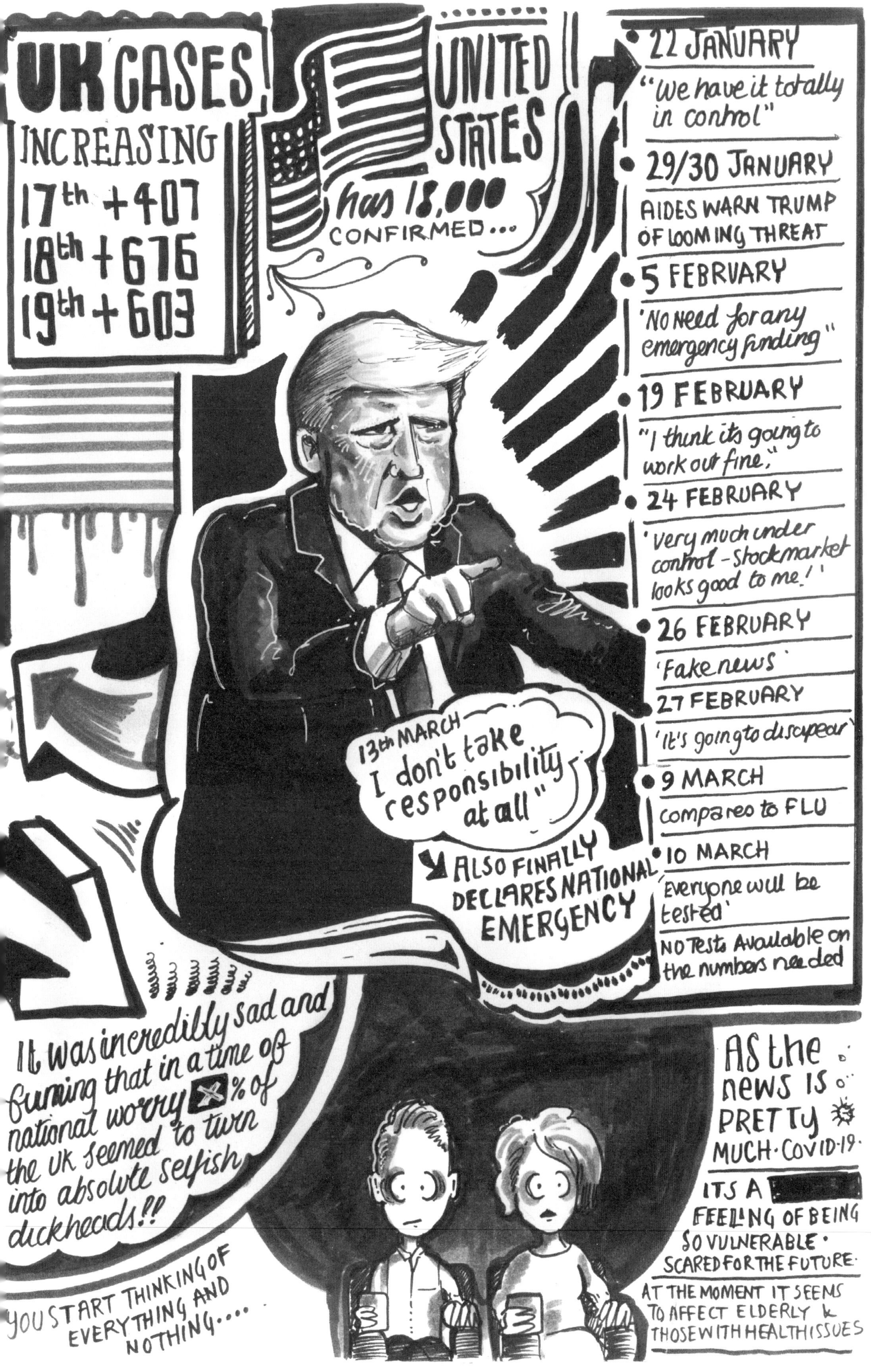
UK CASES INCREASING
17th +407
18th +676
19th +603
UNITED STATES has 18,000 CONFIRMED...
22 JANUARY
"We have it totally in control"
29/30 JANUARY
AIDES WARN TRUMP OF LOOMING THREAT
5 FEBRUARY
'No need for any emergency funding"
19 FEBRUARY
"I think its going to work out fine."
24 FEBRUARY
'Very much under control - Stockmarket looks good to me!'
26 FEBRUARY
'Fake news'
27 FEBRUARY
'It's going to disapear'
9 MARCH
compares to FLU
10 MARCH
Everyone will be tested'
NO Tests Available on the numbers needed
13th MARCH
I don't take responsibility at all"
ALSO FINALLY DECLARES NATIONAL EMERGENCY
It was incredibly sad and fuming that in a time of national worry % of the UK seemed to turn into absolute selfish dickheads!!
AS the news is PRETTY MUCH COVID-19.
ITS A [redacted] FEELING OF BEING SO VULNERABLE. SCARED FOR THE FUTURE.
AT THE MOMENT IT SEEMS TO AFFECT ELDERLY & THOSE WITH HEALTH ISSUES
YOU START THINKING OF EVERYTHING AND NOTHING....

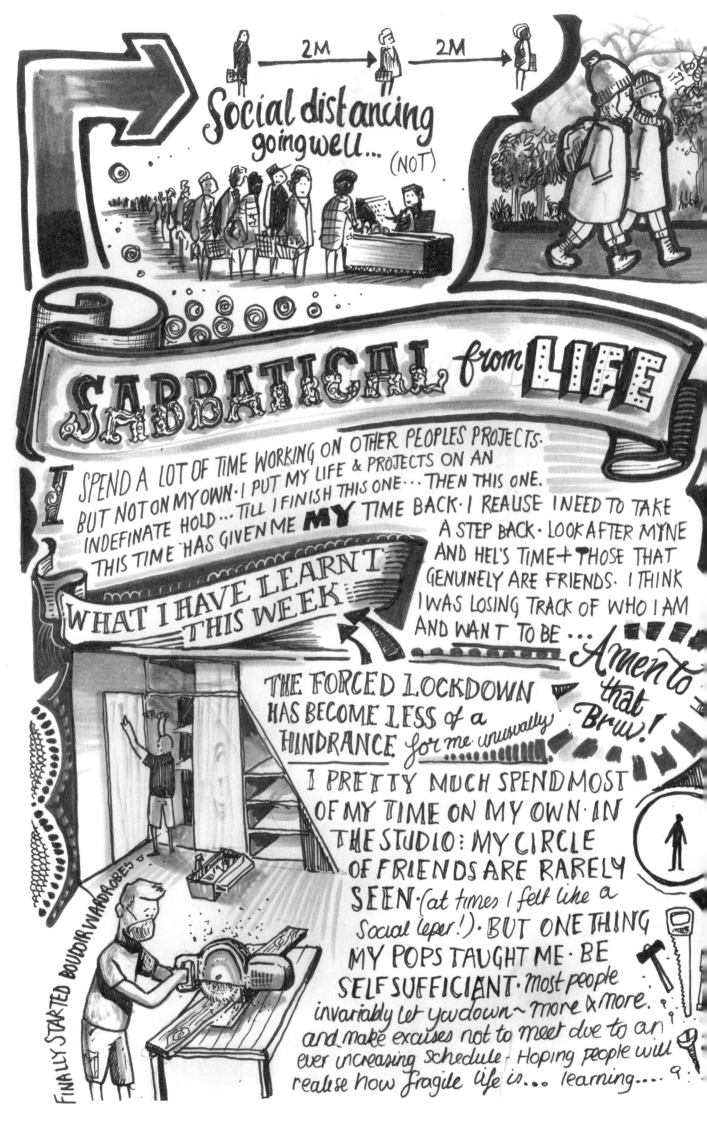

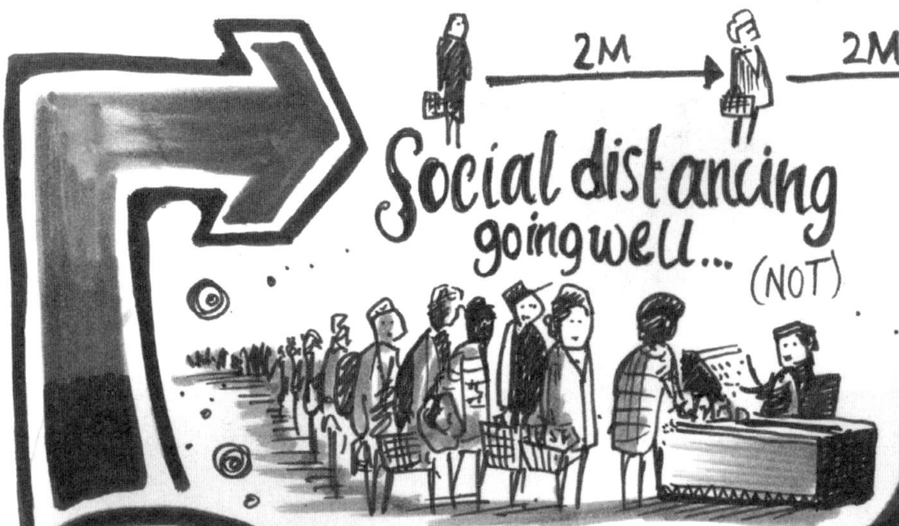
2M
2M
Social distancing
going well... (NOT)

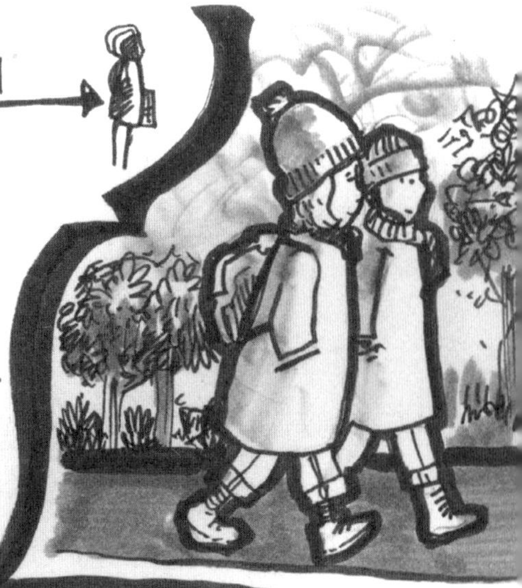

SABBATICAL from LIFE

I SPEND A LOT OF TIME WORKING ON OTHER PEOPLES PROJECTS. BUT NOT ON MY OWN. I PUT MY LIFE & PROJECTS ON AN INDEFINATE HOLD... TILL I FINISH THIS ONE... THEN THIS ONE. THIS TIME HAS GIVEN ME **MY** TIME BACK. I REALISE I NEED TO TAKE A STEP BACK. LOOK AFTER MYNE AND HEL'S TIME + THOSE THAT GENUINELY ARE FRIENDS. I THINK I WAS LOSING TRACK OF WHO I AM AND WANT TO BE...

WHAT I HAVE LEARNT THIS WEEK

Amen to that Bruv!

THE FORCED LOCKDOWN HAS BECOME LESS *of a* HINDRANCE *for me unusually.*

I PRETTY MUCH SPEND MOST OF MY TIME ON MY OWN IN THE STUDIO: MY CIRCLE OF FRIENDS ARE RARELY SEEN. *(at times I felt like a social leper!)*. BUT ONE THING MY POPS TAUGHT ME. BE SELF SUFFICIENT. *Most people invariably let you down ~ more & more. and make excuses not to meet due to an ever increasing schedule. Hoping people will realise how fragile life is... learning....*

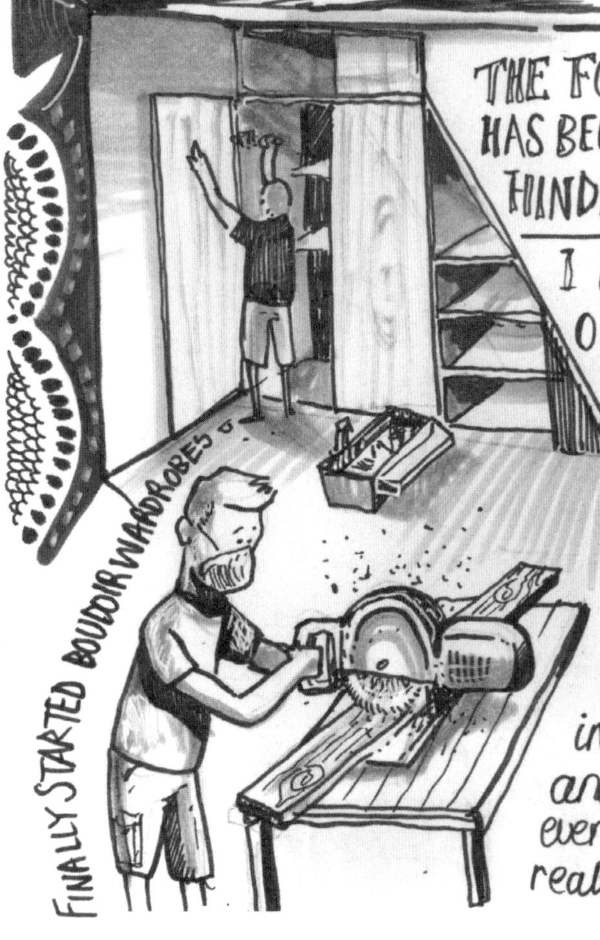
FINALLY STARTED BOUDOIR WARDROBES

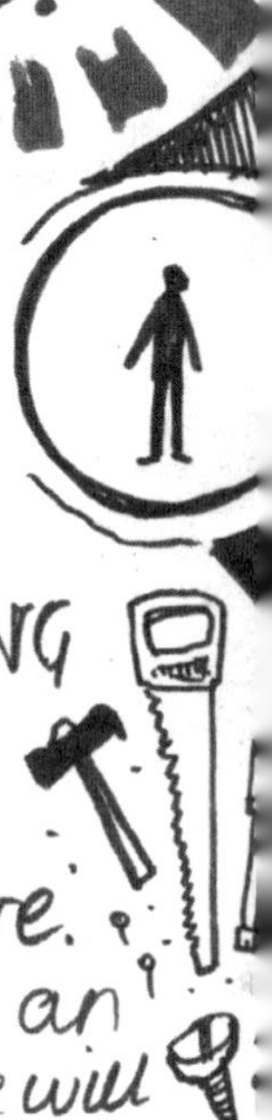

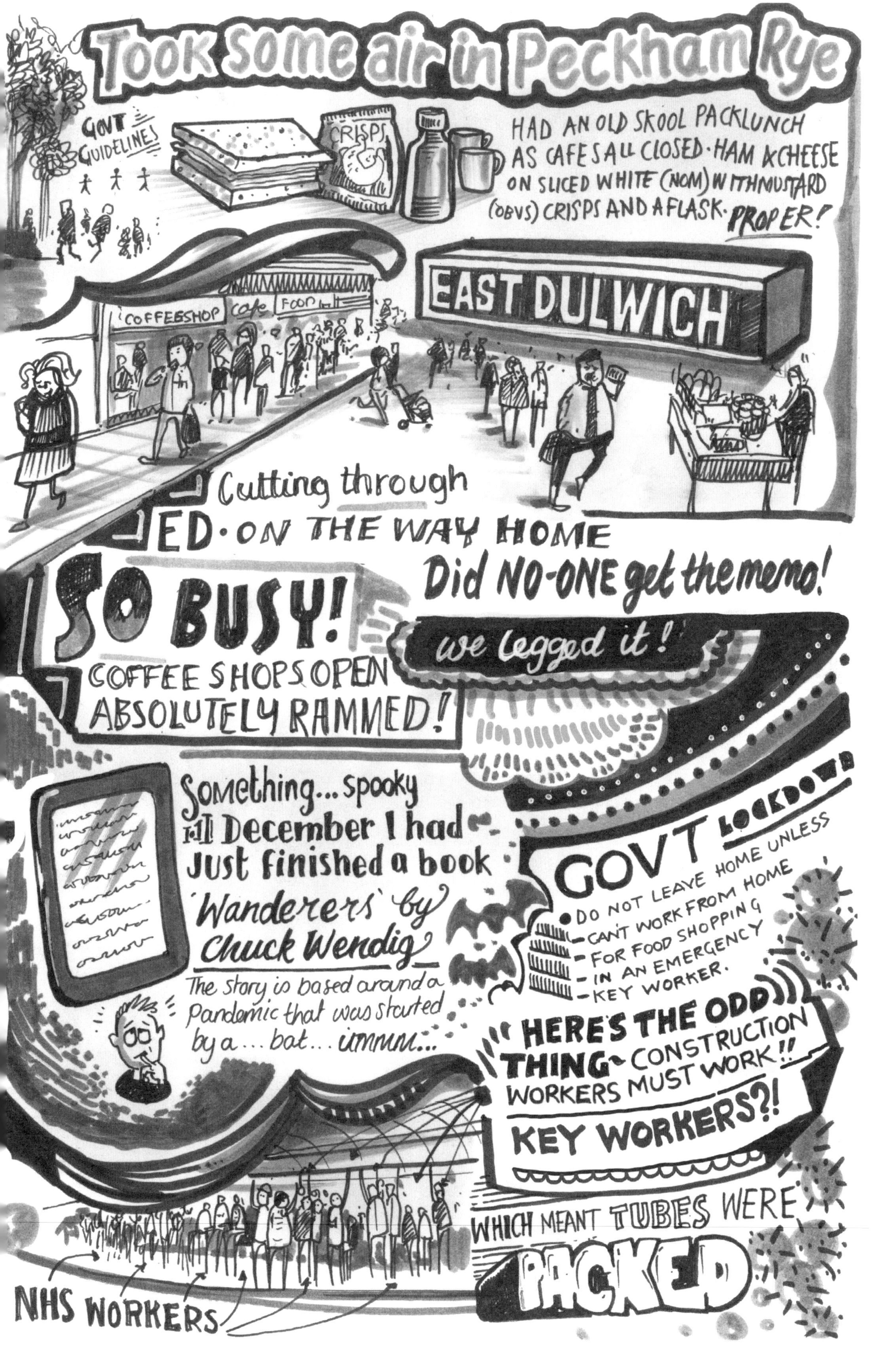

Took some air in Peckham Rye
GOVT GUIDELINES
CRISPS
HAD AN OLD SKOOL PACKLUNCH AS CAFES ALL CLOSED · HAM & CHEESE ON SLICED WHITE (NOM) WITH MUSTARD (OBVS) CRISPS AND A FLASK. PROPER!
COFFEESHOP
Cafe
FOOD
EAST DULWICH
Cutting through
ED · ON THE WAY HOME
SO BUSY!
COFFEE SHOPS OPEN ABSOLUTELY RAMMED!
Did NO-ONE get the memo!
we legged it!
Something... spooky
In December I had just finished a book
'Wanderers' by Chuck Wendig
The story is based around a Pandemic that was started by a... bat... ummm...
LOCKDOWN
GOVT
• DO NOT LEAVE HOME UNLESS
- CAN'T WORK FROM HOME
- FOR FOOD SHOPPING
- IN AN EMERGENCY
- KEY WORKER.
"HERE'S THE ODD THING - CONSTRUCTION WORKERS MUST WORK!!
KEY WORKERS?!
WHICH MEANT TUBES WERE
PACKED
NHS WORKERS

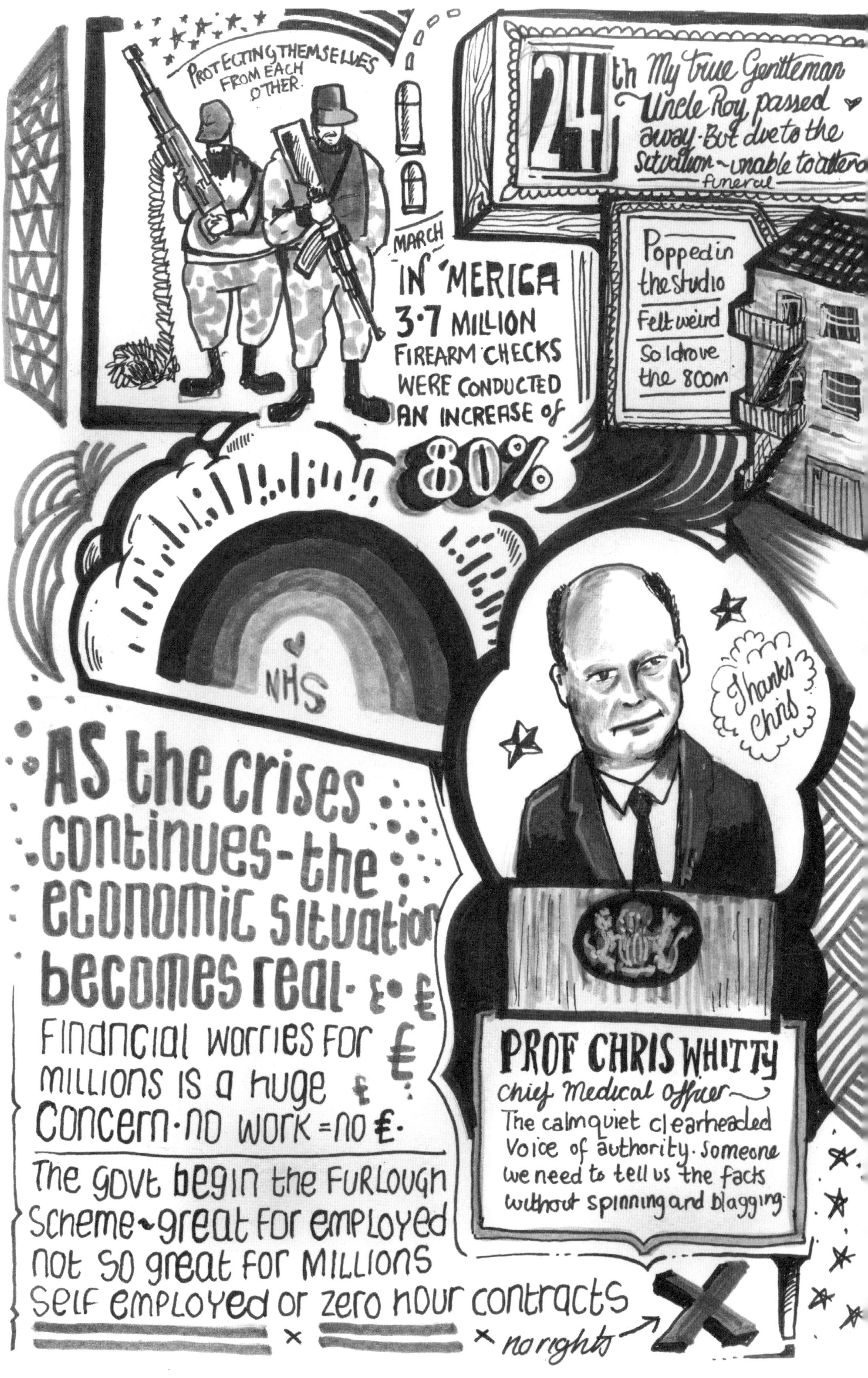

PROTECTING THEMSELVES FROM EACH OTHER
MARCH
IN 'MERICA 3·7 MILLION FIREARM CHECKS WERE CONDUCTED AN INCREASE of 80%
24th My true Gentleman Uncle Roy passed away. But due to the situation ~ unable to attend funeral
Popped in the studio
Felt weird
So I drove the 800m
NHS
Thanks Chris
As the crises continues - the economic situation becomes real. £ € €
Financial worries for millions is a huge concern. no work = no €.
£
The govt begin the FURLOUGH scheme ~ great for employed not so great for millions self employed or zero hour contracts
no rights
PROF CHRIS WHITTY
Chief Medical Officer
The calm quiet clearheaded Voice of authority. Someone we need to tell us the facts without spinning and blagging.

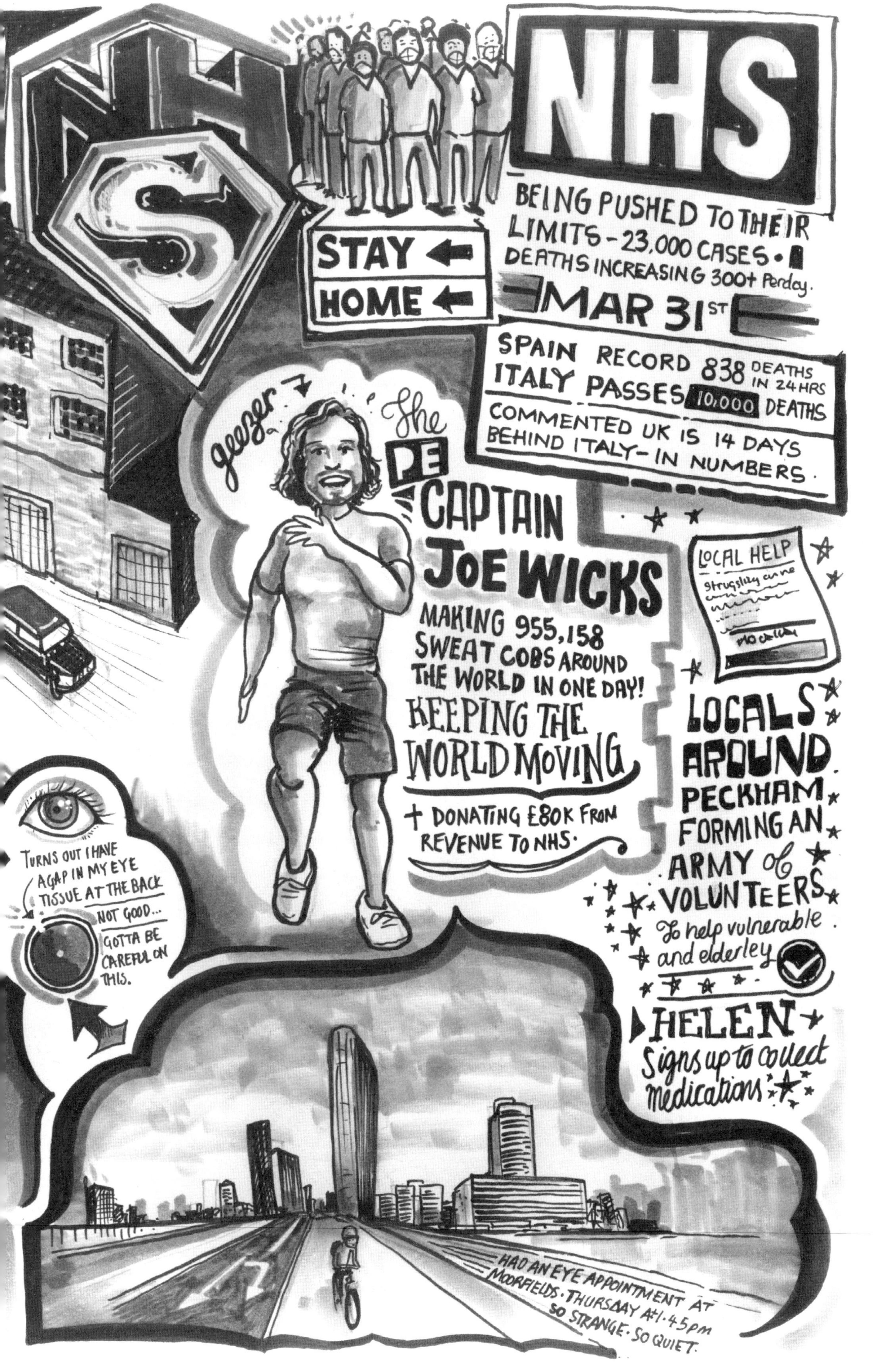
NHS
BEING PUSHED TO THEIR LIMITS - 23,000 CASES • DEATHS INCREASING 300+ Perday.
MAR 31ST
STAY HOME
SPAIN RECORD 838 DEATHS IN 24 HRS
ITALY PASSES 10,000 DEATHS
COMMENTED UK IS 14 DAYS BEHIND ITALY - IN NUMBERS.
geezer
The PE CAPTAIN JOE WICKS
MAKING 955,158 SWEAT COBS AROUND THE WORLD IN ONE DAY!
KEEPING THE WORLD MOVING
+ DONATING £80K FROM REVENUE TO NHS.
LOCAL HELP
LOCALS AROUND PECKHAM FORMING AN ARMY of VOLUNTEERS
To help vulnerable and elderley
HELEN Signs up to collect medications
TURNS OUT I HAVE A GAP IN MY EYE TISSUE AT THE BACK
NOT GOOD...
GOTTA BE CAREFUL ON THIS.
HAD AN EYE APPOINTMENT AT MOORFIELDS. THURSDAY AT 1.45pm
SO STRANGE. SO QUIET.

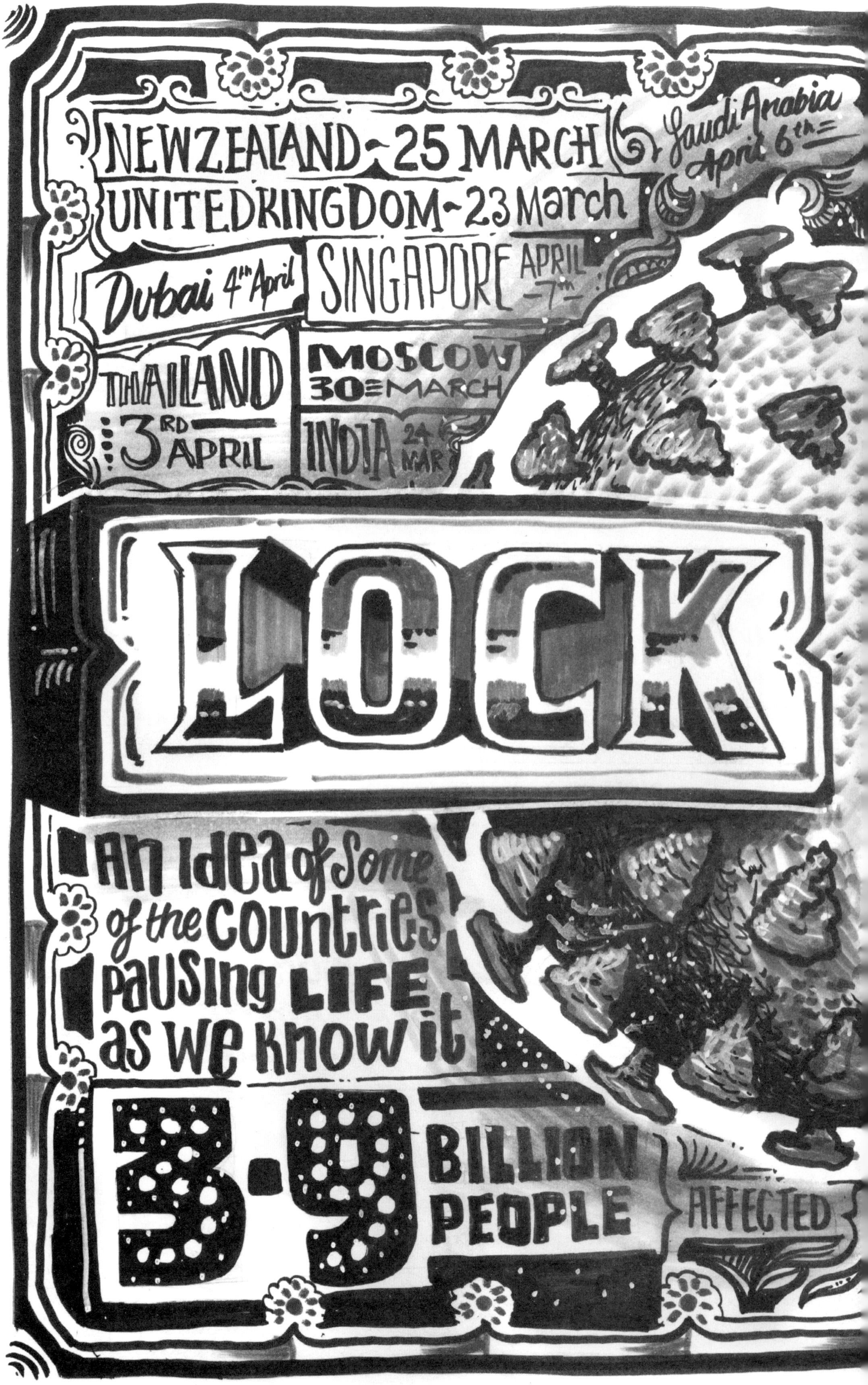

NEWZEALAND ~ 25 MARCH
UNITEDKINGDOM ~ 23 March
Saudi Arabia April 6th
Dubai 4th April
SINGAPORE APRIL 7th
THAILAND 3RD APRIL
MOSCOW 30th MARCH
INDIA 24 MAR
LOCK
An idea of some of the countries pausing LIFE as we know it
3.9 BILLION PEOPLE AFFECTED

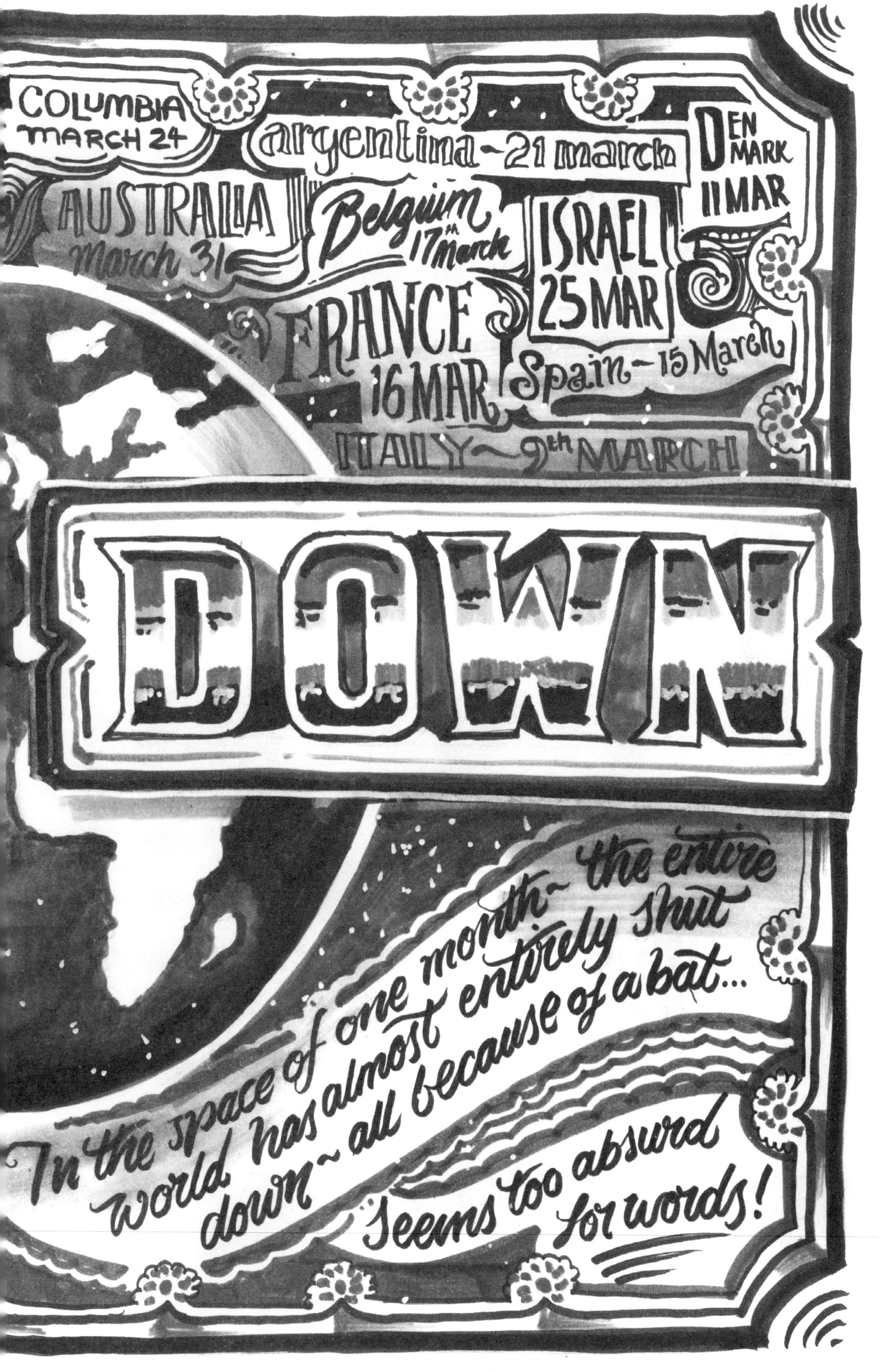
COLUMBIA MARCH 24
argentina ~ 21 march
DEN MARK 11 MAR
AUSTRALIA March 31
Belgium 17th march
ISRAEL 25 MAR
FRANCE 16 MAR
Spain ~ 15 March
ITALY ~ 9th MARCH
DOWN
In the space of one month ~ the entire world has almost entirely shut down ~ all because of a bat...
Seems too absurd for words!

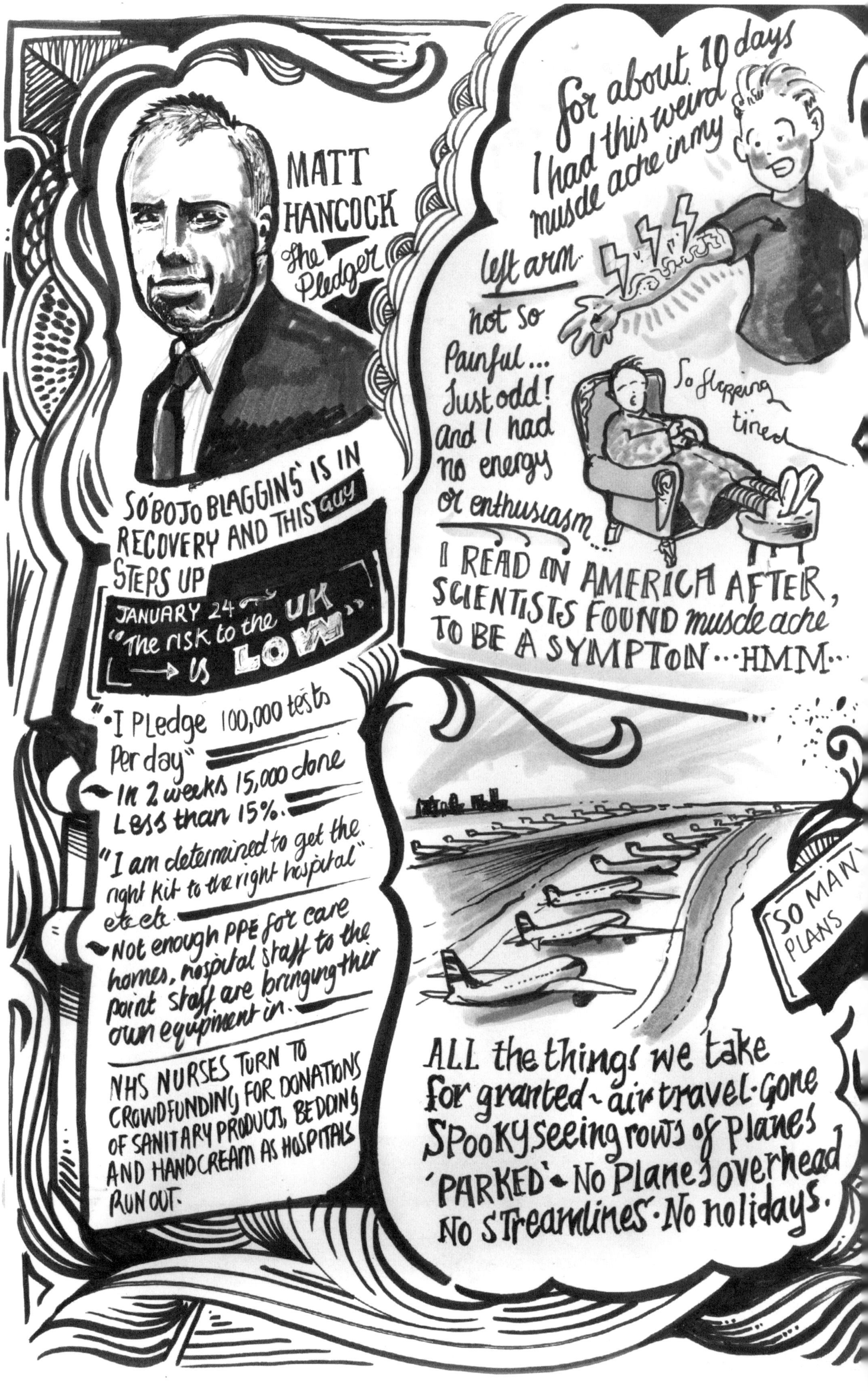

MATT HANCOCK
The Pledger
SO BOJO BLAGGINS IS IN RECOVERY AND THIS GUY STEPS UP
JANUARY 24 "The risk to the UK is LOW"
"I Pledge 100,000 tests per day"
In 2 weeks 15,000 done
Less than 15%.
"I am determined to get the right kit to the right hospital" etc etc
Not enough PPE for care homes, hospital staff to the point staff are bringing their own equipment in.
NHS NURSES TURN TO CROWDFUNDING FOR DONATIONS OF SANITARY PRODUCTS, BEDDING AND HANDCREAM AS HOSPITALS RUN OUT.
For about 10 days I had this weird muscle ache in my left arm
not so Painful... Just odd! and I had no energy or enthusiasm...
So flipping tired
I READ IN AMERICA AFTER, SCIENTISTS FOUND muscle ache TO BE A SYMPTON...HMM...
SO MANY PLANS
ALL the things we take for granted - air travel - Gone
Spooky seeing rows of planes 'PARKED' - No Planes overhead
No Streamlines - No holidays.

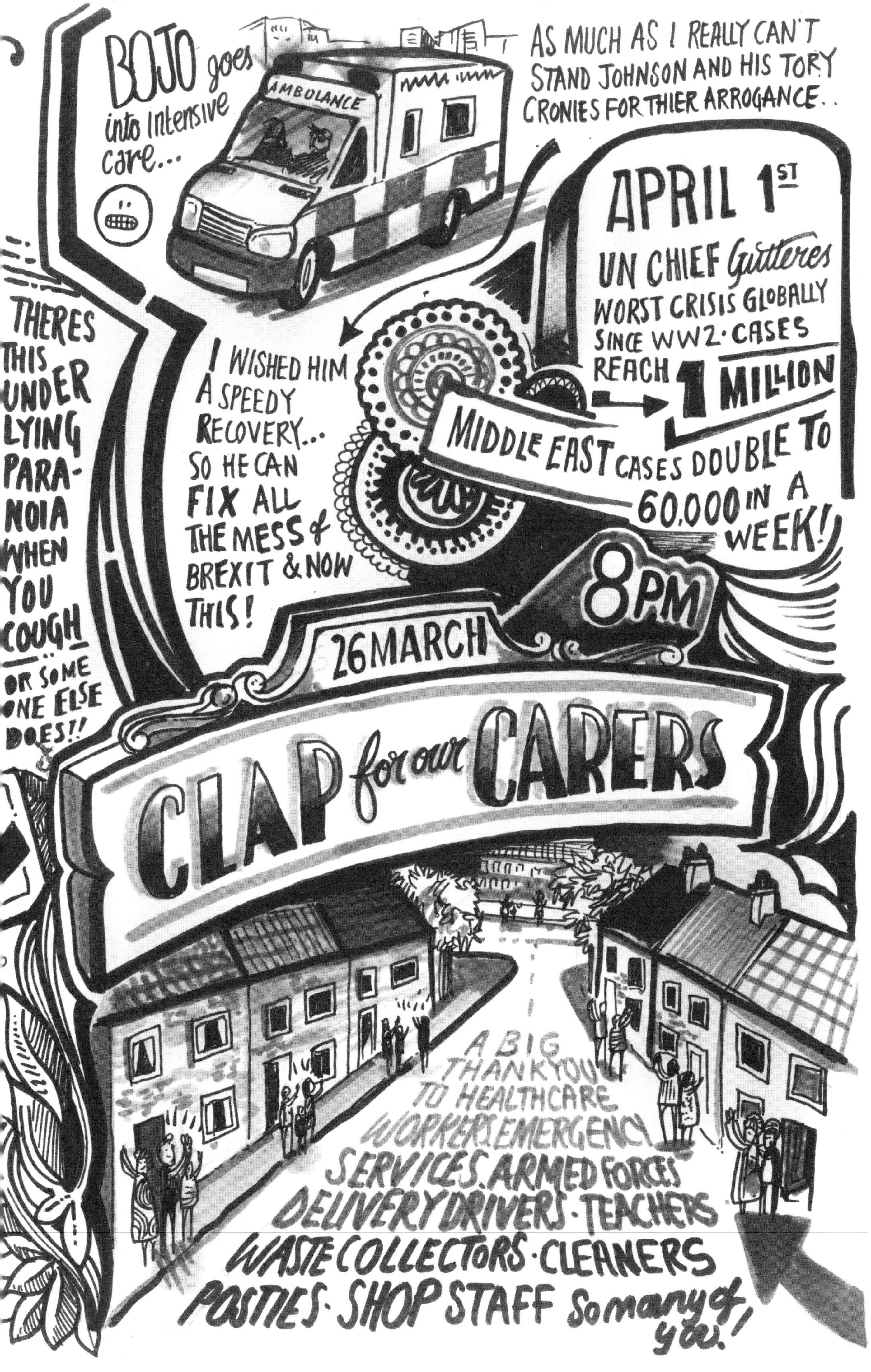
BOJO goes into intensive care...
AMBULANCE
AS MUCH AS I REALLY CAN'T STAND JOHNSON AND HIS TORY CRONIES FOR THIER ARROGANCE..
APRIL 1ST
UN CHIEF Gutteres
WORST CRISIS GLOBALLY SINCE WW2 · CASES REACH → 1 MILLION
THERES THIS UNDERLYING PARANOIA WHEN YOU COUGH... OR SOME ONE ELSE DOES!!
I WISHED HIM A SPEEDY RECOVERY... SO HE CAN FIX ALL THE MESS of BREXIT & NOW THIS!
MIDDLE EAST CASES DOUBLE TO 60,000 IN A WEEK!
8PM
26 MARCH
CLAP for our CARERS
A BIG THANK YOU TO HEALTHCARE WORKERS. EMERGENCY SERVICES. ARMED FORCES DELIVERY DRIVERS · TEACHERS
WASTE COLLECTORS · CLEANERS
POSTIES · SHOP STAFF So many of you!

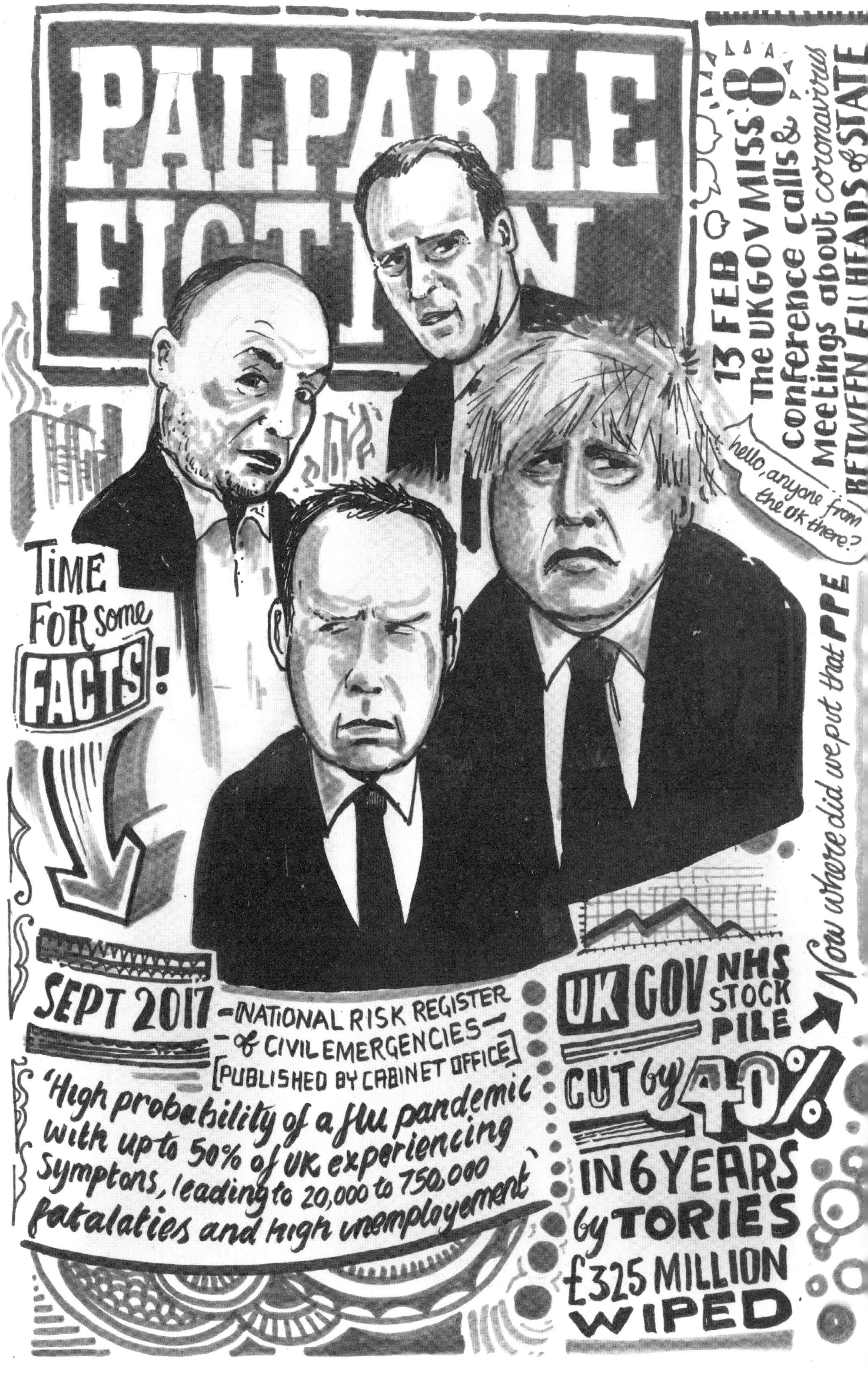
PALPABLE
FICTI N
13 FEB The UKGOV MISS 8 conference calls & meetings about coronavirus BETWEEN EU HEADS of STATE
hello, anyone from the UK there?
TIME FOR some FACTS!
Now where did we put that PPE
SEPT 2017 -NATIONAL RISK REGISTER -of CIVIL EMERGENCIES- [PUBLISHED BY CABINET OFFICE]
'High probability of a flu pandemic with up to 50% of UK experiencing symptons, leading to 20,000 to 750,000 fatalaties and high unemployement'
UK GOV NHS STOCK PILE CUT by 40% IN 6 YEARS by TORIES
£325 MILLION WIPED

21 FEB – **NERVTAG** [NEW AND EMERGING RESPIRATORY VIRUS] [THREAT ADVISORY GROUP]

Concluded a moderate risk after **WHO** *declared a public health emergency of International concern*

12 MARCH BOJO – "BANNING MAJOR EVENTS WILL HAVE LITTLE EFFECT ON THE SPREAD"

"EVERYBODY BE COOL THIS IS A ROBBERY"

AS 1000's **DIE** BOJO goes on **HOLIDAY**

BUT MANAGED TO MISS **5** COBRA MEETINGS ON THE VIRUS

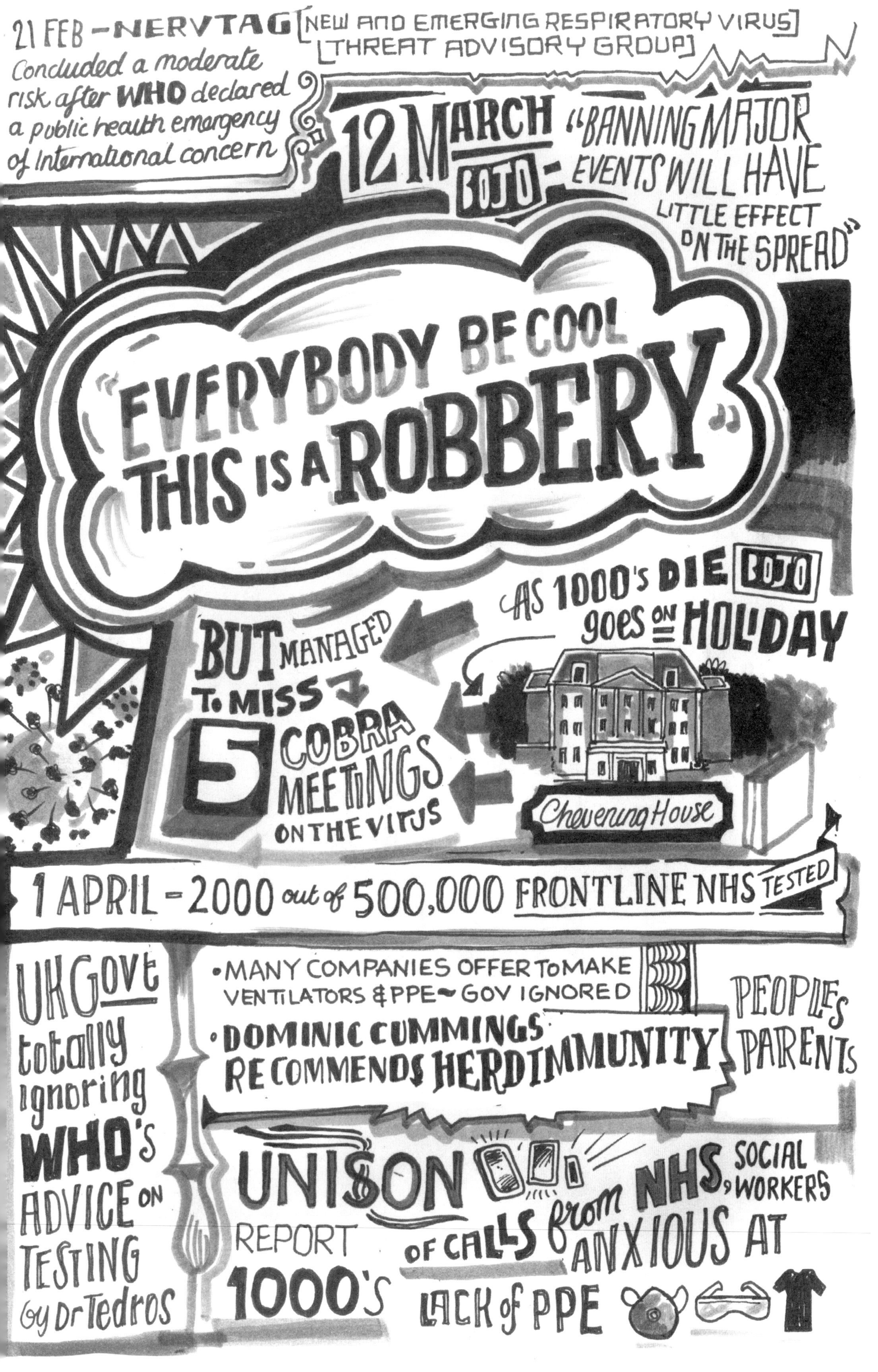

Chevening House

1 APRIL – 2000 *out of* 500,000 FRONTLINE NHS TESTED

UK Govt totally ignoring **WHO**'s ADVICE ON TESTING by Dr Tedros

- MANY COMPANIES OFFER TO MAKE VENTILATORS & PPE ~ GOV IGNORED
- **DOMINIC CUMMINGS RECOMMENDS HERD IMMUNITY**

PEOPLEs PARENTs

UNISON REPORT **1000's** OF CALLS *from* **NHS**, SOCIAL WORKERS ANXIOUS AT LACK of PPE

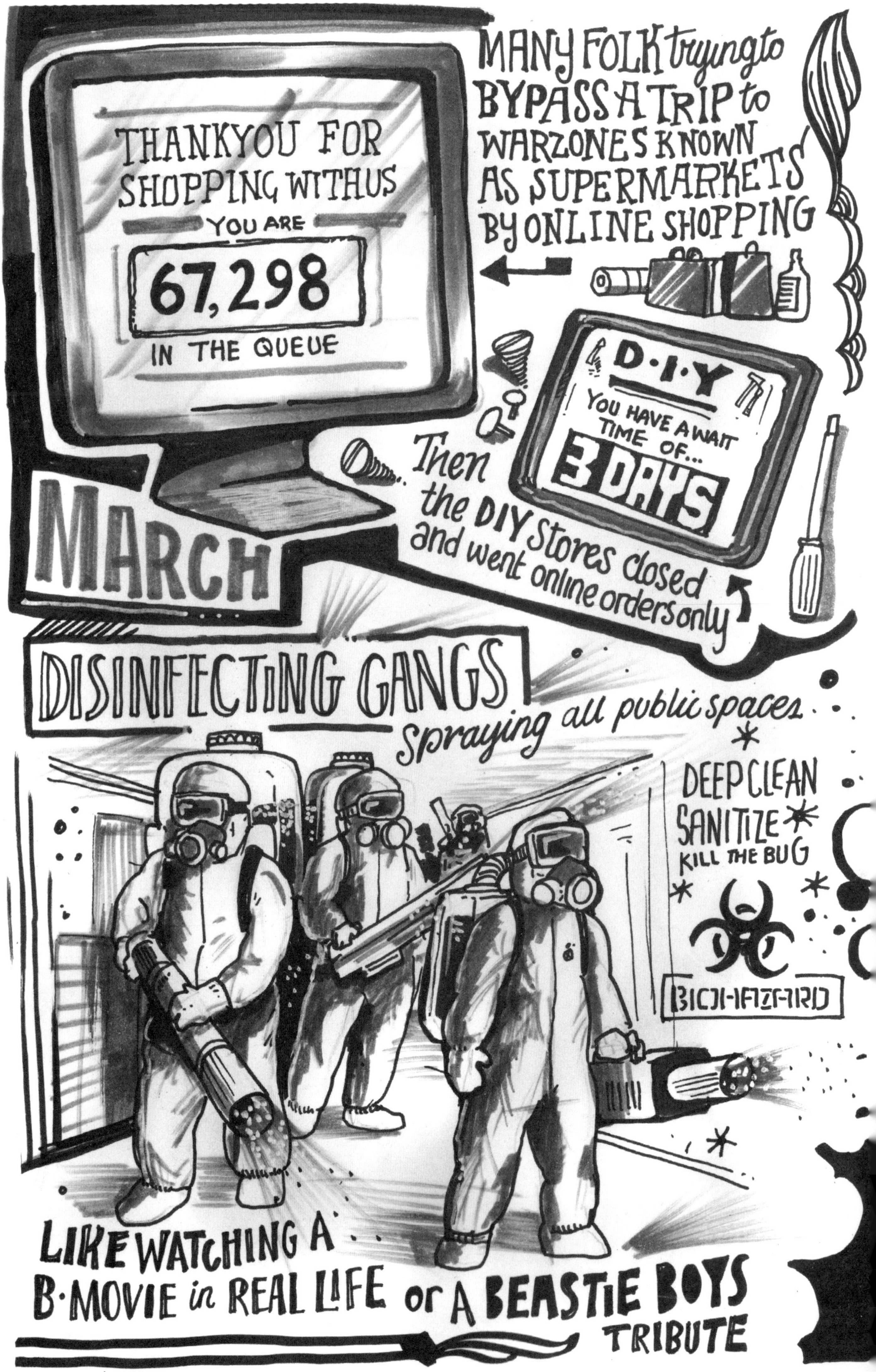
THANKYOU FOR SHOPPING WITH US
YOU ARE
67,298
IN THE QUEUE
MANY FOLK trying to BYPASS A TRIP to WARZONES KNOWN AS SUPERMARKETS BY ONLINE SHOPPING
D·I·Y
YOU HAVE A WAIT TIME OF...
3 DAYS
Then the DIY Stores closed and went online orders only
MARCH
DISINFECTING GANGS
spraying all public spaces
DEEP CLEAN
SANITIZE
KILL THE BUG
BIOHAZARD
LIKE WATCHING A B·MOVIE in REAL LIFE or A BEASTIE BOYS TRIBUTE

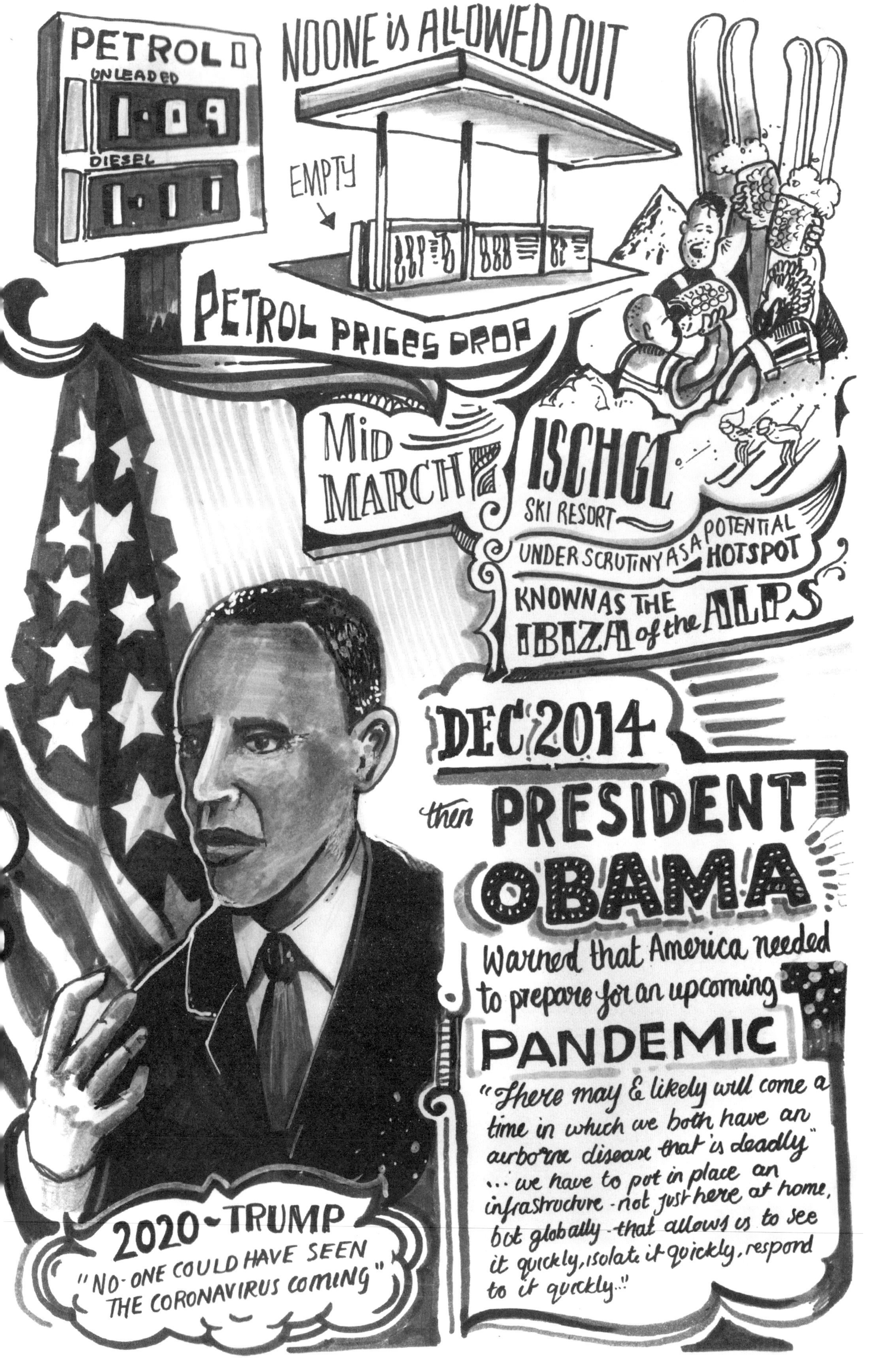
PETROL
UNLEADED
1·09
DIESEL
1·11
NOONE is ALLOWED OUT
EMPTY
PETROL PRICES DROP
Mid MARCH
ISCHGL
SKI RESORT
UNDER SCRUTINY AS A POTENTIAL HOTSPOT
KNOWN AS THE IBIZA of the ALPS
DEC 2014
then PRESIDENT OBAMA
Warned that America needed to prepare for an upcoming
PANDEMIC
"There may & likely will come a time in which we both have an airborne disease that is deadly" ... we have to put in place an infrastructure - not just here at home, but globally - that allows us to see it quickly, isolate it quickly, respond to it quickly..."
2020 - TRUMP
"NO-ONE COULD HAVE SEEN THE CORONAVIRUS COMING"

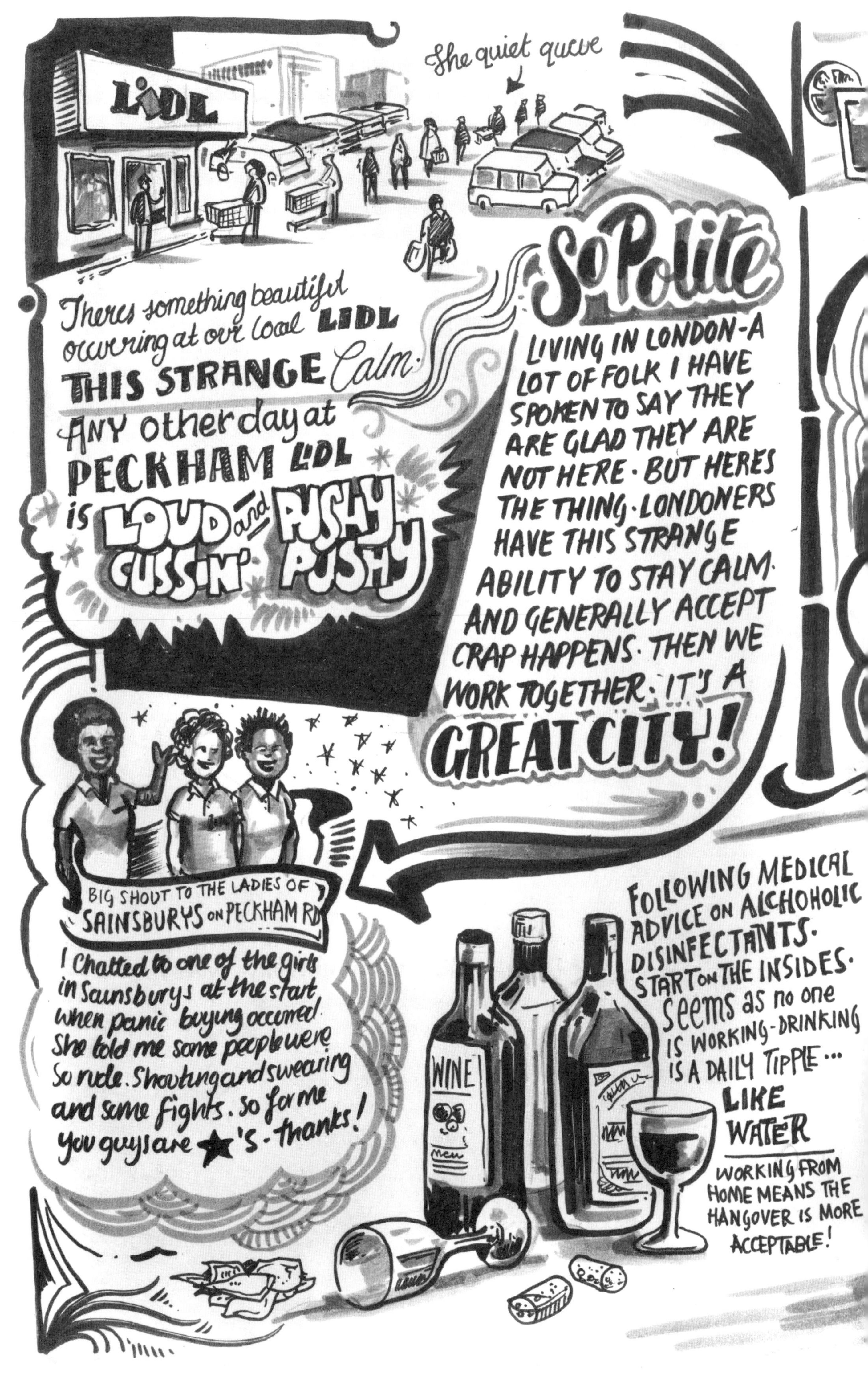

The quiet queue
LIDL
Theres something beautiful occurring at our local LIDL
THIS STRANGE Calm.
ANY other day at PECKHAM LIDL is LOUD and PUSHY
CUSSIN' PUSHY
So Polite
LIVING IN LONDON - A LOT OF FOLK I HAVE SPOKEN TO SAY THEY ARE GLAD THEY ARE NOT HERE. BUT HERES THE THING. LONDONERS HAVE THIS STRANGE ABILITY TO STAY CALM. AND GENERALLY ACCEPT CRAP HAPPENS. THEN WE WORK TOGETHER. IT'S A
GREAT CITY!
BIG SHOUT TO THE LADIES OF SAINSBURYS ON PECKHAM RD
I Chatted to one of the girls in Sainsburys at the start when panic buying occurred. She told me some people were so rude. Shouting and swearing and some fights. So for me you guys are ★'s - thanks!
FOLLOWING MEDICAL ADVICE ON ALCHOHOLIC DISINFECTANTS. START ON THE INSIDES.
Seems as no one is WORKING - DRINKING IS A DAILY TIPPLE...
LIKE WATER
WINE
WORKING FROM HOME MEANS THE HANGOVER IS MORE ACCEPTABLE!

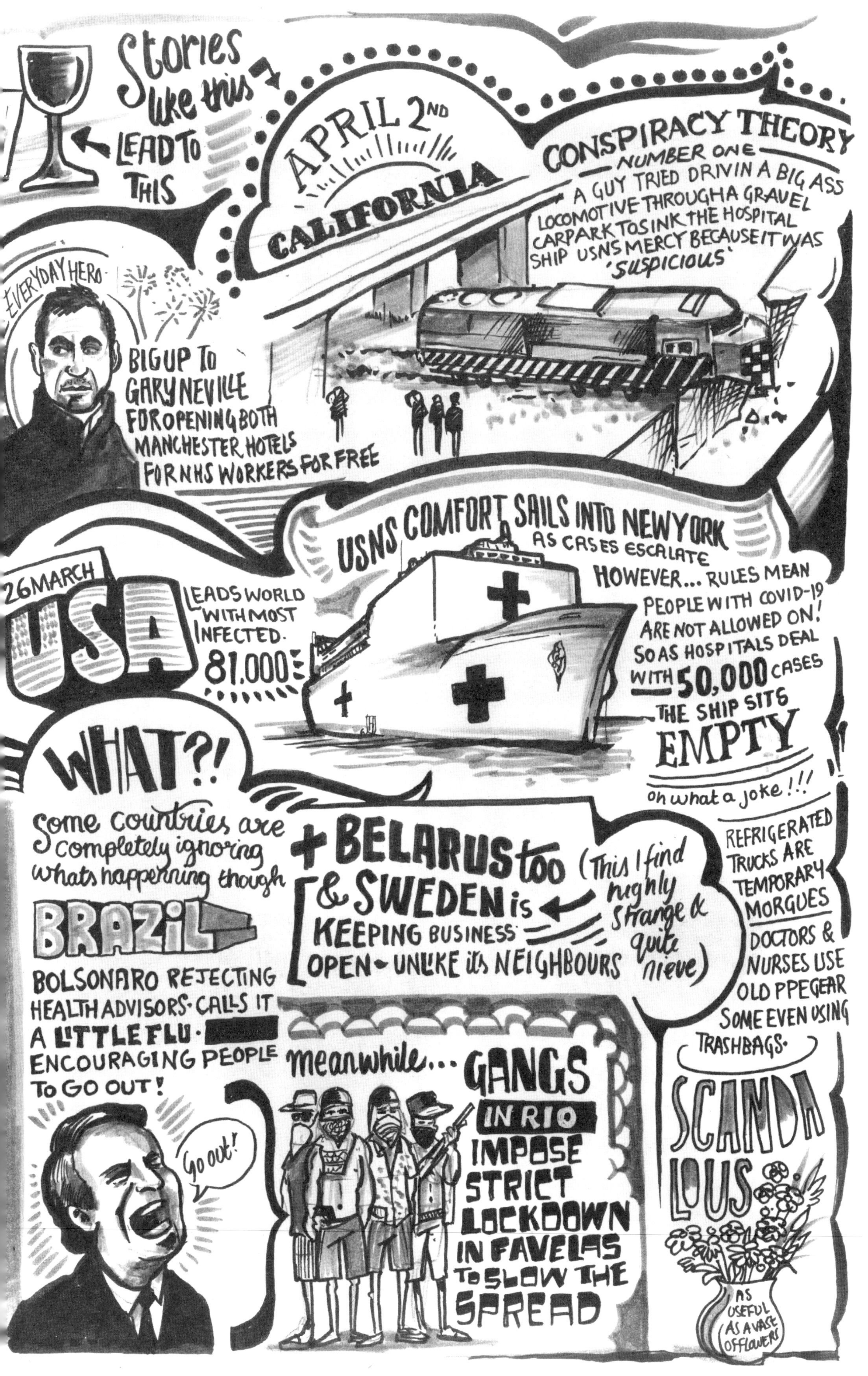

Stories like this LEAD TO THIS
APRIL 2ND
CALIFORNIA
CONSPIRACY THEORY
— NUMBER ONE —
A GUY TRIED DRIVIN A BIG ASS LOCOMOTIVE THROUGH A GRAVEL CARPARK TO SINK THE HOSPITAL SHIP USNS MERCY BECAUSE IT WAS 'SUSPICIOUS'
EVERYDAY HERO
BIG UP TO GARY NEVILLE FOR OPENING BOTH MANCHESTER HOTELS FOR NHS WORKERS FOR FREE
USNS COMFORT SAILS INTO NEW YORK
AS CASES ESCALATE
26 MARCH
USA
LEADS WORLD WITH MOST INFECTED.
81,000
HOWEVER... RULES MEAN PEOPLE WITH COVID-19 ARE NOT ALLOWED ON! SO AS HOSPITALS DEAL WITH 50,000 CASES THE SHIP SITS EMPTY
oh what a joke!!!
WHAT?!
Some countries are completely ignoring whats happerning though
BRAZIL
BOLSONARO REJECTING HEALTH ADVISORS · CALLS IT A LITTLE FLU · [redacted] ENCOURAGING PEOPLE TO GO OUT!
Go out!
+ BELARUS too
& SWEDEN is KEEPING BUSINESS OPEN ~ UNLIKE its NEIGHBOURS
(This I find highly strange & quite nieve)
meanwhile... GANGS IN RIO IMPOSE STRICT LOCKDOWN IN FAVELAS TO SLOW THE SPREAD
REFRIGERATED TRUCKS ARE TEMPORARY MORGUES
DOCTORS & NURSES USE OLD PPE GEAR SOME EVEN USING TRASHBAGS.
SCANDALOUS
AS USEFUL AS A VASE OF FLOWERS

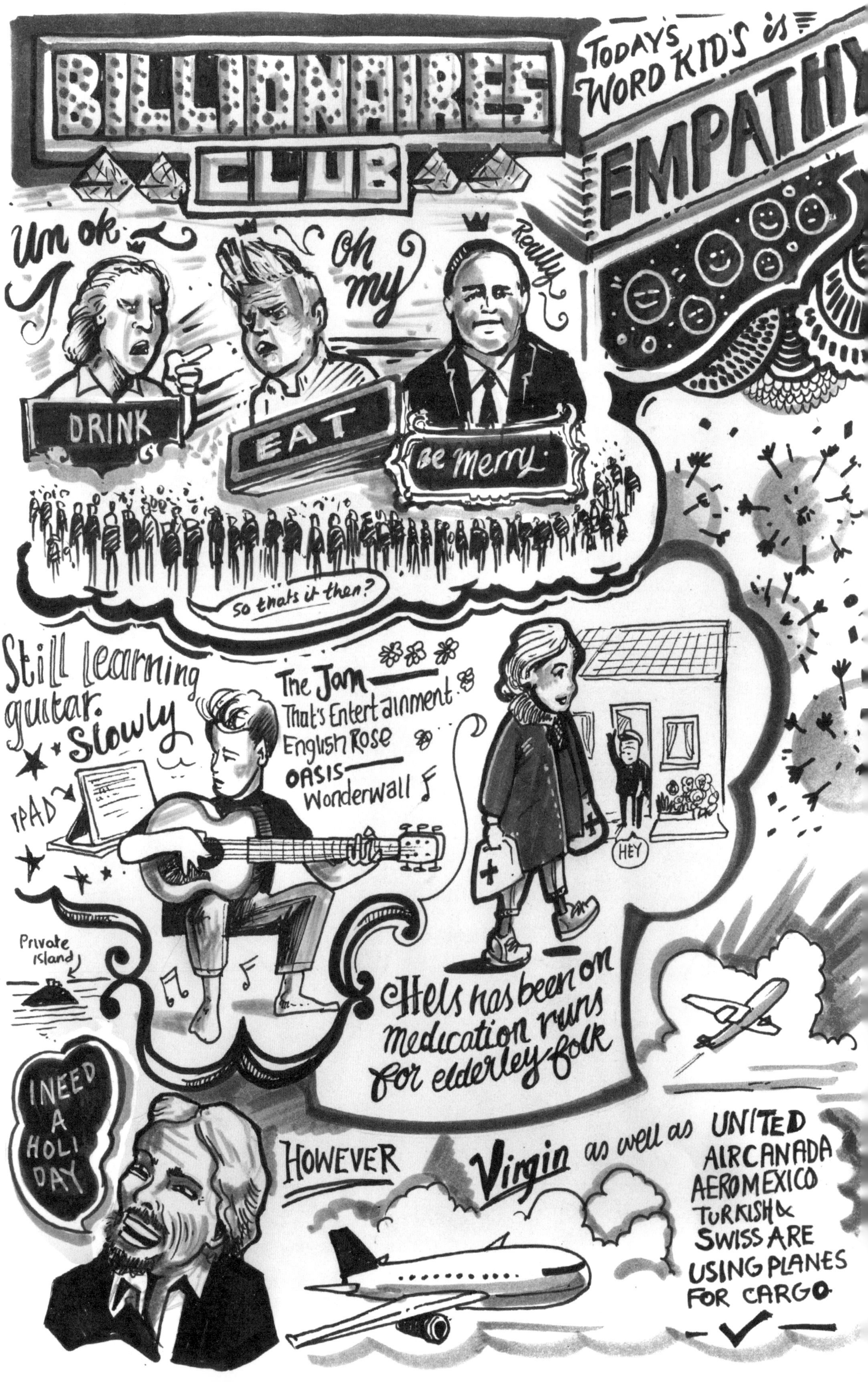
BILLIONAIRES CLUB
TODAY'S WORD KID'S is EMPATHY
Um ok
Oh my
Really
DRINK
EAT
Be Merry
So thats it then?
Still learning guitar. Slowly
The Jam
That's Entertainment
English Rose
OASIS
Wonderwall
IPAD
HEY
Private island
Hels has been on medication runs for elderley folk
I NEED A HOLIDAY
HOWEVER Virgin as well as UNITED AIRCANADA AEROMEXICO TURKISH & SWISS ARE USING PLANES FOR CARGO

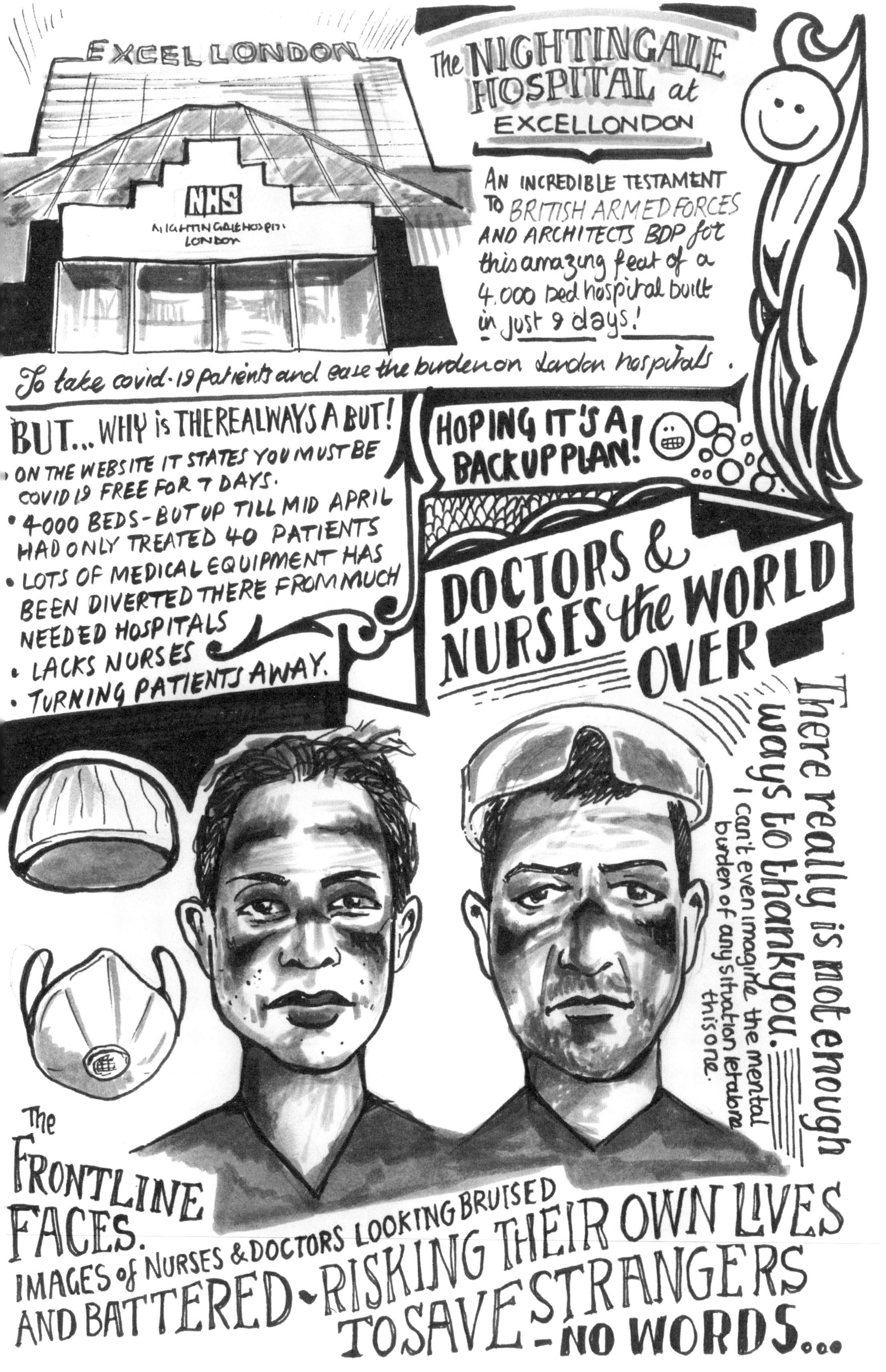

EXCEL LONDON
NHS
NIGHTINGALE HOSPITAL LONDON
The NIGHTINGALE HOSPITAL at EXCELLONDON
AN INCREDIBLE TESTAMENT TO BRITISH ARMED FORCES AND ARCHITECTS BDP for this amazing feat of a 4,000 bed hospital built in just 9 days!
To take covid-19 patients and ease the burden on London hospitals.
BUT... WHY is THERE ALWAYS A BUT!
• ON THE WEBSITE IT STATES YOU MUST BE COVID 19 FREE FOR 7 DAYS.
• 4000 BEDS - BUT UP TILL MID APRIL HAD ONLY TREATED 40 PATIENTS
• LOTS OF MEDICAL EQUIPMENT HAS BEEN DIVERTED THERE FROM MUCH NEEDED HOSPITALS
• LACKS NURSES
• TURNING PATIENTS AWAY.
HOPING IT'S A BACKUP PLAN!
DOCTORS & NURSES the WORLD OVER
There really is not enough ways to thankyou.
I can't even imagine the mental burden of any situation letalone this one.
The FRONTLINE FACES.
IMAGES of NURSES & DOCTORS LOOKING BRUISED AND BATTERED - RISKING THEIR OWN LIVES TO SAVE STRANGERS - NO WORDS...

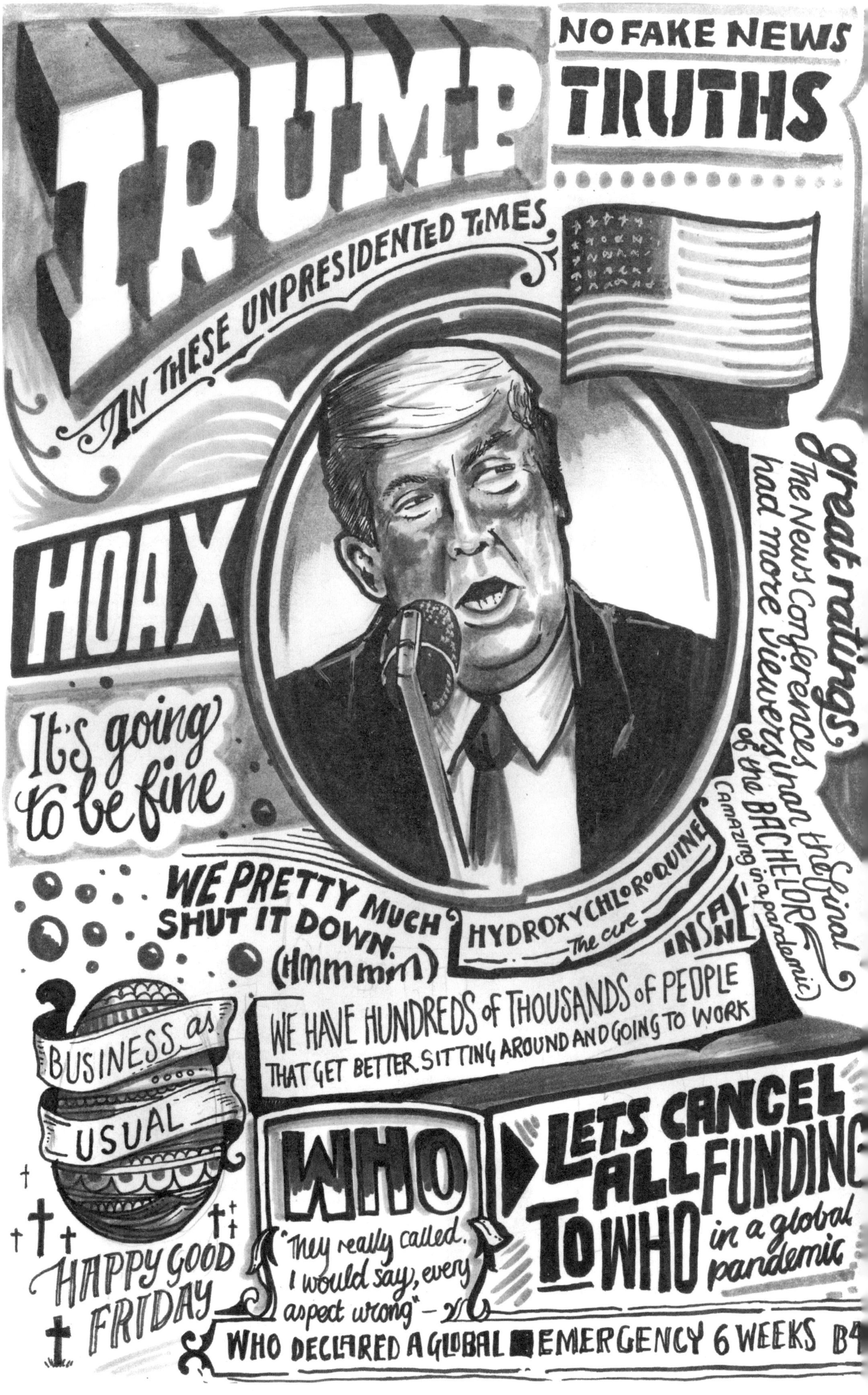

TRUMP
NO FAKE NEWS
TRUTHS
IN THESE UNPRESIDENTED TIMES
HOAX
It's going to be fine
great ratings
The News Conferences had more viewers than the final of the BACHELOR
(amazing in a pandemic)
WE PRETTY MUCH SHUT IT DOWN.
(Hmmmm)
HYDROXYCHLOROQUINE
The cure
INSANE
WE HAVE HUNDREDS of THOUSANDS of PEOPLE
THAT GET BETTER. SITTING AROUND AND GOING TO WORK
BUSINESS as USUAL
HAPPY GOOD FRIDAY
WHO
"They really called. I would say, every aspect wrong" –
LETS CANCEL ALL FUNDING TO WHO
in a global pandemic
WHO DECLARED A GLOBAL EMERGENCY 6 WEEKS B4

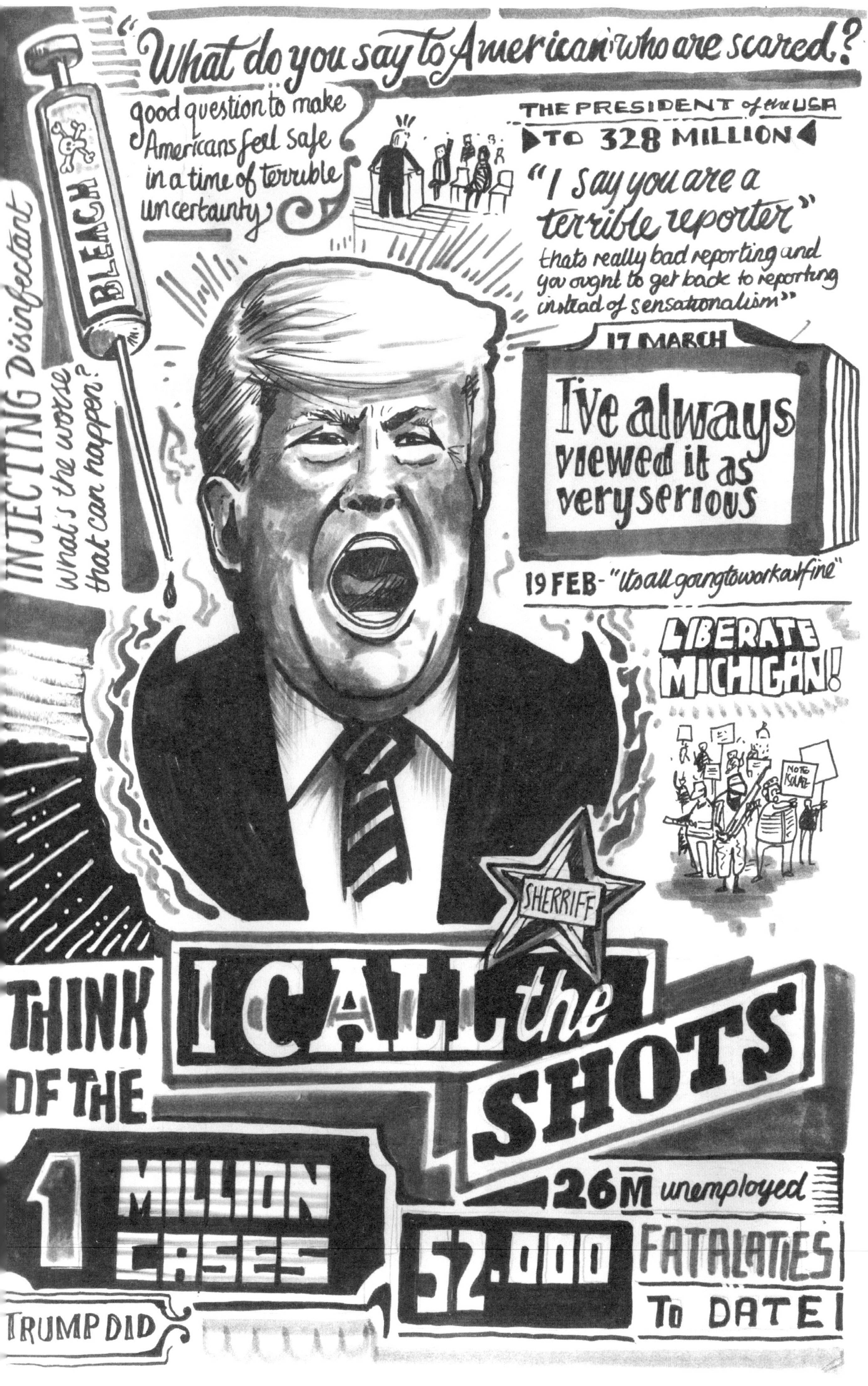
"What do you say to American who are scared?
good question to make Americans feel safe in a time of terrible uncertainty
THE PRESIDENT of the USA
TO 328 MILLION
"I say you are a terrible reporter" thats really bad reporting and you ought to get back to reporting instead of sensationalism"
17 MARCH
I've always viewed it as very serious
19 FEB - "Its all going to work out fine"
LIBERATE MICHIGAN!
NO TO ISOLATE
BLEACH
INJECTING Disinfectant
What's the worse that can happen?
SHERRIFF
I CALL the SHOTS
THINK OF THE
1 MILLION CASES
TRUMP DID
26M unemployed
52.000 FATALATIES TO DATE!

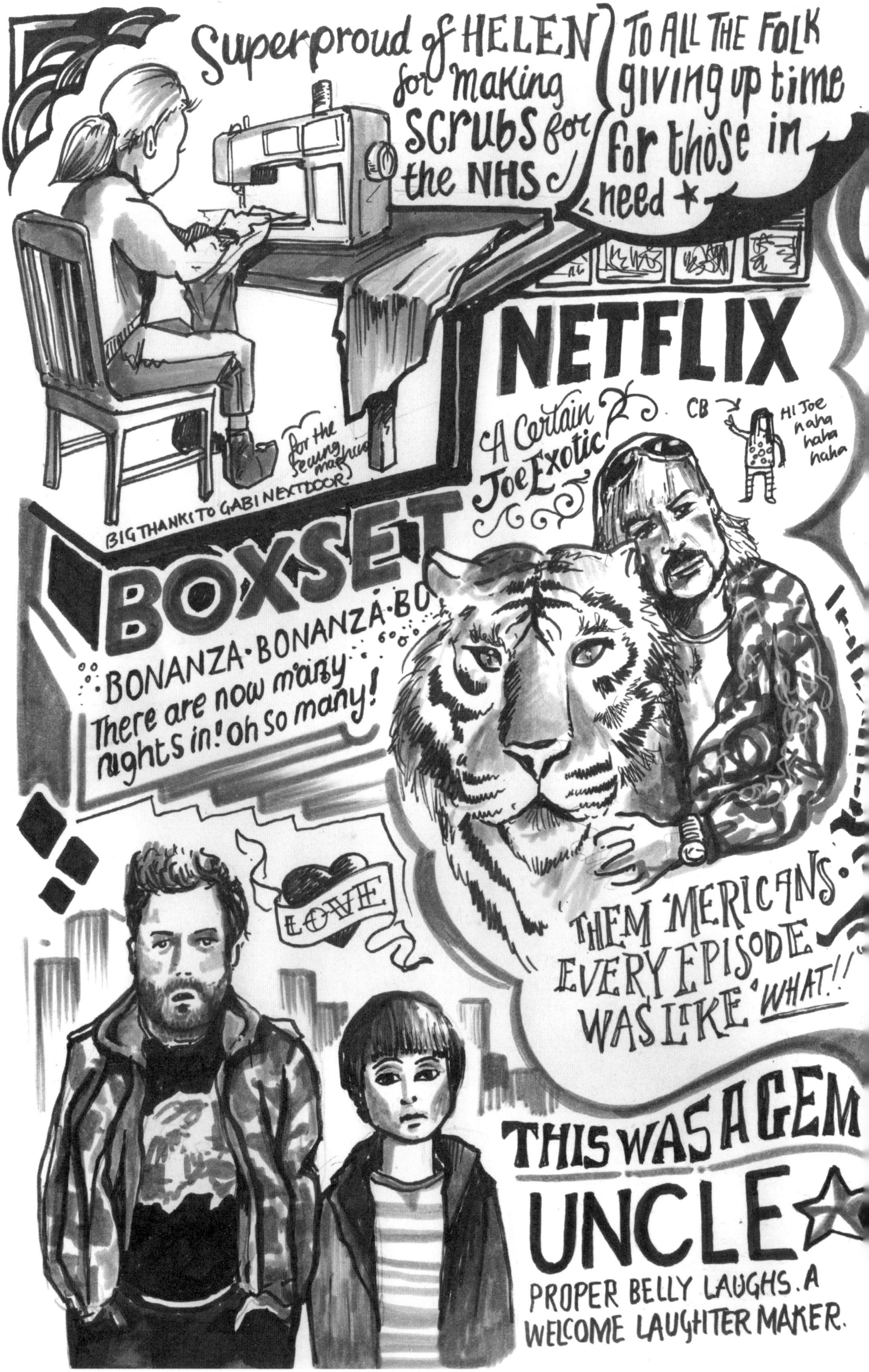
Superproud of HELEN for making scrubs for the NHS
To all the folk giving up time for those in need
for the sewing machine
BIG THANKS TO GABI NEXT DOOR
NETFLIX
A Certain Joe Exotic
CB
Hi Joe haha haha haha
BOXSET
BONANZA·BONANZA·BO
There are now many nights in! Oh so many!
LOVE
THEM 'MERICANS. EVERY EPISODE WAS LIKE 'WHAT!!'
THIS WAS A GEM
UNCLE
PROPER BELLY LAUGHS. A WELCOME LAUGHTER MAKER.

TAIWAN

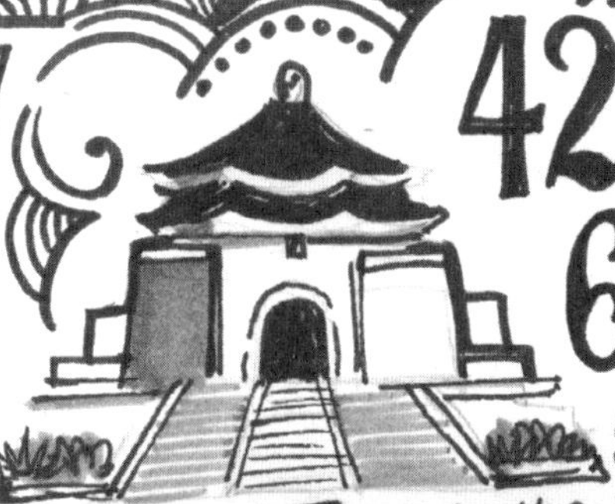

420 CASES

6 DEATHS

AMAZING!!!

A Super Strict approach has benefitted noend

- PASSENGERS ARRIVING - HANDOVER MOBILES SO THEY CAN BE TRACKED & ISOLATED.
- FINES FOR VIOLATING QUARANTINE - $3,333 to $333,333!
- SPECIALCABS FOR ARRIVING PASSENGERS
- CLOSING BORDERS TO CHINA IMMEDIATELY
- NO INTERNATIONAL TOURISTS.
- HEALTH MONITORING } STRAIGHT AWAY.
- CONTACT TRACING

Due to the SARS crisis Taiwan were way ahead of controlling quickly

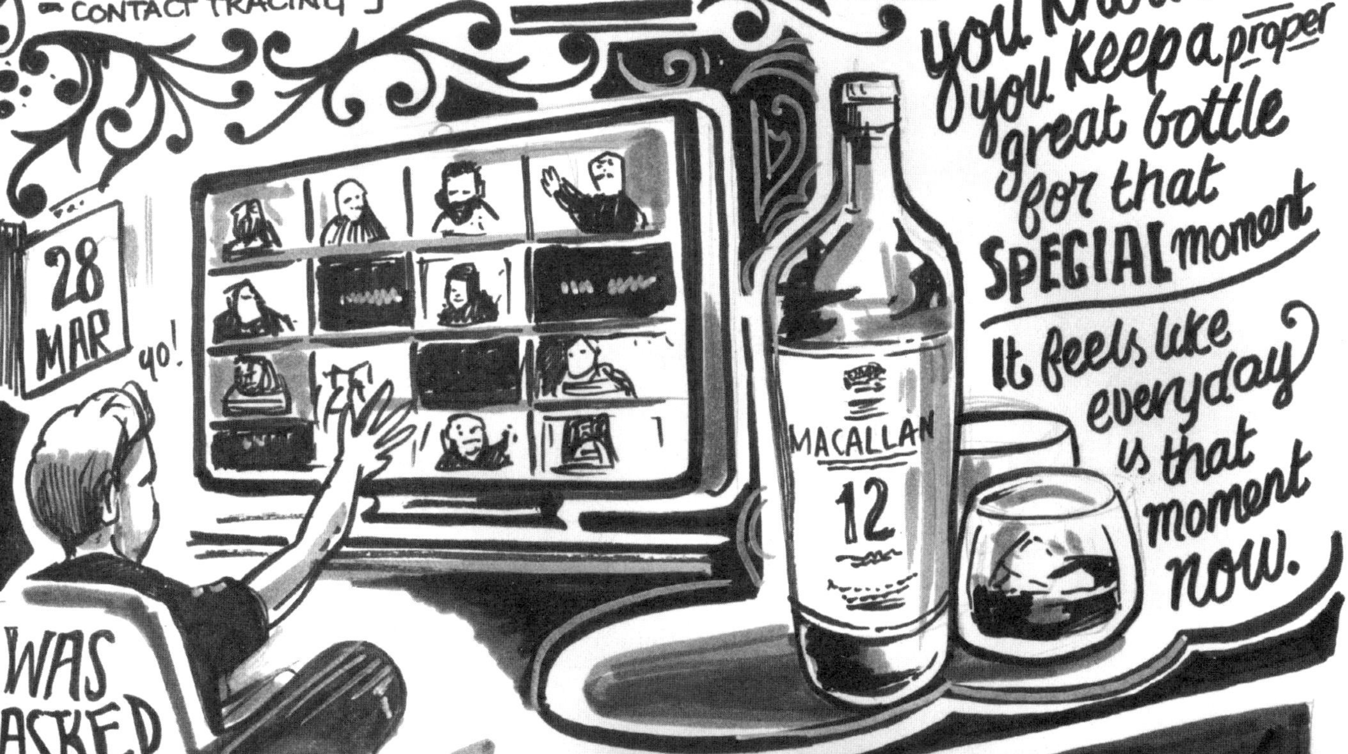

28 MAR
yo!
MACALLAN
12

you know when you keep a proper great bottle for that SPECIAL moment

It feels like everyday is that moment now.

WAS ASKED by the LOVELY TOM·S to be a GUEST SPEAKER to his ART STUDENTS IN NEW YORK

7 APR

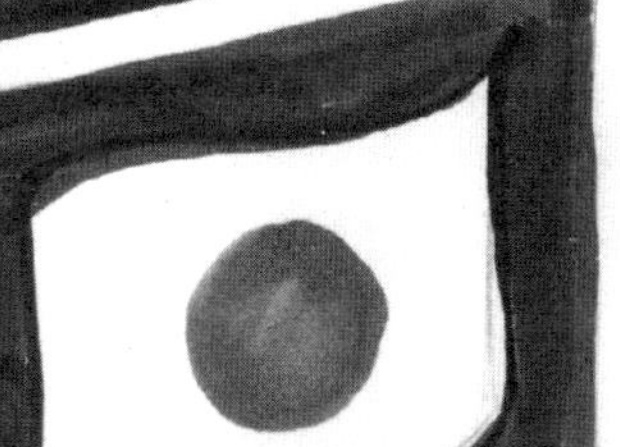

JAPAN

DECLARE A STATE OF EMERGENCY

after a sharp rise in cases

2020 OLYMPICS CANCELLED TILL 2021

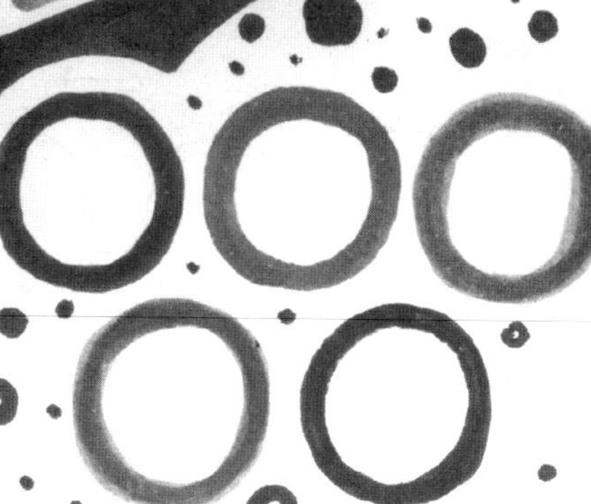

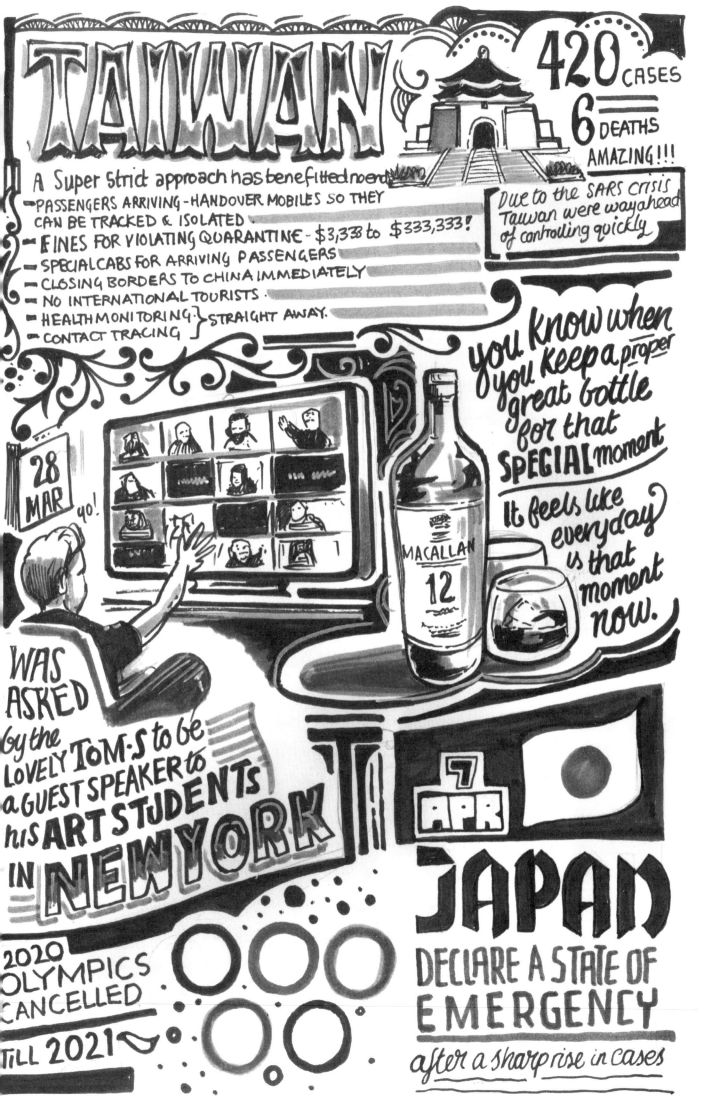

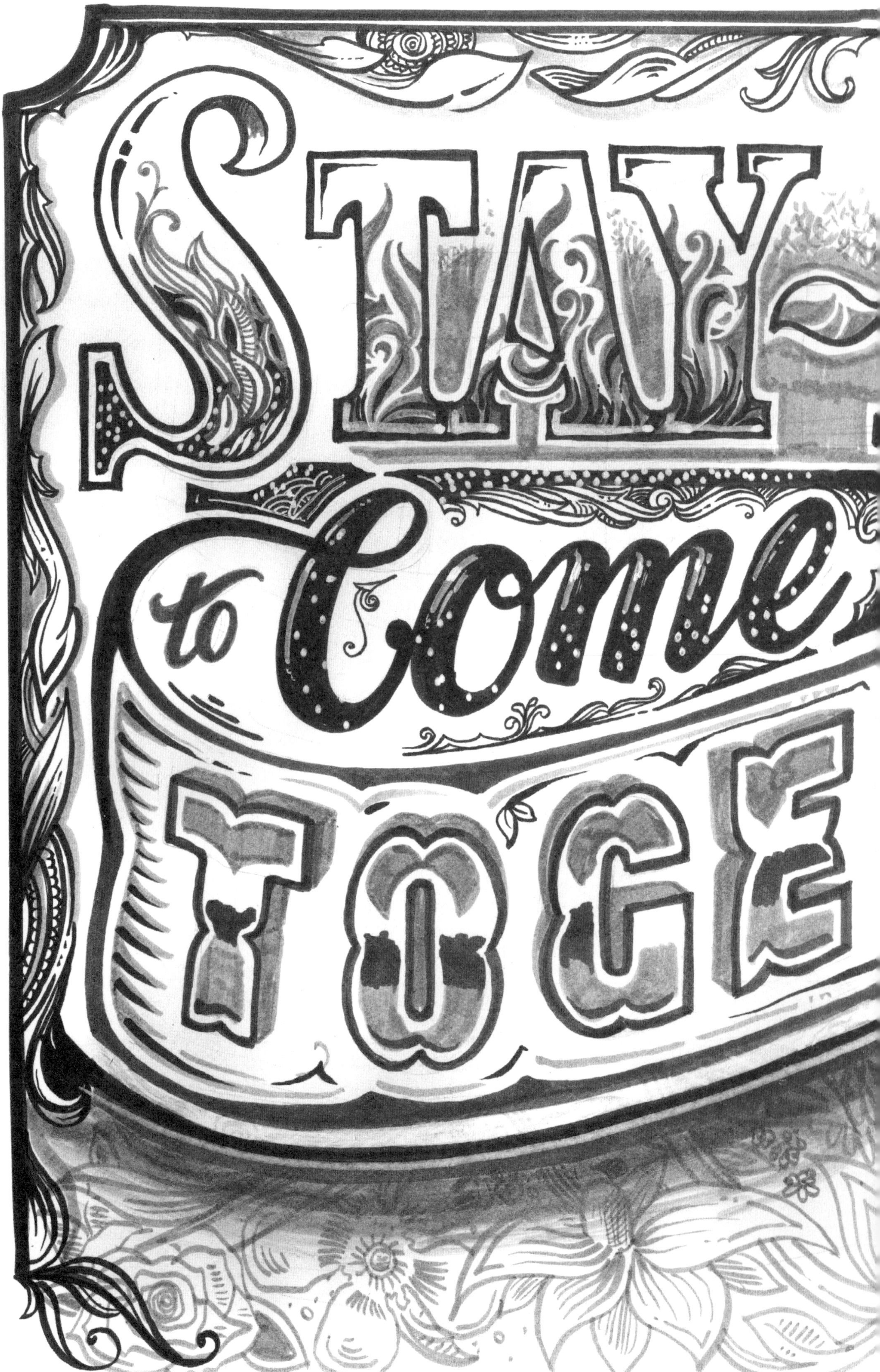
STAY
to Come
TOGE

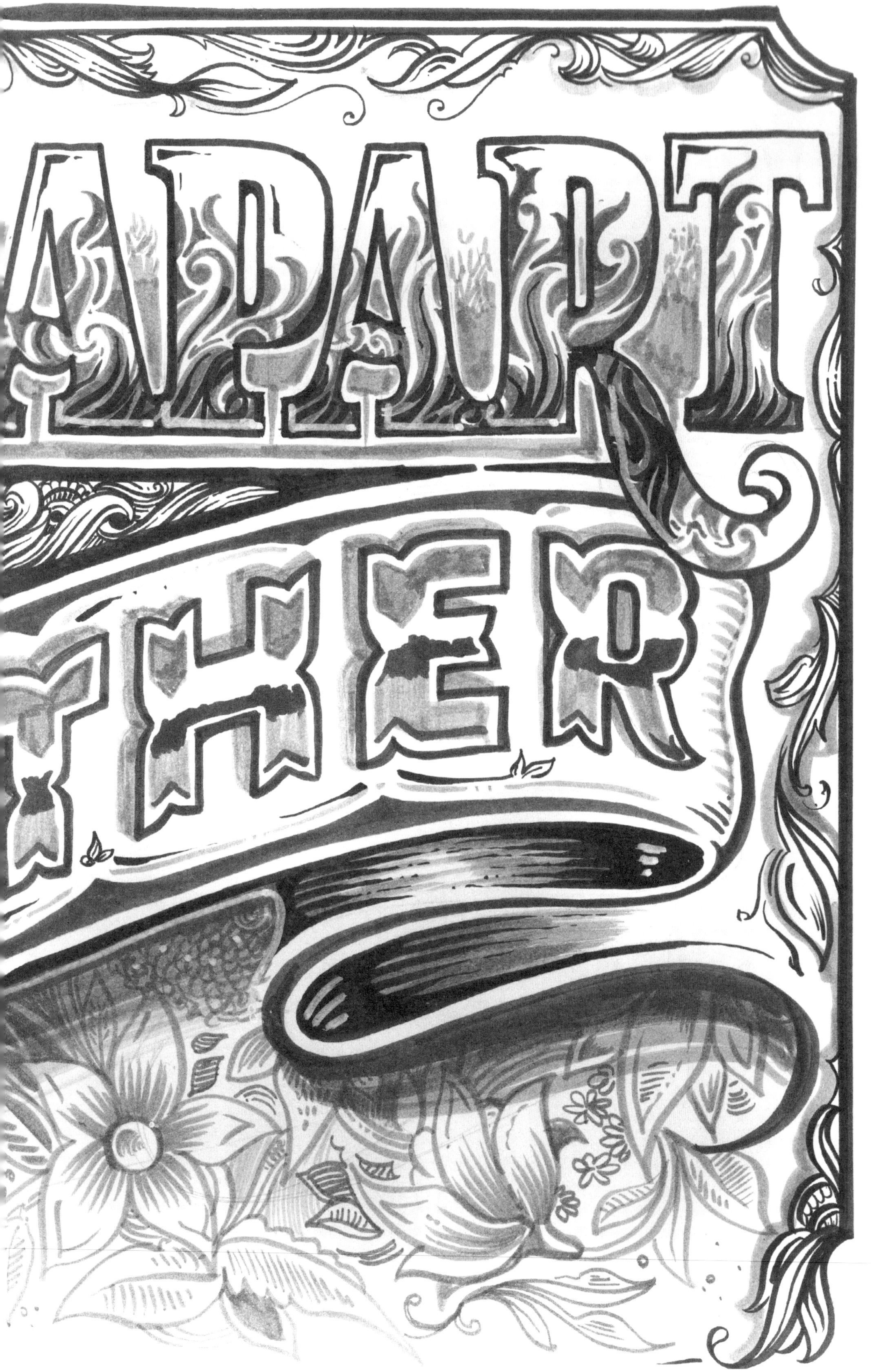
APART
THER

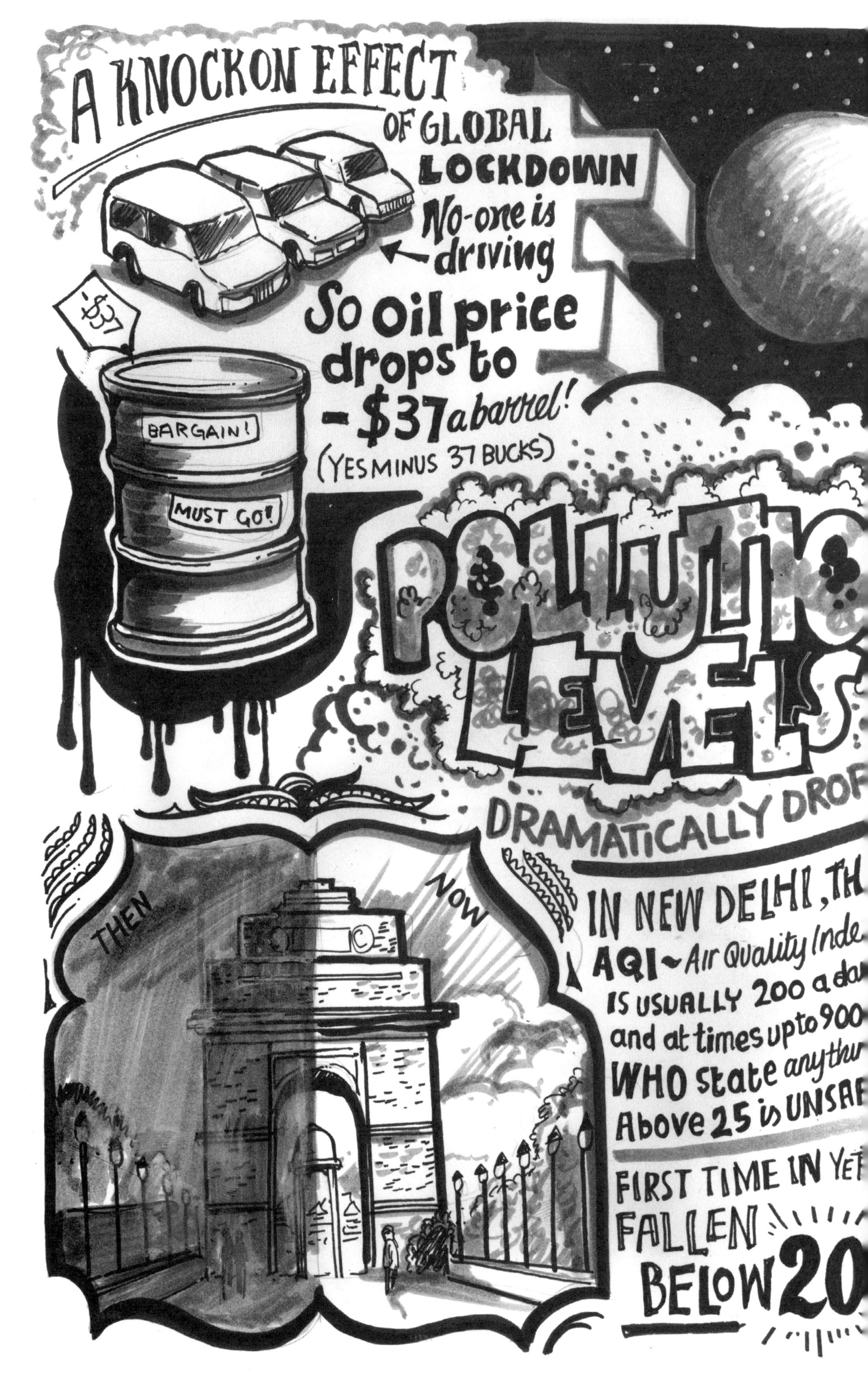

A KNOCKON EFFECT
OF GLOBAL LOCKDOWN
No-one is driving
-$37
So Oil price drops to -$37 a barrel!
(YES MINUS 37 BUCKS)
BARGAIN!
MUST GO!
POLLUTIO
LEVELS
DRAMATICALLY DROP
THEN
NOW
IN NEW DELHI, TH
AQI ~ Air Quality Inde
IS USUALLY 200 a da
and at times up to 900
WHO state anythi
Above 25 is UNSAF
FIRST TIME IN YE
FALLEN
BELOW 20

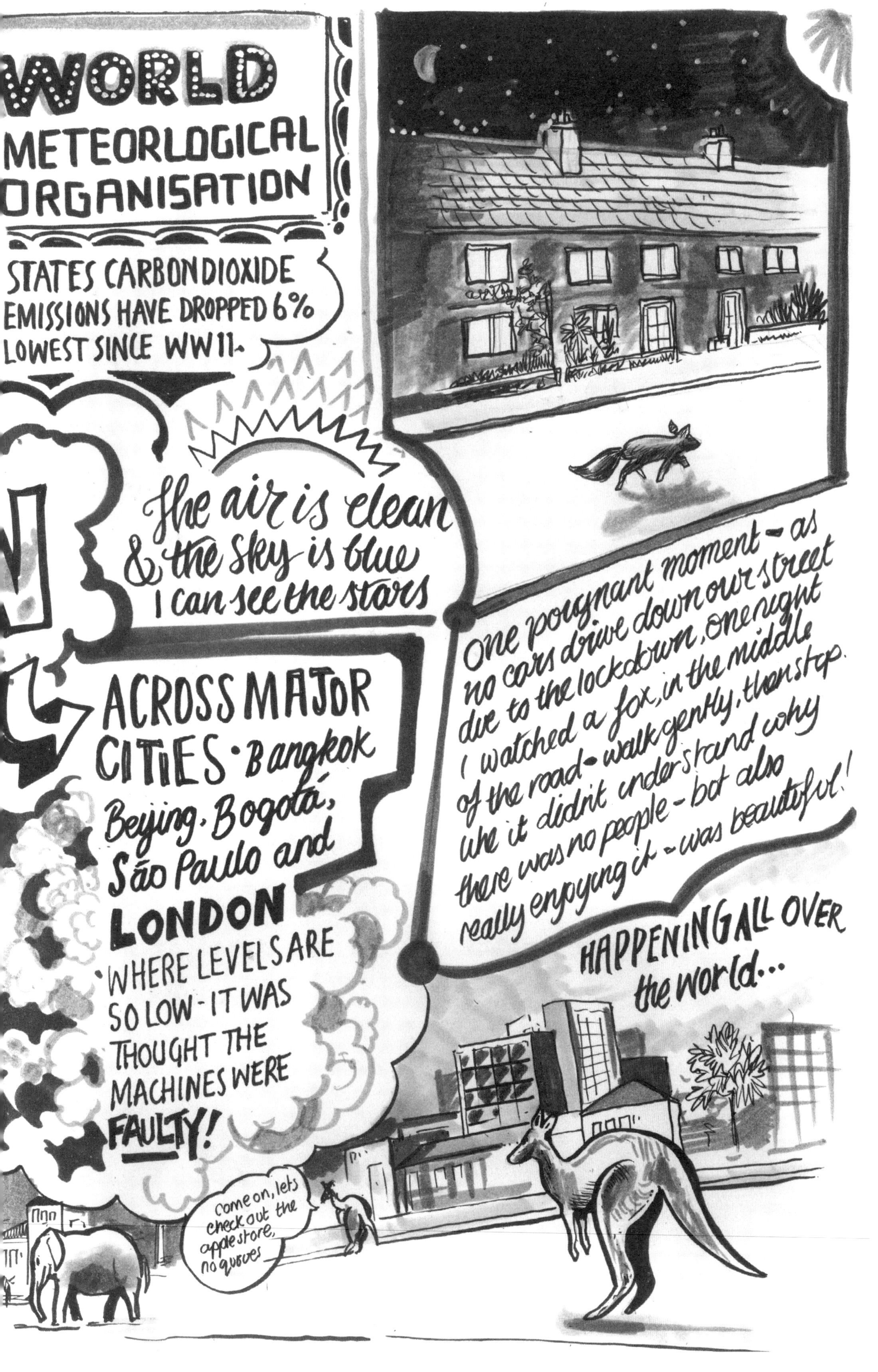
WORLD METEOROLGICAL ORGANISATION
STATES CARBONDIOXIDE EMISSIONS HAVE DROPPED 6% LOWEST SINCE WW11.
The air is clean & the sky is blue I can see the stars
ACROSS MAJOR CITIES · Bangkok Beijing. Bogotá, São Paulo and LONDON WHERE LEVELS ARE SO LOW - IT WAS THOUGHT THE MACHINES WERE FAULTY!
One poignant moment - as no cars drive down our street due to the lockdown, one night I watched a fox, in the middle of the road - walk gently, then stop. Like it didn't understand why there was no people - but also really enjoying it - was beautiful!
HAPPENING ALL OVER the world...
Come on, lets check out the apple store, no queues

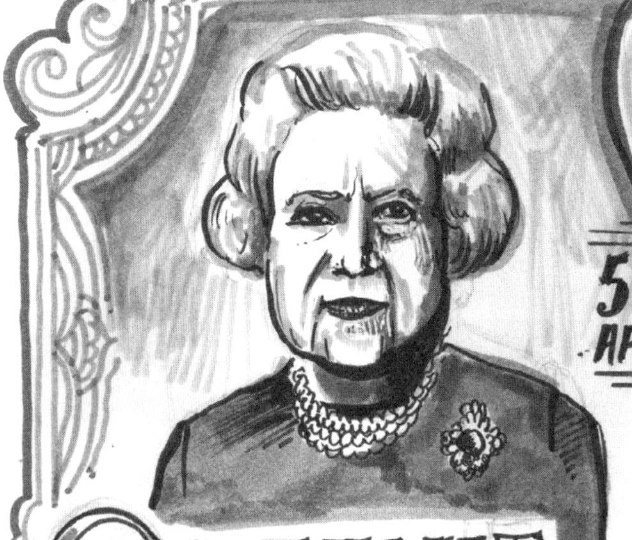

5th APRIL

QUEENIE addresses the Nation

WE WILL MEET AGAIN

5th ADDRESS IN 68 YEARS

The Gov has introduced a FURLOUGH SCHEM FOR THOSE employed. UP TO £2,500 Per Month of 80% of PEOPLES WAGES.

I HOWEVER AS THE DIRECTOR & SOLE EMPLOYEE of A Ltd COMPANY AM ENTITLED to... **ZERO**

AFTER 36 YEARS, PAID £400,000 IN TAX & VAT AND NOTHING

Yeah thanks Rishi!!

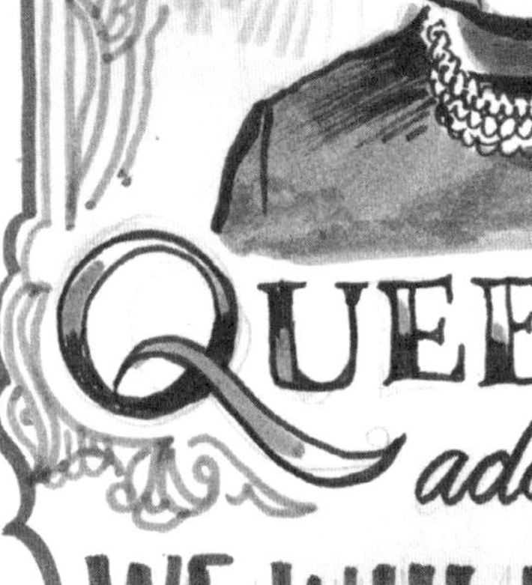

Football TOOK A KICK IN AS TOP CLUBS **FURLOUGH** STAFF but PAY PLAYERS FULL PAY

BOO

Some players Paid upto £3M

MAN UTD STRIKER MARCUS RASHFORD *Good Guy*

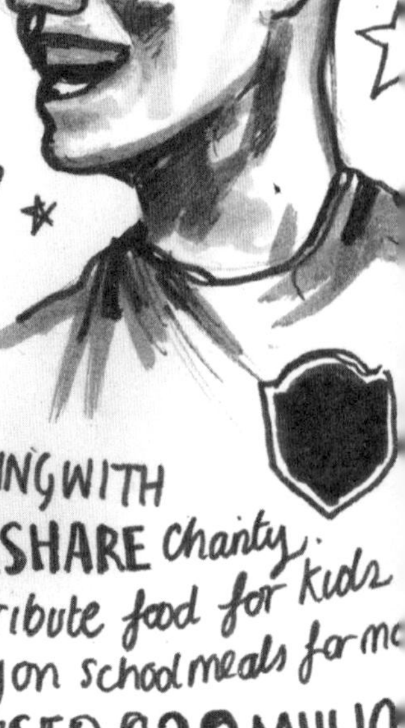

Some footballers refuse to take paycut to help in UK. Meanwhile BARCA in Spain take a 70% Paycut and make additional payments to nonplaying staff & JUVENTAS have frozen thier pay for 4 MONTHS

WORKING WITH FARESHARE Charity to distribute food for kids who rely on school meals for mo food. RAISED £20 MILLIO

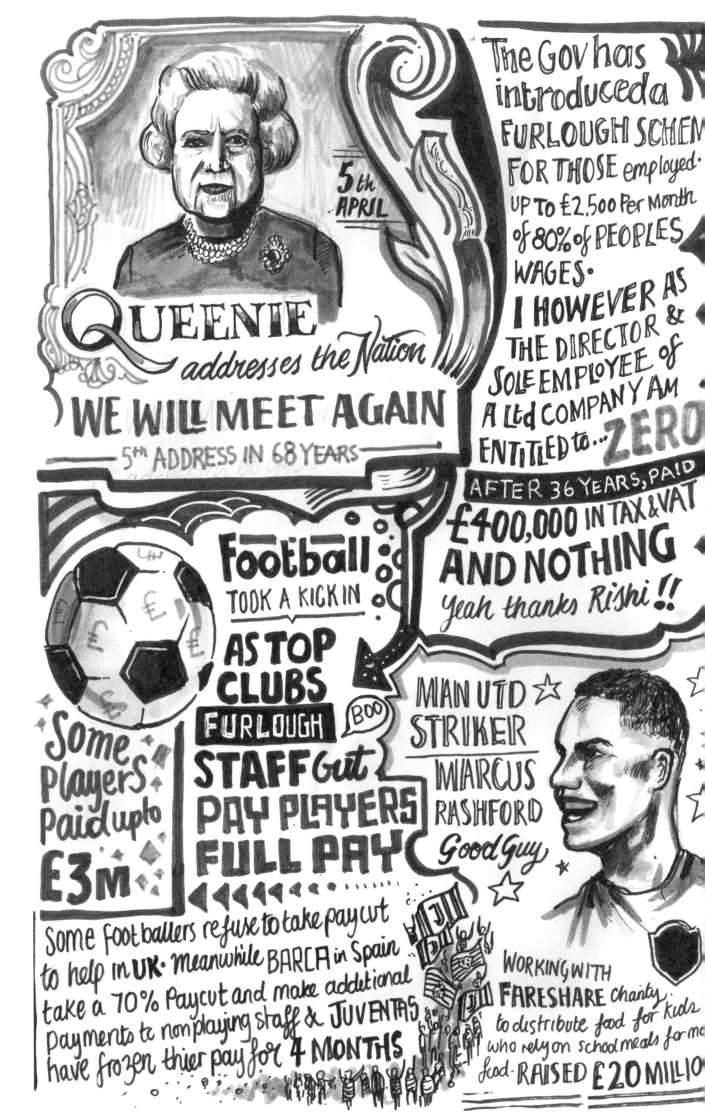

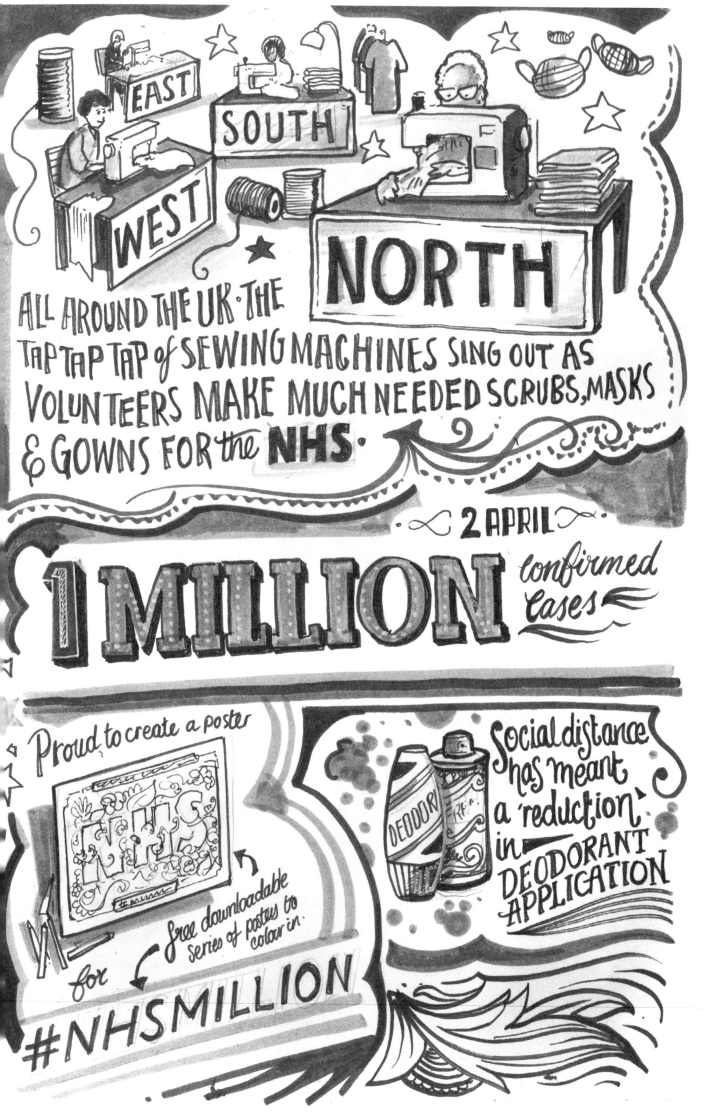

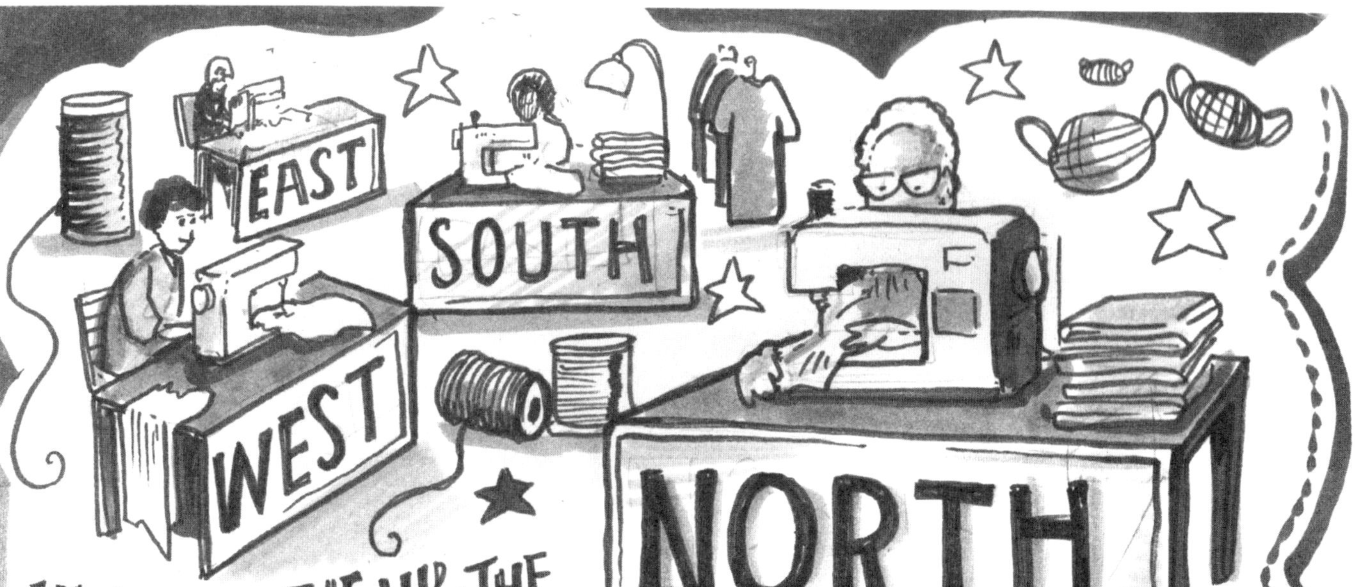
EAST
SOUTH
WEST
NORTH

ALL AROUND THE UK · THE TAP TAP TAP of SEWING MACHINES SING OUT AS VOLUNTEERS MAKE MUCH NEEDED SCRUBS, MASKS & GOWNS FOR the **NHS** ·

2 APRIL

1 MILLION *confirmed cases*

Proud to create a poster

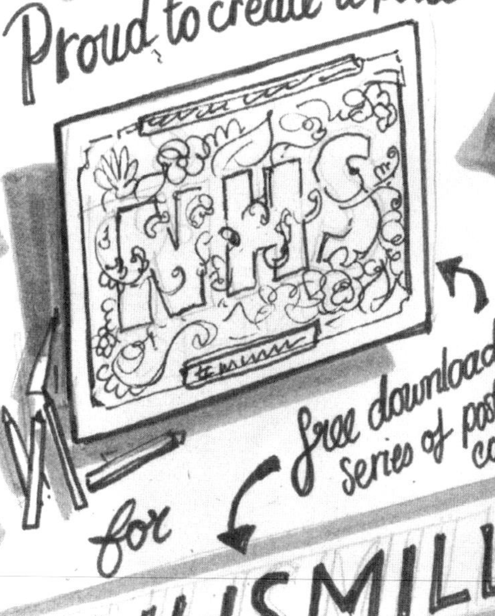
NHS

free downloadable series of posters to colour in

for

#NHSMILLION

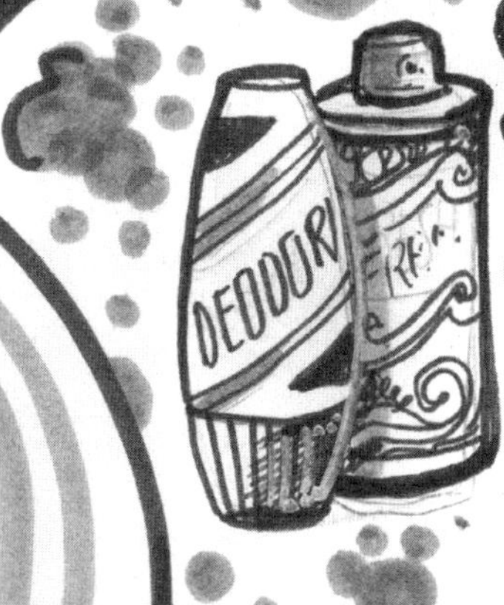

Social distance has meant a 'reduction' in DEODORANT APPLICATION

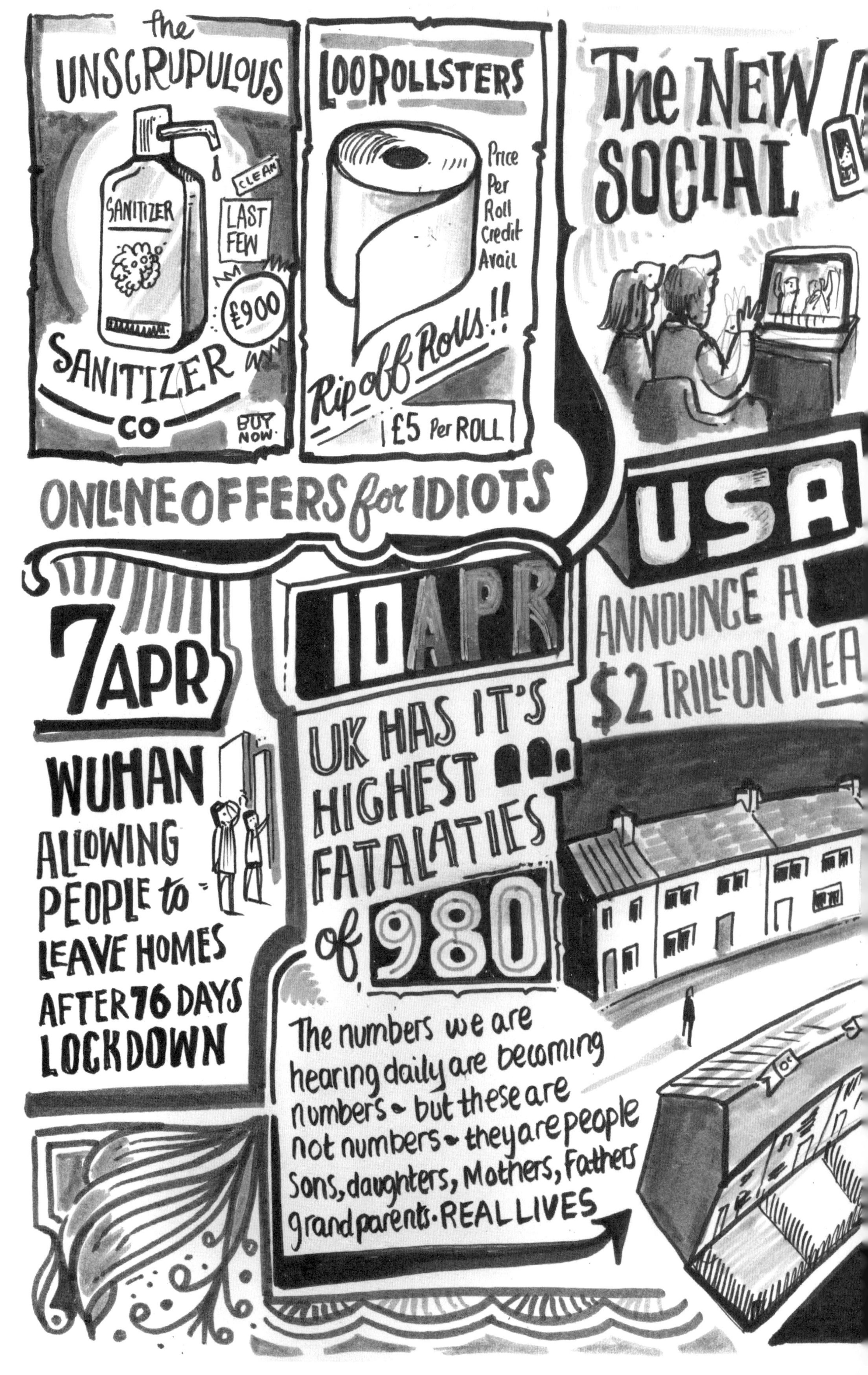
the UNSCRUPULOUS
SANITIZER
CLEAN
LAST FEW
£900
SANITIZER CO
BUY NOW.
LOO ROLLSTERS
Price Per Roll Credit Avail
Rip off Rolls!!
£5 Per ROLL
ONLINE OFFERS for IDIOTS
The NEW SOCIAL
USA
ANNOUNCE A $2 TRILLION MEA
7 APR
WUHAN ALLOWING PEOPLE to LEAVE HOMES AFTER 76 DAYS LOCKDOWN
10 APR
UK HAS IT'S HIGHEST FATALATIES of 980
The numbers we are hearing daily are becoming numbers - but these are not numbers - they are people
Sons, daughters, Mothers, Fathers grandparents. REAL LIVES

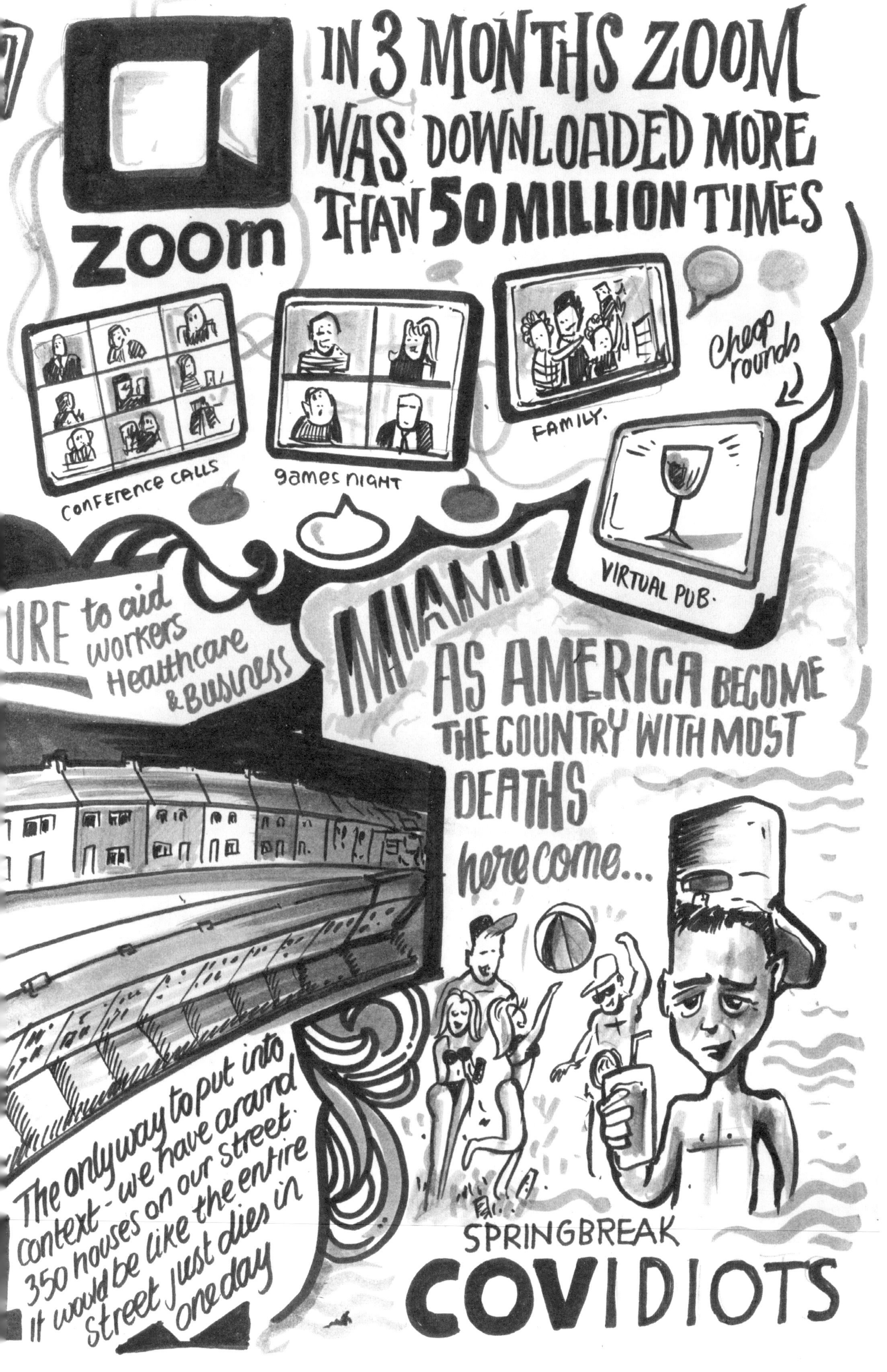

IN 3 MONTHS ZOOM WAS DOWNLOADED MORE THAN 50 MILLION TIMES
zoom
conference calls
games night
FAMILY.
Cheap rounds
VIRTUAL PUB.
URE to aid workers Healthcare & Business
MIAMI
AS AMERICA BECOME THE COUNTRY WITH MOST DEATHS
here come...
The only way to put into context - we have arand 350 houses on our street. It would be like the entire street just dies in one day
SPRINGBREAK
COVIDIOTS

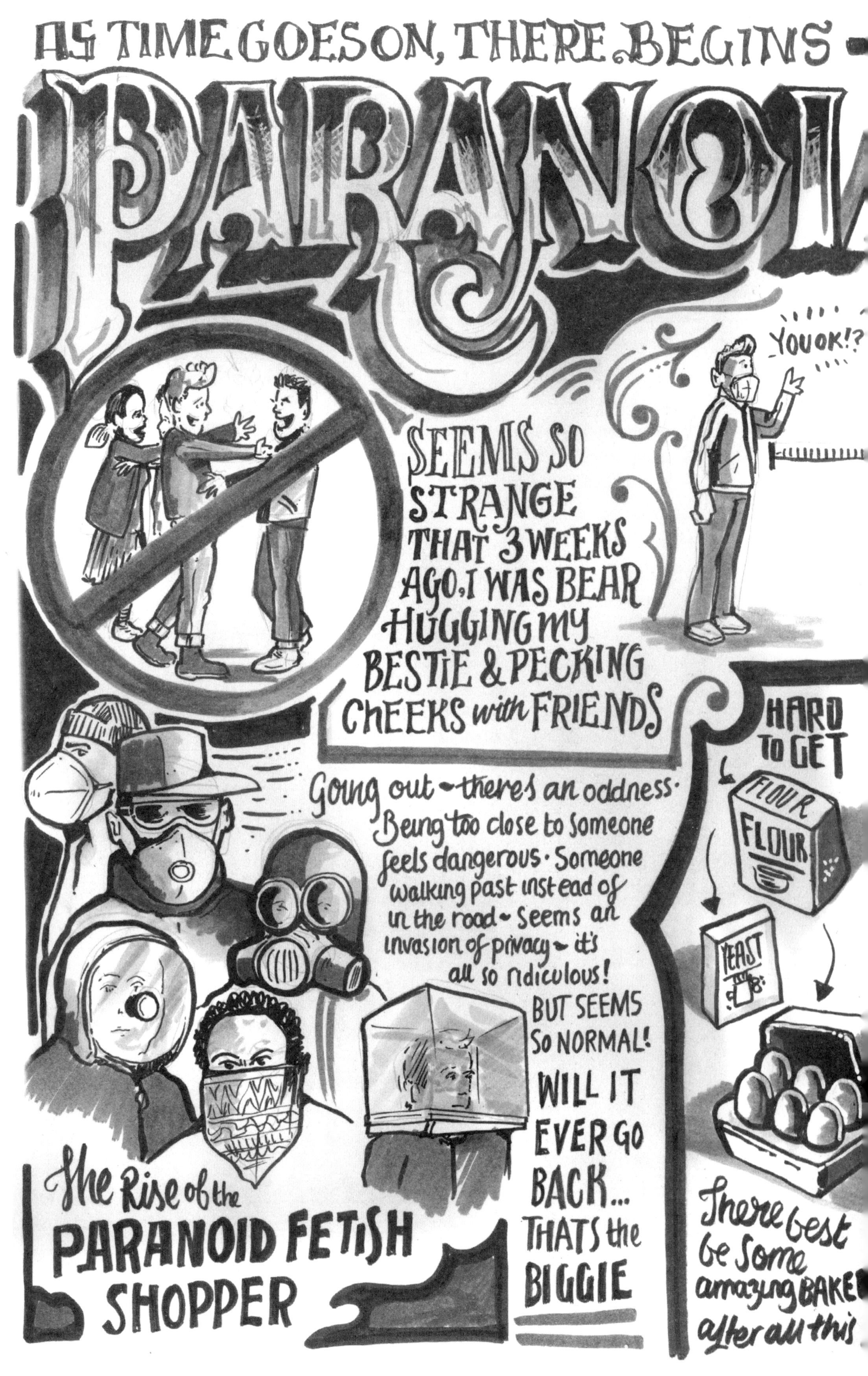
AS TIME GOES ON, THERE BEGINS -
PARANOI
YOU OK!?
SEEMS SO STRANGE THAT 3 WEEKS AGO, I WAS BEAR HUGGING MY BESTIE & PECKING CHEEKS with FRIENDS
HARD TO GET
FLOUR
FLOUR
YEAST
Going out - there's an oddness. Being too close to someone feels dangerous. Someone walking past instead of in the road - seems an invasion of privacy - it's all so ridiculous!
BUT SEEMS SO NORMAL!
WILL IT EVER GO BACK... THATS the BIGGIE
The Rise of the PARANOID FETISH SHOPPER
There best be some amazing BAKE after all this

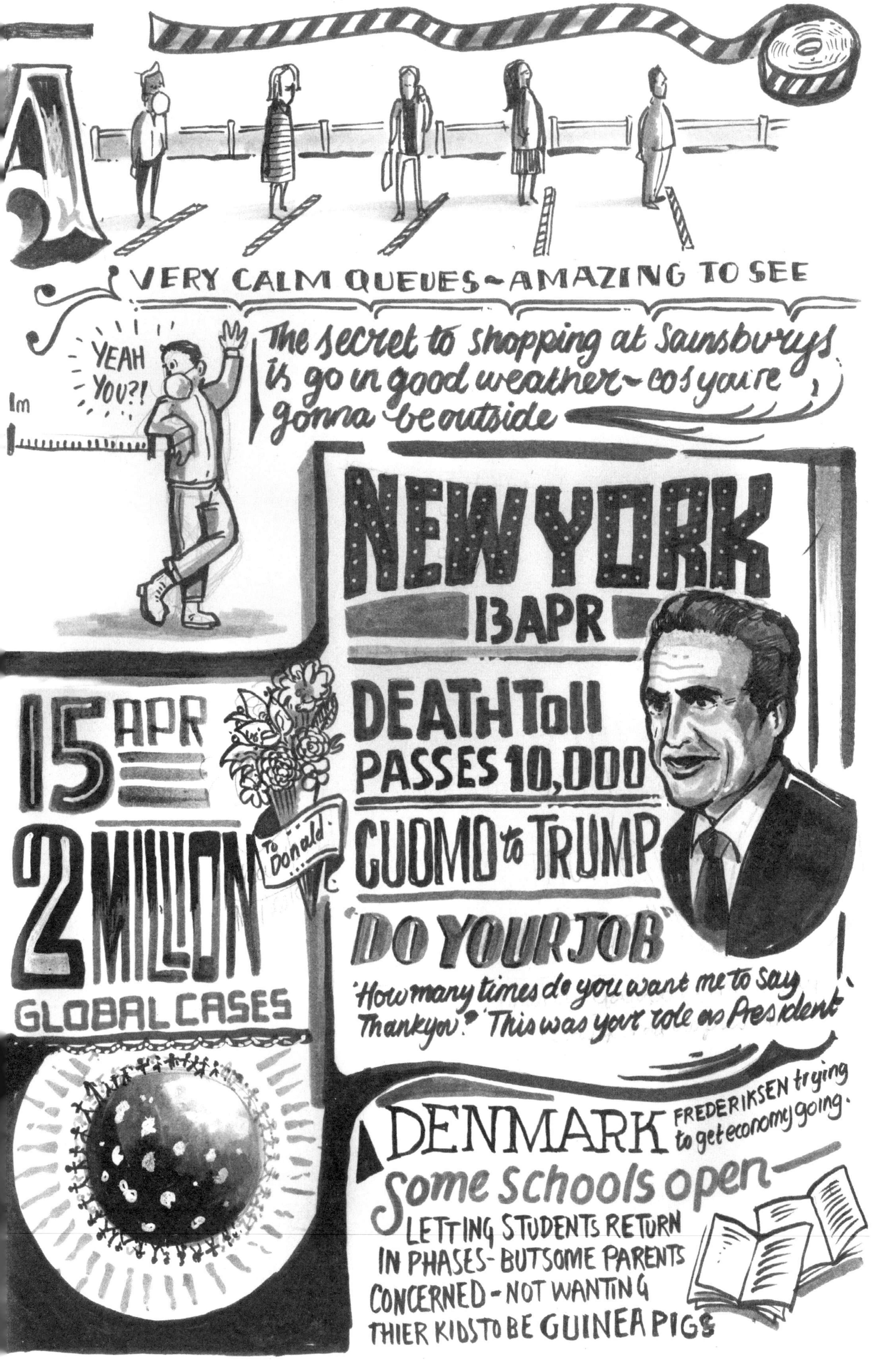
VERY CALM QUEUES ~ AMAZING TO SEE
YEAH YOU?!
1m
The secret to shopping at Sainsburys is go in good weather ~ cos you're gonna be outside
NEW YORK
13 APR
DEATH Toll PASSES 10,000
CUOMO to TRUMP
"DO YOUR JOB"
'How many times do you want me to say Thankyou?' 'This was your role as President'
15 APR
2 MILLION
GLOBAL CASES
To Donald
DENMARK
FREDERIKSEN trying to get economy going.
Some Schools open
LETTING STUDENTS RETURN IN PHASES - BUT SOME PARENTS CONCERNED - NOT WANTING THIER KIDS TO BE GUINEA PIGS

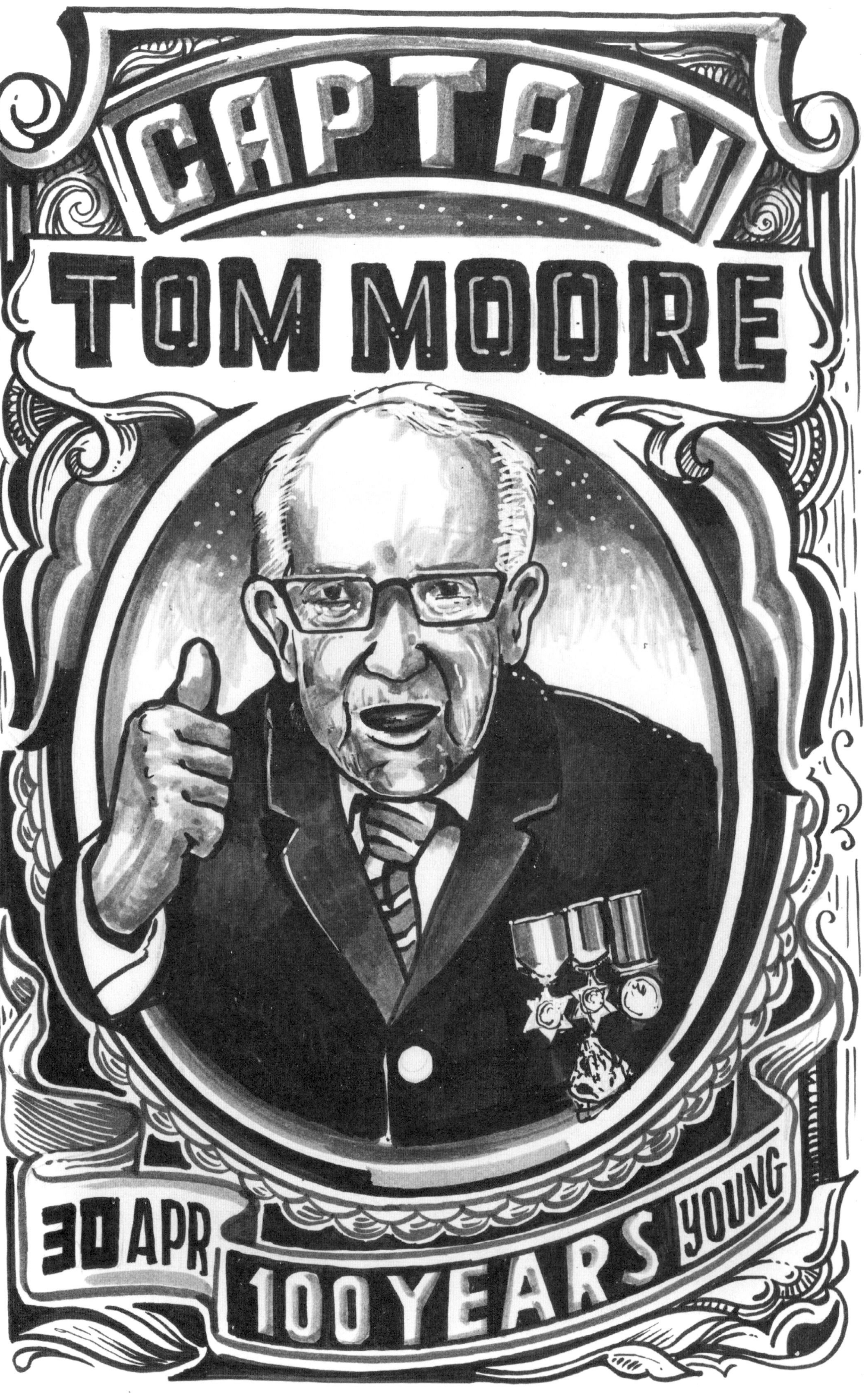
CAPTAIN
TOM MOORE
30 APR
100 YEARS
YOUNG

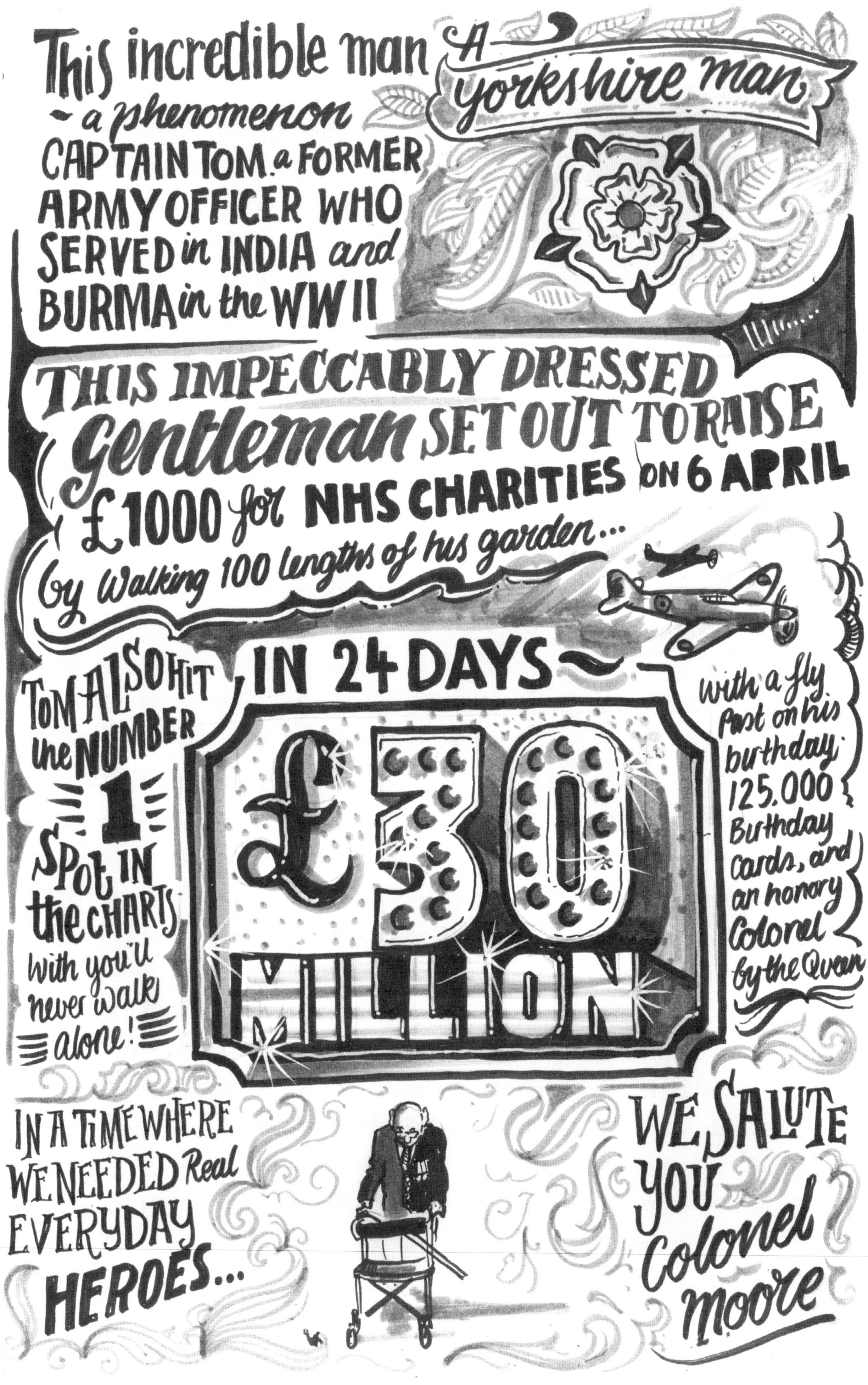
This incredible man
a phenomenon
CAPTAIN TOM a FORMER ARMY OFFICER WHO SERVED in INDIA and BURMA in the WW II
A yorkshire man
THIS IMPECCABLY DRESSED gentleman SET OUT TO RAISE £1000 for NHS CHARITIES ON 6 APRIL
by Walking 100 lengths of his garden...
IN 24 DAYS
£30 MILLION
TOM ALSO HIT the NUMBER 1 SPOT IN the CHARTS
with you'll never walk alone!
with a fly Past on his birthday. 125.000 Birthday cards, and an honory Colonel by the Queen
IN A TIME WHERE WE NEEDED Real EVERYDAY HEROES...
WE SALUTE YOU Colonel Moore

FILM RELEASE TIMINGS ARE MOVE FORWARD

AND SHOWN ONLINE FOR AROUND £15. WHICH INITIALLY SEEMS HIGH. TILL YOU WORK THAT IS THE COST of 1 TICKET AT THE CINEMA (+ homemade icecream & popcorn!)

POPCORN HOME

+ EVERYONES AT HOME.

TROLLS MADE $100 million IN 3 WEEKS from DIGITAL RENTAL

LITERALLY, A CAPTIVE AUDIENCE

MAKING FRESH PASTA FROM JUST SEMOLINA & WATER

NOM NOM

UK EXTENDS LOCKDOWN by A FURTHER 3 WEEKS 16th

NO SKOOL

AS ALL SCHOOLS HAVE CLOSED. THE PARENTS ARE NOW THE NEW TEACHERS

+ WHEN SOME PARENTS TRY & GRASP TRIGONOMETRY, SCIENCE & HISTORY, LONG FORGOTTEN. AS WELL AS REFEREEING SIBLING BATTLES & WORKING FROM HOME

$+$ $-$ 6 $\times$ $\times$ 4 $\div$ 1 3 $=$ 5 7

$\cdot 9$ 16

15

$\cdot 529$

$333 \cdot 3$

SARDINE FAMILY OF FIVE

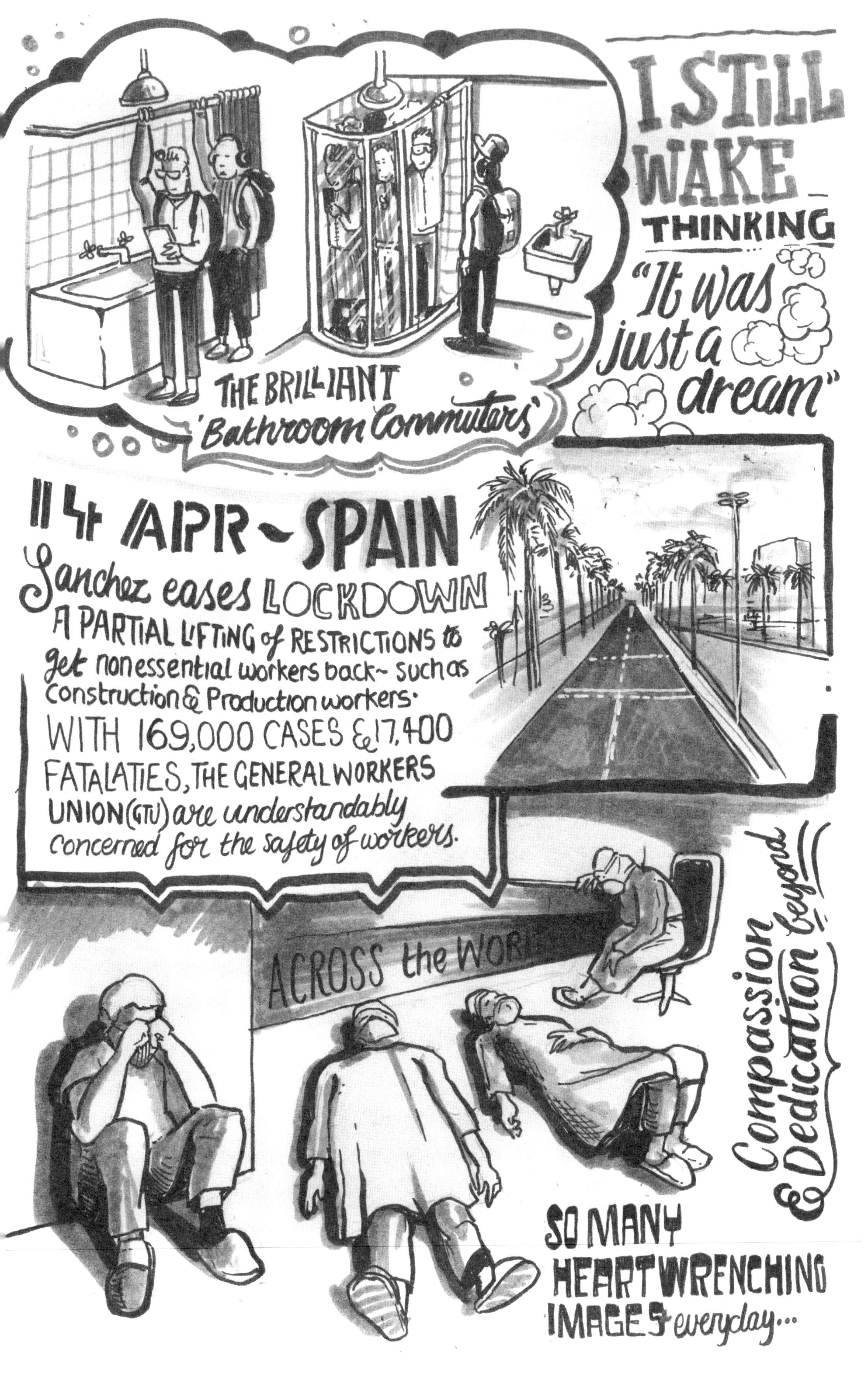

THE BRILLIANT
'Bathroom Commuters'
I STILL WAKE THINKING
"It was just a dream"
14 APR ~ SPAIN
Sanchez eases LOCKDOWN
A PARTIAL LIFTING of RESTRICTIONS to get nonessential workers back~ such as construction & Production workers.
WITH 169,000 CASES & 17,400 FATALATIES, THE GENERAL WORKERS UNION (GTU) are understandably concerned for the safety of workers.
ACROSS the
Compassion & Dedication beyond
SO MANY HEARTWRENCHING IMAGES everyday...

HAVING HAD A MULTITUDE of JOBS FROM A DELIVERY DRIVER & POSTMAN for the ROYAL MAIL

TO CLEANING COUNCIL OFFICES & CABINS ON A CRUISESHIP

I have A SOFT SPOT

UNSUNG HEROES

Thankyou.

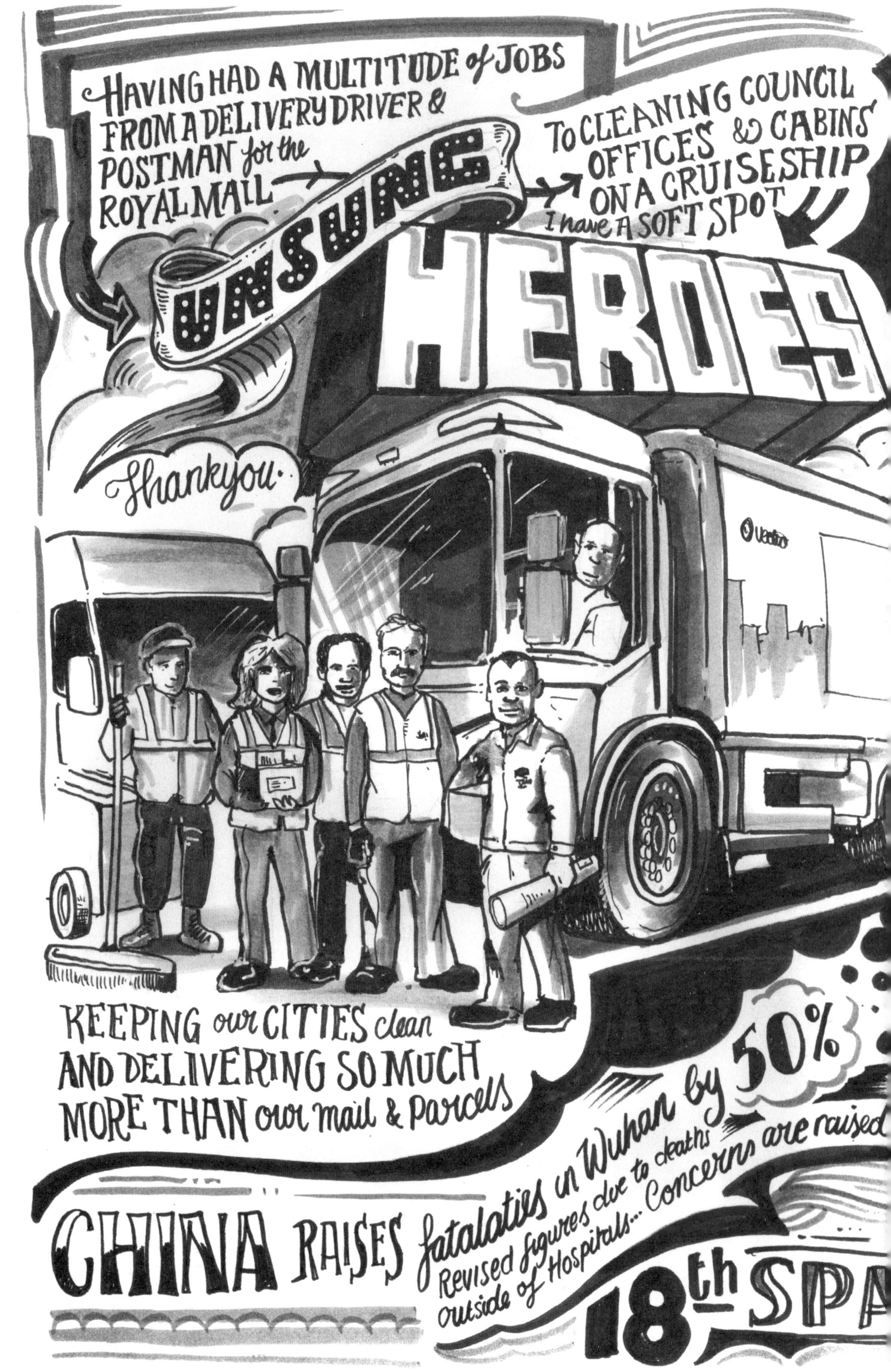

KEEPING our CITIES clean AND DELIVERING SO MUCH MORE THAN our mail & parcels

CHINA RAISES fatalaties in Wuhan by 50%

Revised figures due to deaths outside of Hospitals... Concerns are raised

18th SPA

APR 15

2 Million CASES GLOBALLY

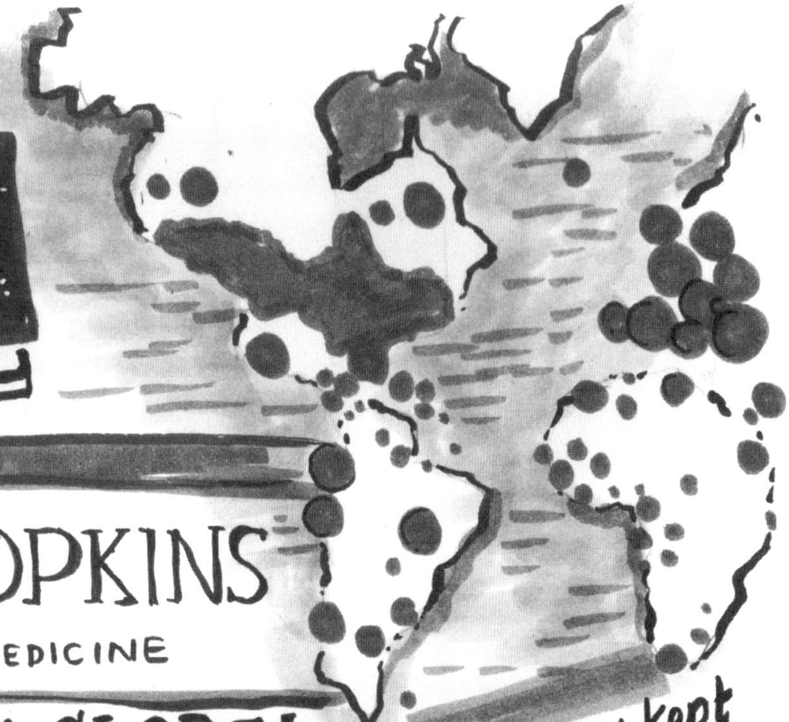

JOHNS HOPKINS
UNIVERSITY of MEDICINE

EXPERTS in GLOBAL PUBLIC HEALTH, INFECTIOUS DISEASE and emergency preparedness.

These guys kept us informed of all the facts and figures daily ☆

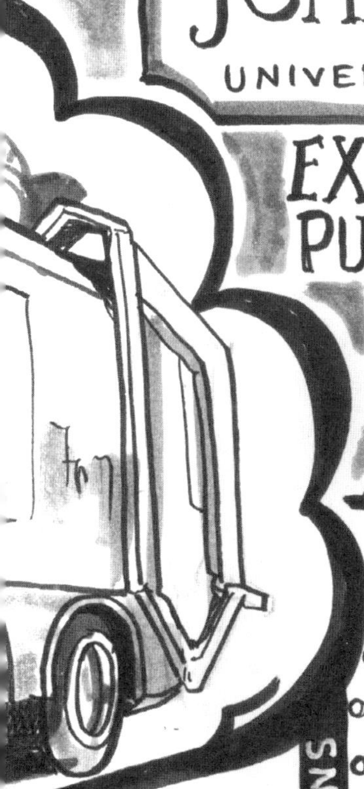

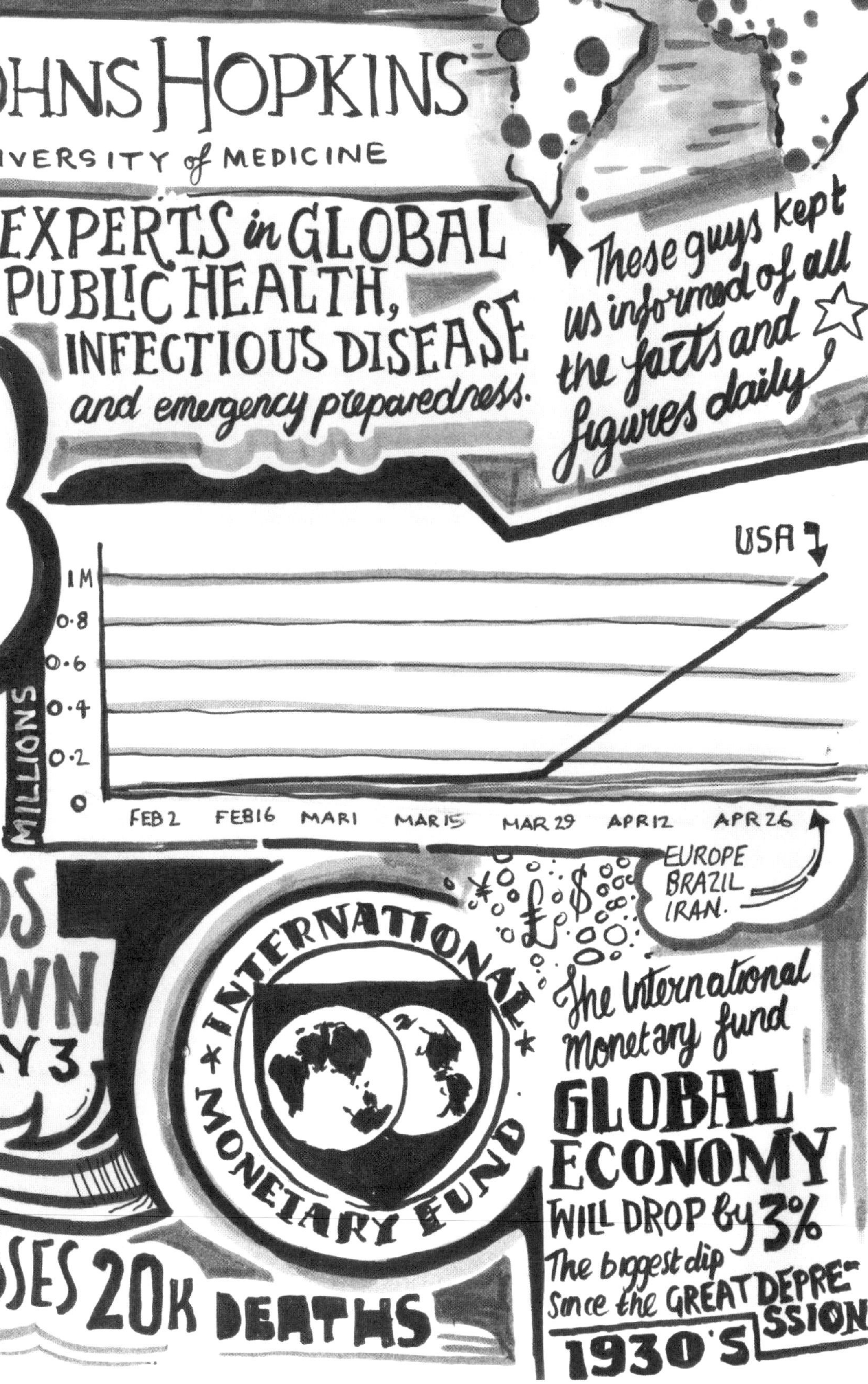
USA
MILLIONS
1M
0.8
0.6
0.4
0.2
0
FEB 2
FEB 16
MAR 1
MAR 15
MAR 29
APR 12
APR 26
EUROPE
BRAZIL
IRAN.

14 APRIL
INDIA EXTENDS LOCKDOWN TILL MAY 3

INTERNATIONAL MONETARY FUND

The International Monetary fund
GLOBAL ECONOMY
WILL DROP by 3%
The biggest dip since the GREAT DEPRESSION 1930'S

N PASSES 20K DEATHS

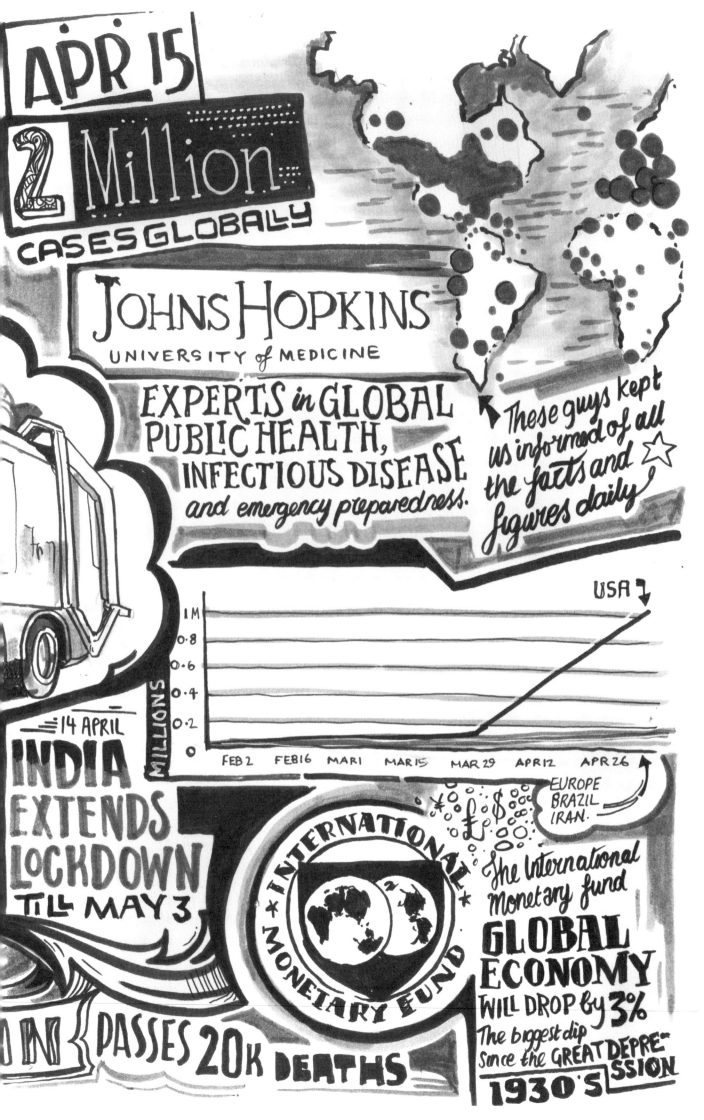

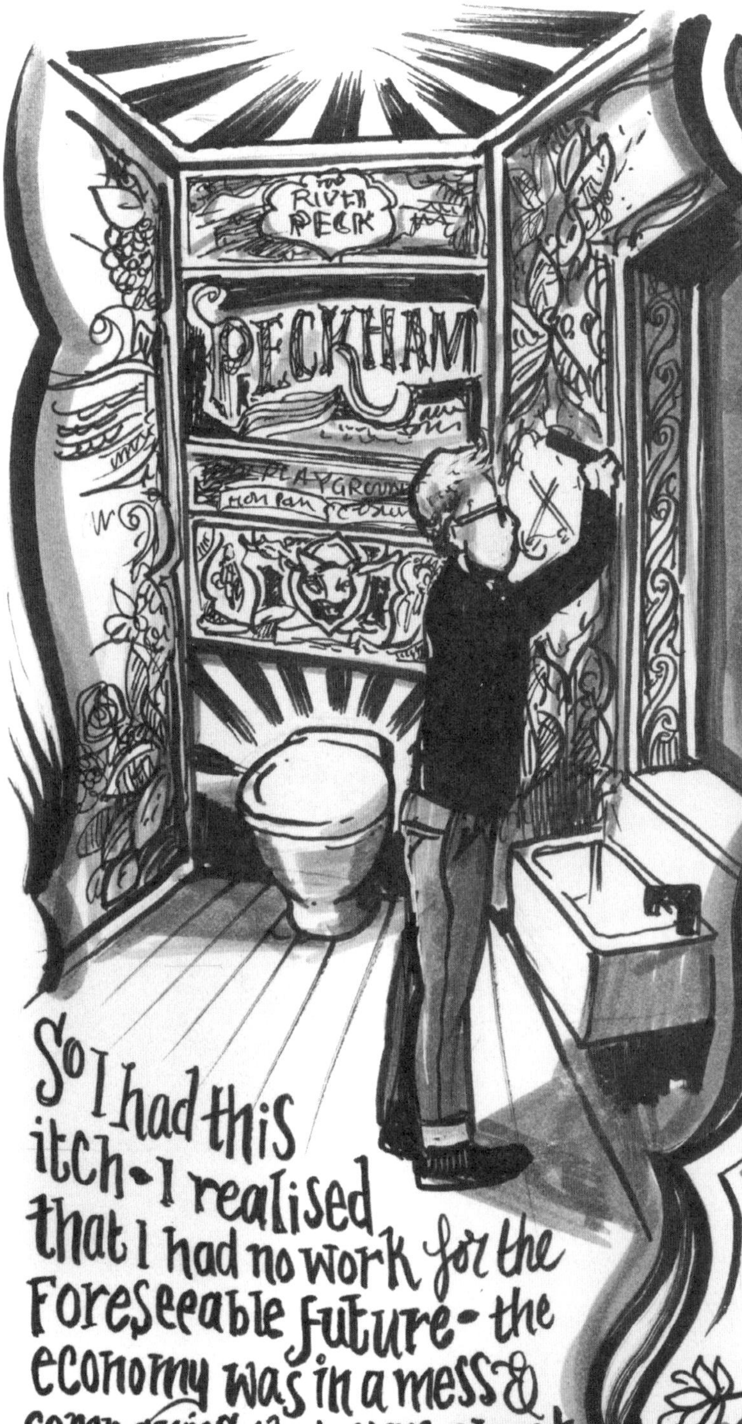
RIVER PECK
PECKHAM
PLAYGROUND

So I had this itch. I realised that I had no work for the foreseeable future – the economy was in a mess & companies that were almost clients would have a long process to get any sense of normality.

AND I really wanted to INK!

So it was a joy when Hels said I can ink the downstairs loo!

I have to say of all the jobs (!) I have done, this was by far the most time consuming and difficult to do. BUT OH WHAT A LOO!

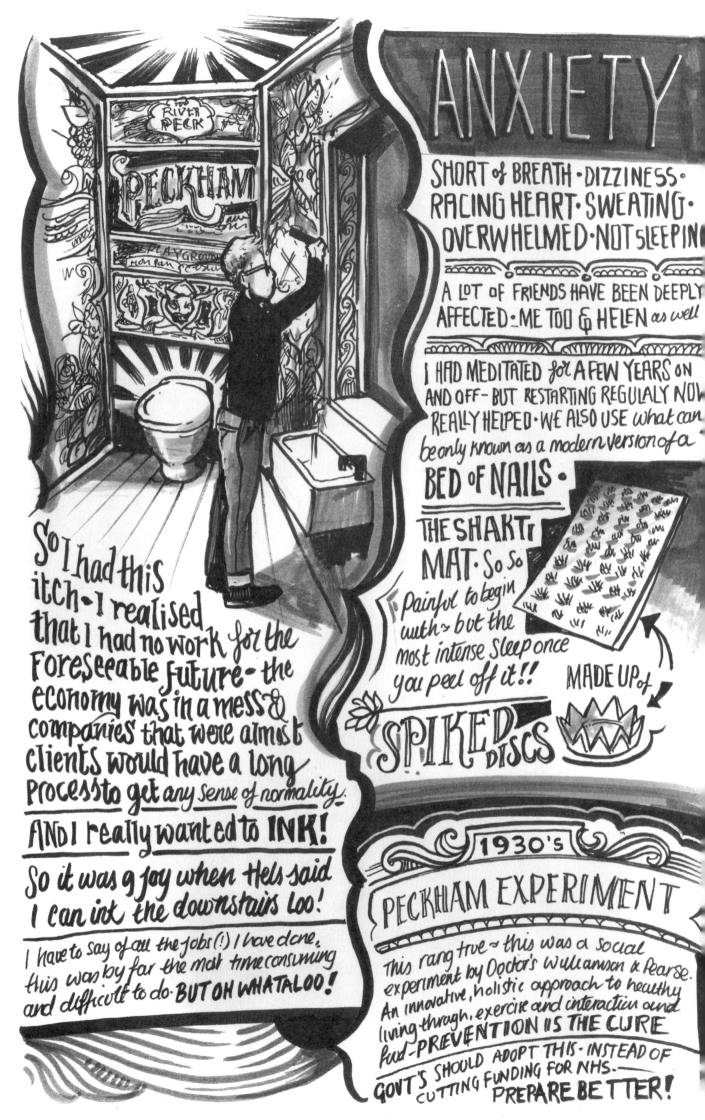

ANXIETY

SHORT of BREATH • DIZZINESS • RACING HEART • SWEATING • OVERWHELMED • NOT SLEEPING

A LOT OF FRIENDS HAVE BEEN DEEPLY AFFECTED – ME TOO & HELEN as well

I HAD MEDITATED for A FEW YEARS ON AND OFF – BUT RESTARTING REGULALY NOW REALLY HELPED • WE ALSO USE what can be only known as a modern version of a BED OF NAILS •

THE SHAKTI MAT • So So painful to begin with ~ but the most intense sleep once you peel off it!!

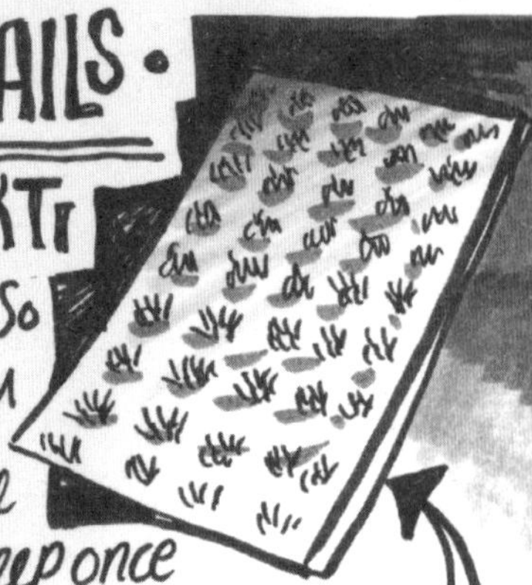

MADE UP of SPIKED DISCS

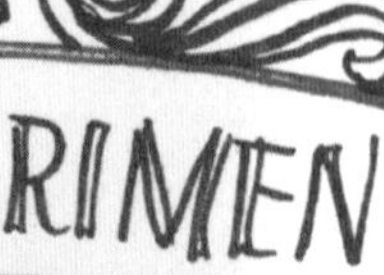

1930's PECKHAM EXPERIMENT

This rang true ~ this was a social experiment by Doctor's Williamson & Pearse. An innovative, holistic approach to healthy living through exercise and interaction and food – PREVENTION IS THE CURE

GOVT'S SHOULD ADOPT THIS – INSTEAD OF CUTTING FUNDING FOR NHS. — PREPARE BETTER!

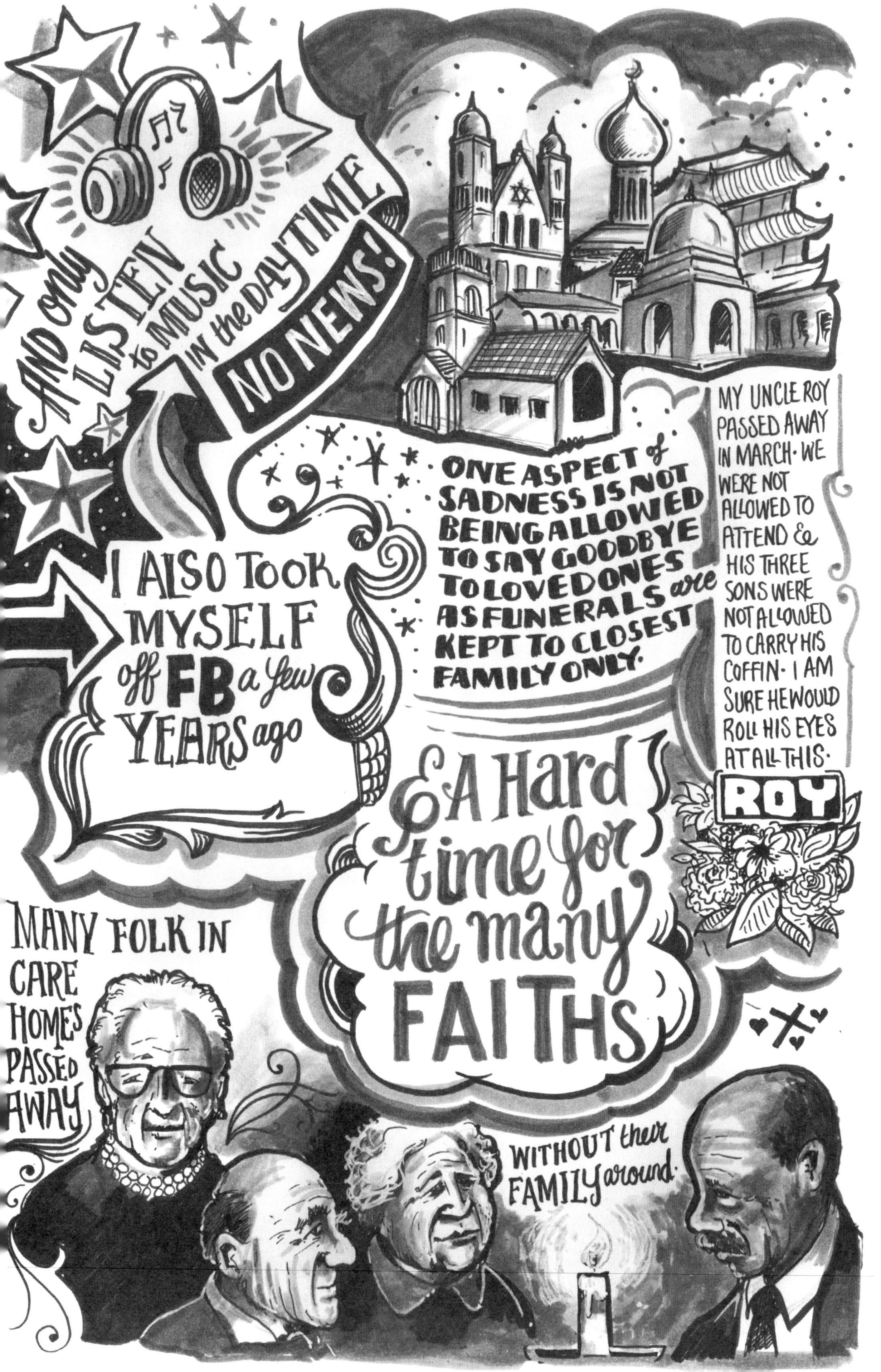

AND only LISTEN to MUSIC in the DAYTIME
NO NEWS!
I ALSO TOOK MYSELF off FB a few YEARS ago
ONE ASPECT of SADNESS IS NOT BEING ALLOWED TO SAY GOODBYE TO LOVED ONES AS FUNERALS are KEPT TO CLOSEST FAMILY ONLY.
MY UNCLE ROY PASSED AWAY IN MARCH. WE WERE NOT ALLOWED TO ATTEND & HIS THREE SONS WERE NOT ALLOWED TO CARRY HIS COFFIN. I AM SURE HE WOULD ROLL HIS EYES AT ALL THIS.
ROY
A Hard time for the many FAITHS
MANY FOLK IN CARE HOMES PASSED AWAY
WITHOUT their FAMILY around.

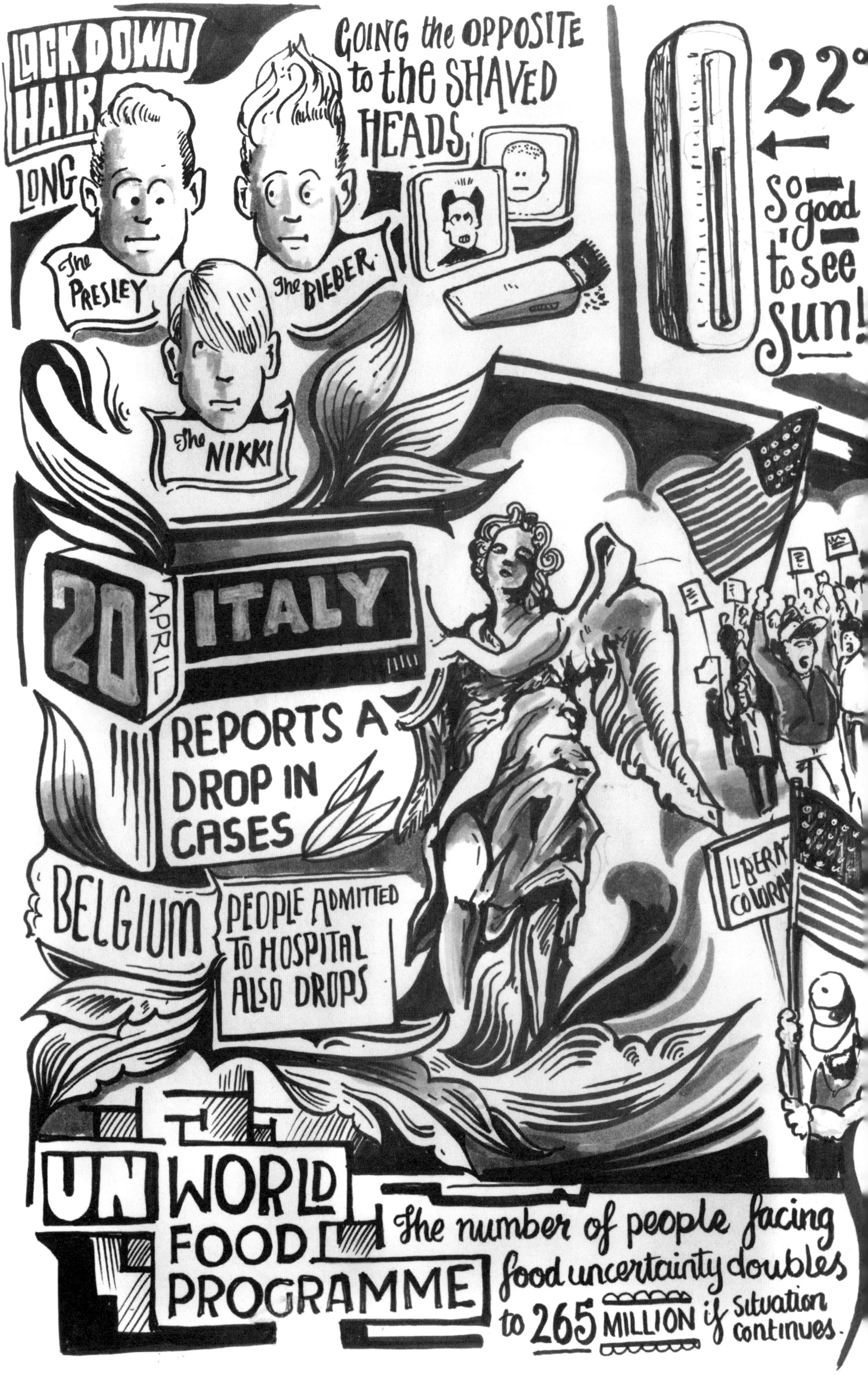

LOCKDOWN HAIR
LONG
GOING the OPPOSITE to the SHAVED HEADS
The PRESLEY
The BIEBER
The NIKKI
22°
So good to see sun!
20 APRIL
ITALY
REPORTS A DROP IN CASES
BELGIUM
PEOPLE ADMITTED TO HOSPITAL ALSO DROPS
UN WORLD FOOD PROGRAMME
The number of people facing food uncertainty doubles to 265 MILLION if situation continues.

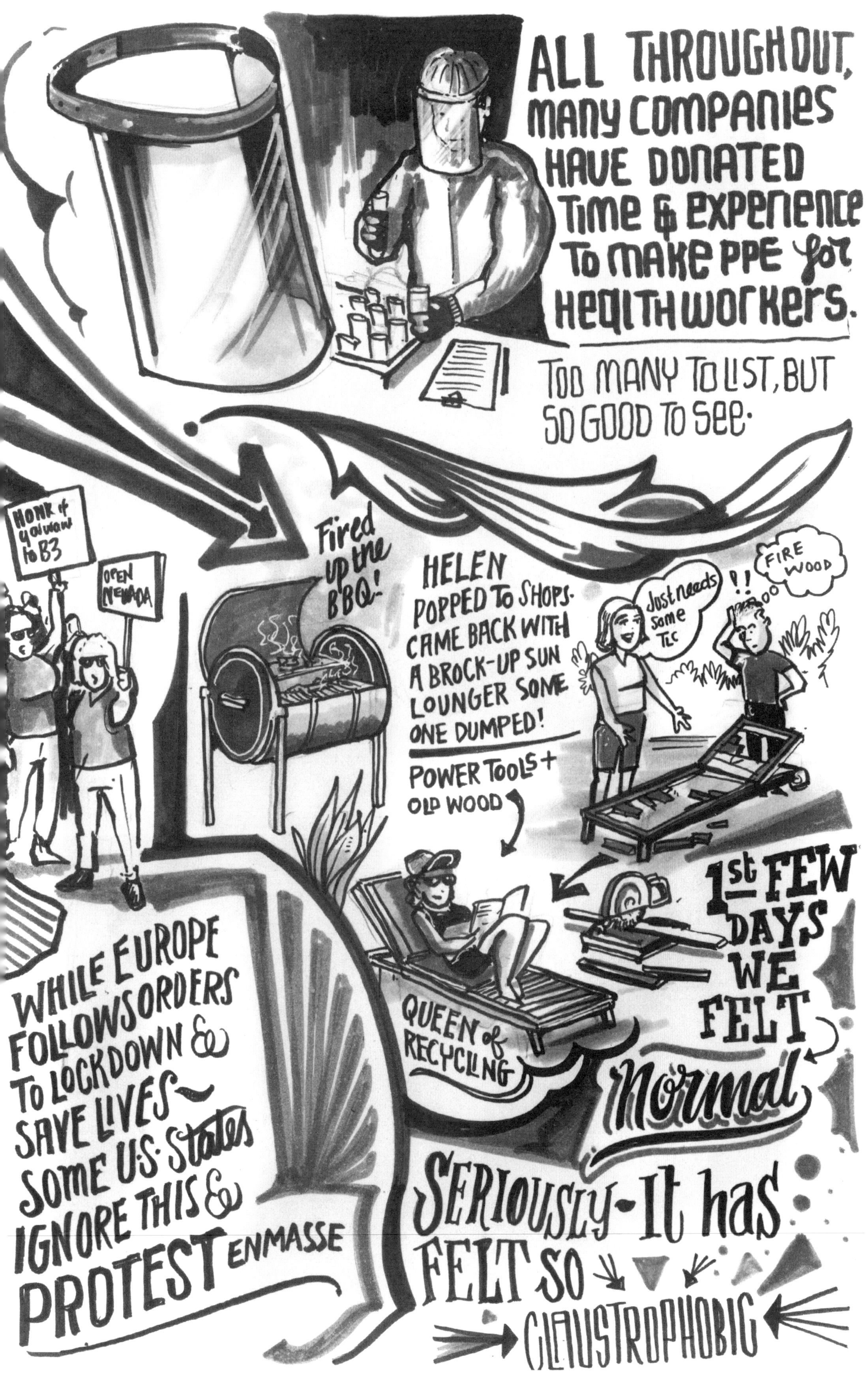
ALL THROUGHOUT, MANY COMPANIES HAVE DONATED TIME & EXPERIENCE TO MAKE PPE for HEALTH WORKERS.
TOO MANY TO LIST, BUT SO GOOD TO SEE.
HONK if you want to B3
OPEN NEVADA
Fired up the BBQ!
HELEN POPPED TO SHOPS. CAME BACK WITH A BROCK-UP SUN LOUNGER SOME ONE DUMPED!
Just needs some TLC
!!
FIRE WOOD
POWER TOOLS + OLD WOOD
QUEEN of RECYCLING
1st FEW DAYS WE FELT normal
WHILE EUROPE FOLLOWS ORDERS TO LOCKDOWN & SAVE LIVES – SOME U.S. States IGNORE THIS & PROTEST EN MASSE
SERIOUSLY – It has FELT SO CLAUSTROPHOBIC

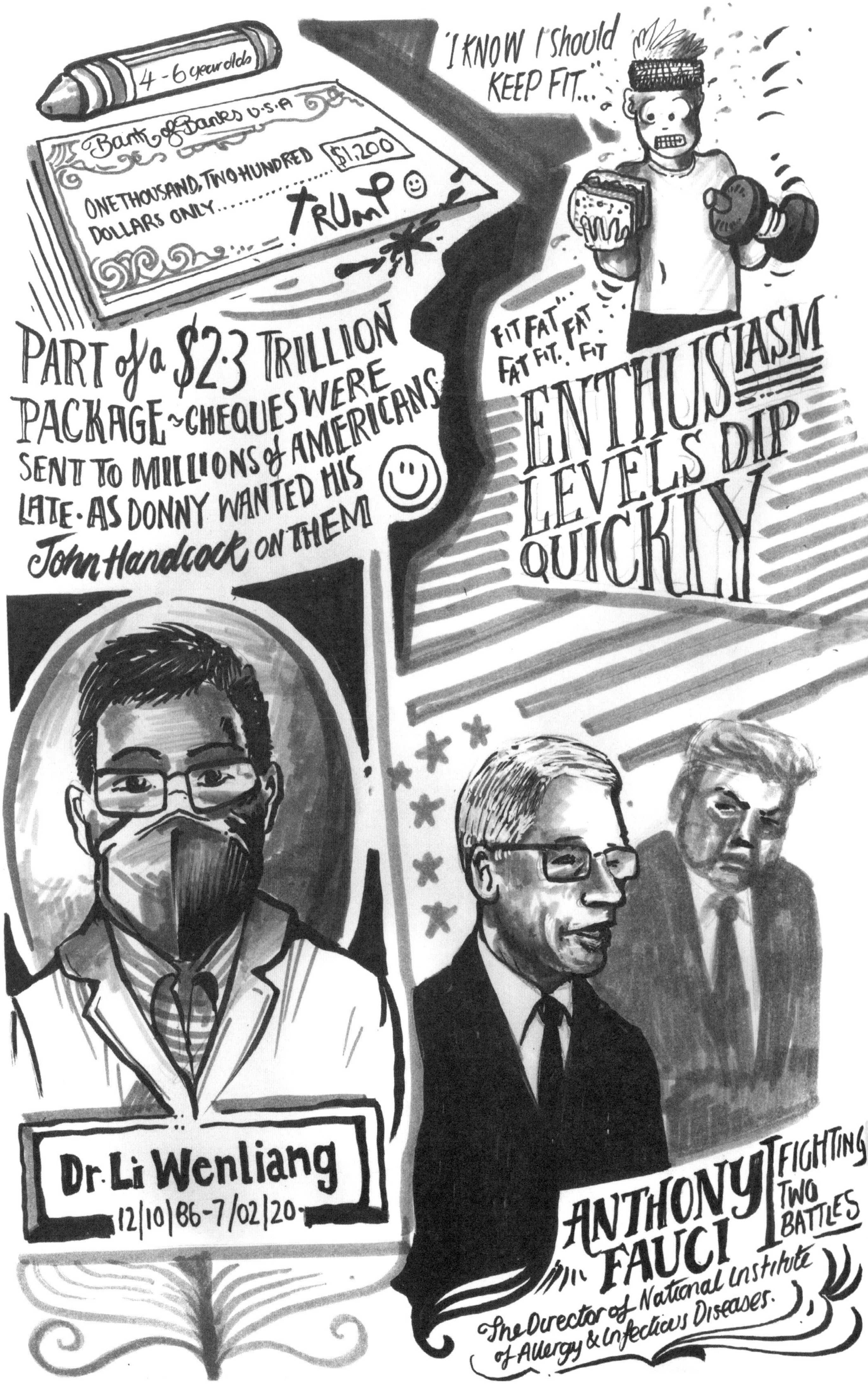
4-6 year olds
Bank of Banks U.S.A
$1,200
ONE THOUSAND, TWO HUNDRED
DOLLARS ONLY
TRUMP
PART of a $2.3 TRILLION PACKAGE ~ CHEQUES WERE SENT TO MILLIONS of AMERICANS LATE. AS DONNY WANTED HIS John Handcock ON THEM
'I KNOW I should KEEP FIT...'
FIT FAT... FAT FIT. FAT FIT
ENTHUSIASM LEVELS DIP QUICKLY
Dr. Li Wenliang
12/10/86-7/02/20
ANTHONY FAUCI
FIGHTING TWO BATTLES
The Director of National Institute of Allergy & Infectious Diseases.

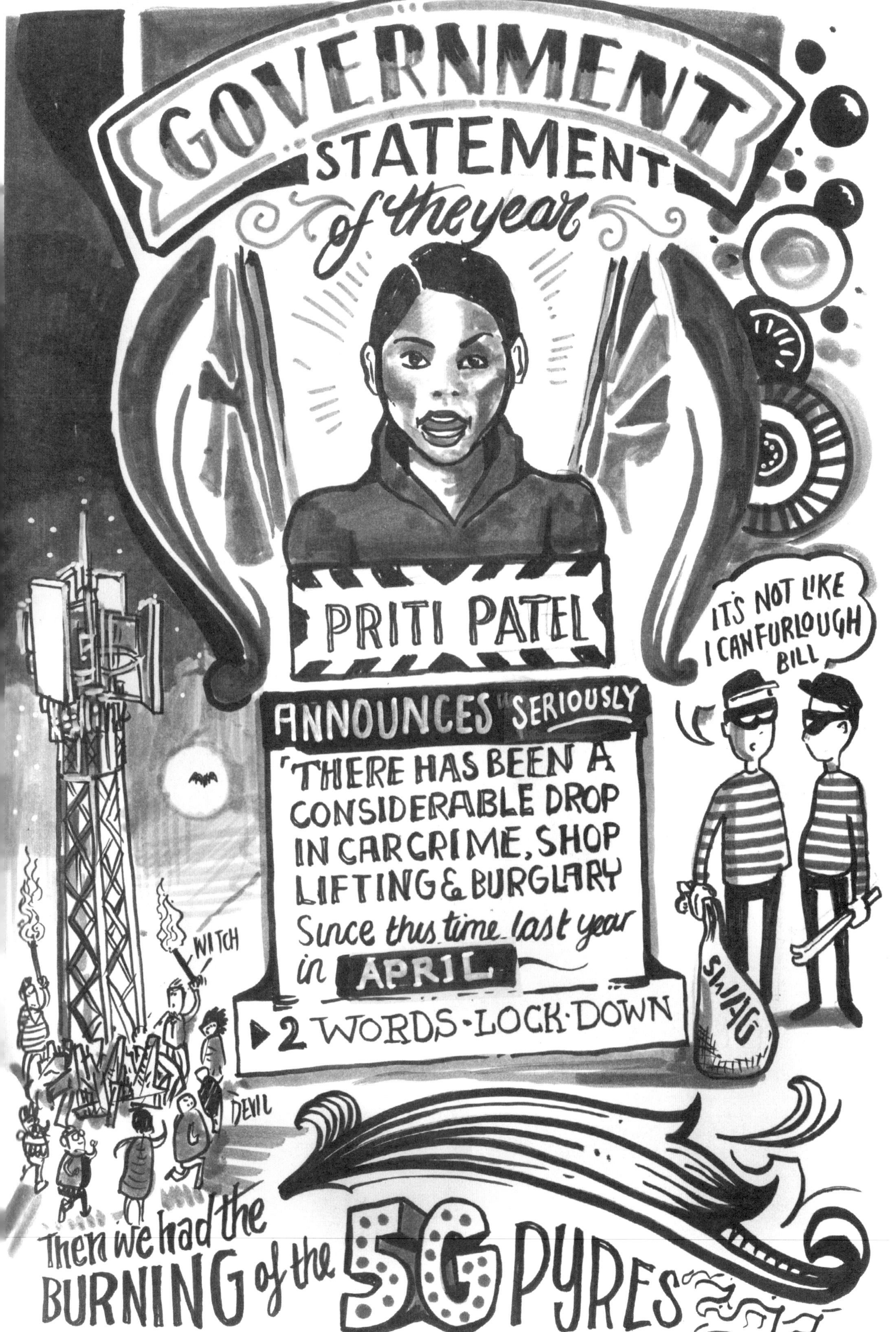

GOVERNMENT STATEMENT of the year
PRITI PATEL
ANNOUNCES "SERIOUSLY
"THERE HAS BEEN A CONSIDERABLE DROP IN CAR CRIME, SHOP LIFTING & BURGLARY Since this time last year in APRIL
2 WORDS - LOCK - DOWN
IT'S NOT LIKE I CAN FURLOUGH BILL
SWAG
WITCH
DEVIL
Then we had the BURNING of the 5G PYRES

LETS TALK ABOUT P-P-E

LETS TALK ABOUT YOU & ME

ALL THE GOOD THINGS & THE BAD THINGS THAT WE SEE.

PERSONAL PROTECTIVE EQUIPMENT

MOST PEOPLE HAD NEVER HEARD OF PPE; UP UNTIL 2 MONTHS AGO. IT HAS BECOME NOW PART of OUR DAILY CONVERSATIONS. PPE is A BASIC REQUIREMENT & NEED for THOSE WORKING IN THE FRONTLINE of any EMERGENCY & NON EMERGENCY SITUATION.

A BASIC REQUIREMENT to protect the health of those

WHO LOOK AFTER OTHERS

ALL 400,000 GOWNS FAIL UK STANDARDS

UK EMERGENCY STOCKPILE INC PPE CUT BY 40% IN 6 YEARS

Many companies in the UK offered their services to make PPE ~ BUT THE GOV IGNORED THESE

SO THESE companies SHIPPED THEIR EQUIPMENT & SUPPLIES ABROAD

SO, ON APRIL 17 - the GOV ORDER PPE from TURKEY. BUT did they? somebody did - or didnt... who knows. IT WAS SUPPOSED TO BE DELIVERED ON 19th APR.

FINALLY ARRIVES ON 22ND APRIL.

5 WEEKS after the → LOCKDOWN

TO BE CHECKED.

7 MAY

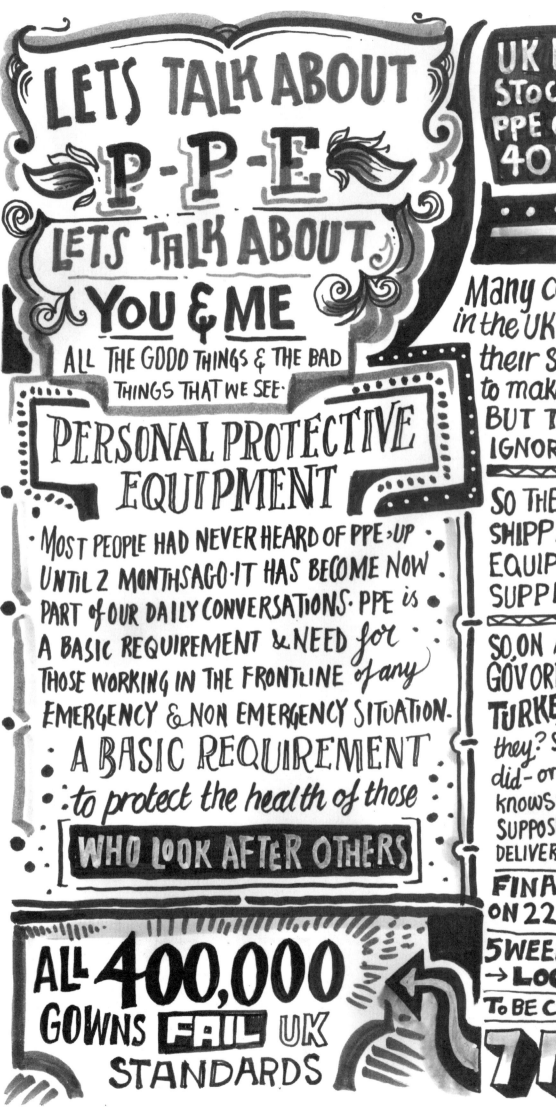

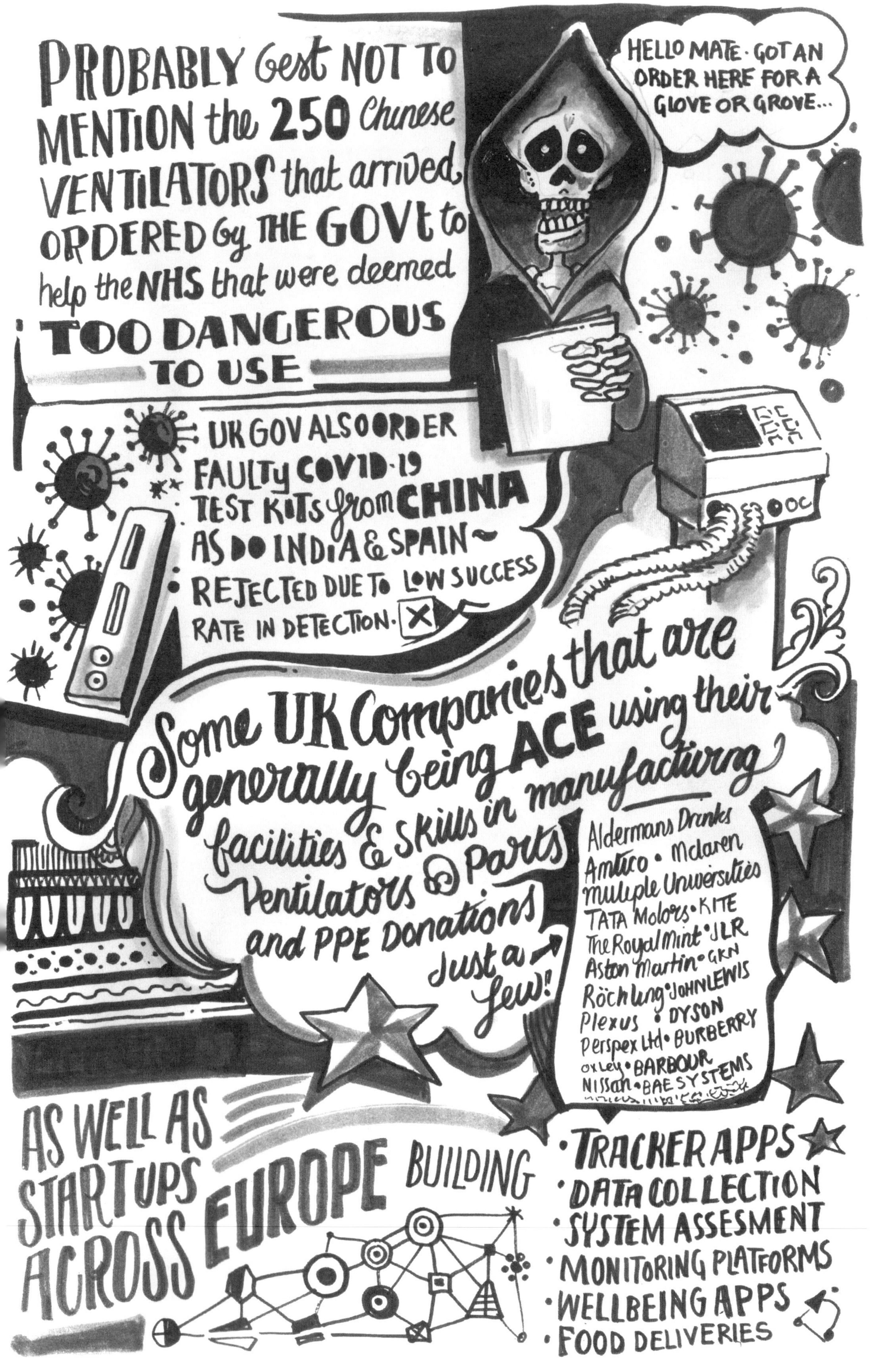
PROBABLY best NOT TO MENTION the 250 Chinese VENTILATORS that arrived, ORDERED by THE GOVt to help the NHS that were deemed TOO DANGEROUS TO USE
HELLO MATE · GOT AN ORDER HERE FOR A GLOVE OR GROVE...
UK GOV ALSO ORDER FAULTY COVID-19 TEST KITS from CHINA AS DO INDIA & SPAIN ~ REJECTED DUE TO LOW SUCCESS RATE IN DETECTION. ☒
Some UK Companies that are generally being ACE using their facilities & skills in manufacturing Ventilators & Parts and PPE Donations
Just a few!
Aldermans Drinks
Amtico • Mclaren
multiple Universities
TATA Motors • KITE
The Royal Mint • JLR
Aston Martin • GKN
Röchling • JOHN LEWIS
Plexus • DYSON
Perspex Ltd • BURBERRY
Oxley • BARBOUR
NISSAN • BAE SYSTEMS
AS WELL AS STARTUPS ACROSS EUROPE BUILDING
• TRACKER APPS
• DATA COLLECTION
• SYSTEM ASSESMENT
• MONITORING PLATFORMS
• WELLBEING APPS
• FOOD DELIVERIES

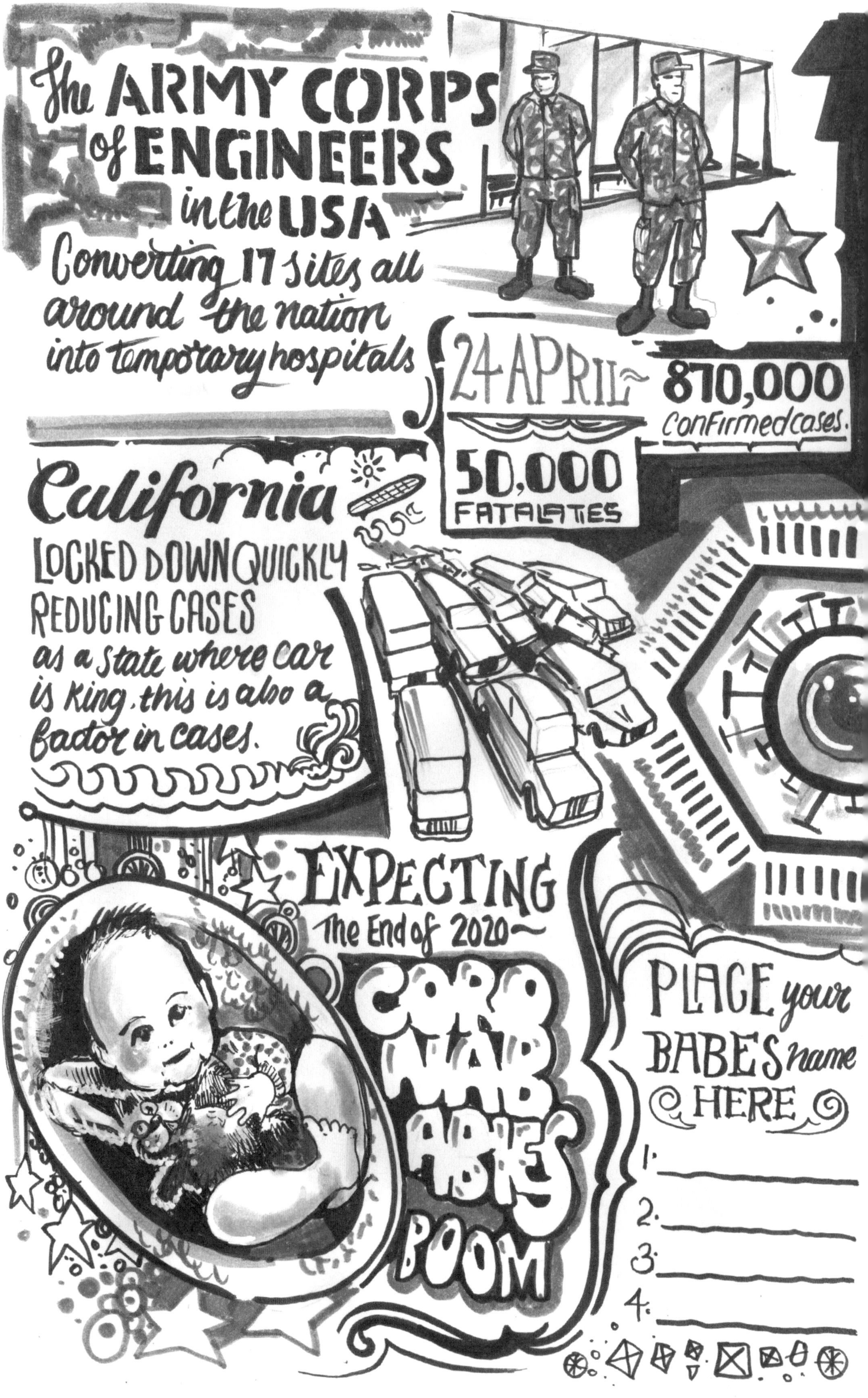

The ARMY CORPS of ENGINEERS in the USA
Converting 17 sites all around the nation into temporary hospitals
24 APRIL
870,000 Confirmed cases.
50,000 FATALATIES
California
LOCKED DOWN QUICKLY REDUCING CASES
as a state where car is king, this is also a factor in cases.
EXPECTING The End of 2020
CORONA BABIES BOOM
PLACE your BABES name HERE
1.
2.
3.
4.

I GUESS THIS is A DRY RUN to RETIRING as a COUPLE ~ IF YOU CAN STILL LAUGH after 2 MONTHS LOCKED IN ~ Surely a good sign...

Some thing secret

EXTRAMARITAL DATING APPs (there are such things) REPORT AN INCREASE of 70%

NOT SURE HOW THIS WORKS A LA SOCIAL DISTANCING

A harrowing aspect to the LOCKDOWN

DOMESTIC ABUSE HELPLINES SEE A RISE of 25%

BE KIND

my friend in NICE told me, she has a friend who has had CHRONIC BACKPAIN for years. AGONISING. when LOCKDOWN happened in PARIS. He went back to his parents. on 3 WEEKS of NOT COMMUTING 2 HOURS A DAY~ WORKING AT HOME + MUMS HOME COOKING NO PAIN

30th APRIL

Some stats.

FRENCH GDP DROPS by 5.8%

ITALY also follows at -4.7%

Spain records lowest daily death toll → FATALATIES of 24,543

GERMANY unemployed raises by 373,000 to 2.64M

USA -NUMBER of CASES TOP **1.M** - A ⅓ of all → GLOBAL INFECTIONS AS DEATHS RATE RISES to **57,000**

MILLION INFECTED
209,000 DEATHS
+ 885,000 Recoveries

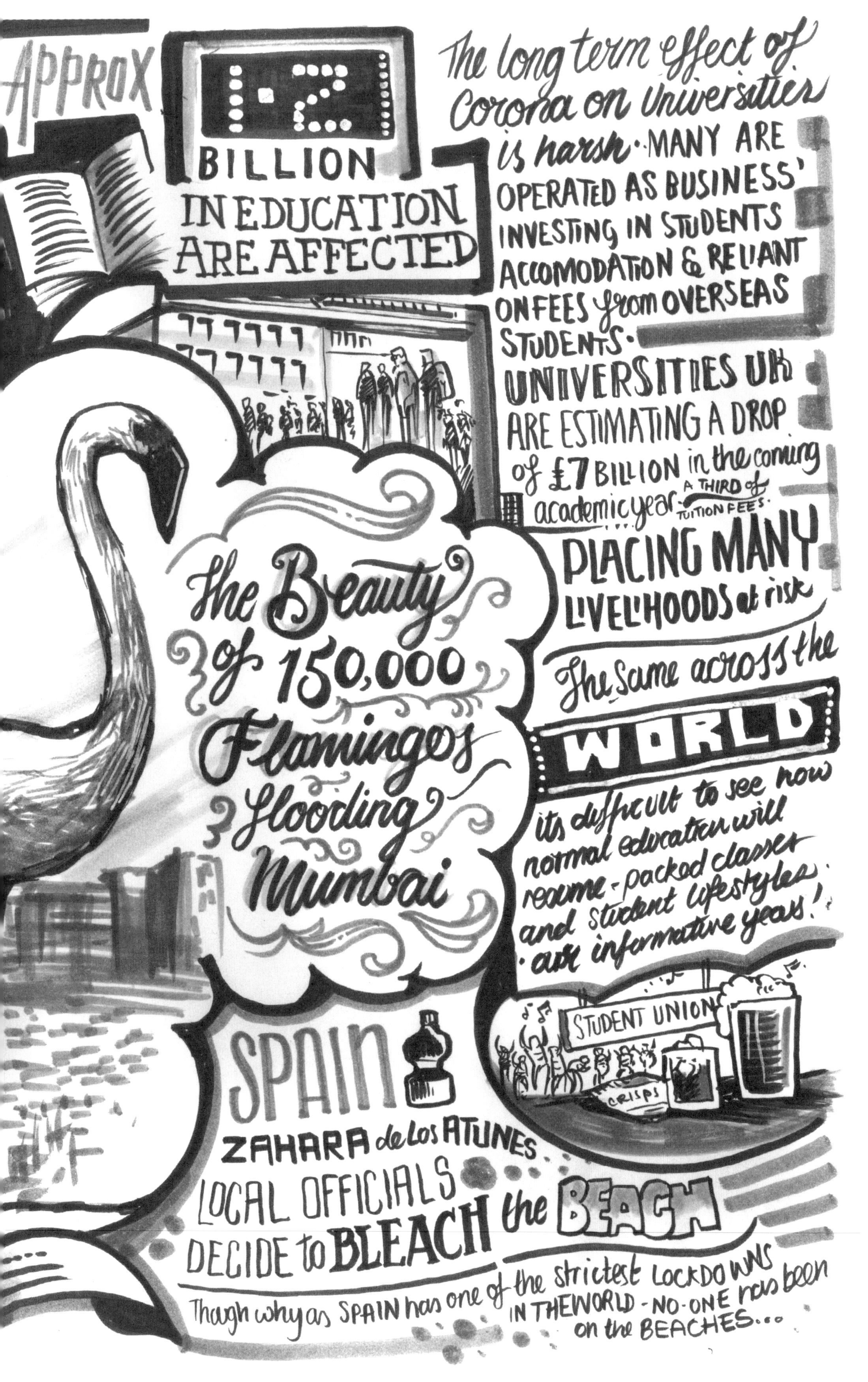

APPROX
1.2
BILLION
IN EDUCATION ARE AFFECTED
The long term effect of Corona on Universities is harsh. MANY ARE OPERATED AS BUSINESS' INVESTING IN STUDENTS ACCOMODATION & RELIANT ON FEES from OVERSEAS STUDENTS.
UNIVERSITIES UK ARE ESTIMATING A DROP of £7 BILLION in the coming academic year... A THIRD of TUITION FEES.
PLACING MANY LIVELIHOODS at risk
The same across the WORLD
its difficult to see how normal education will resume - packed classes and student lifestyles are informative years!
STUDENT UNION
CRISPS
The Beauty of 150,000 Flamingos flooding Mumbai
SPAIN
ZAHARA de LOS ATUNES
LOCAL OFFICIALS DECIDE to BLEACH the BEACH
Though why as SPAIN has one of the strictest LOCKDOWNS IN THE WORLD - NO-ONE has been on the BEACHES...

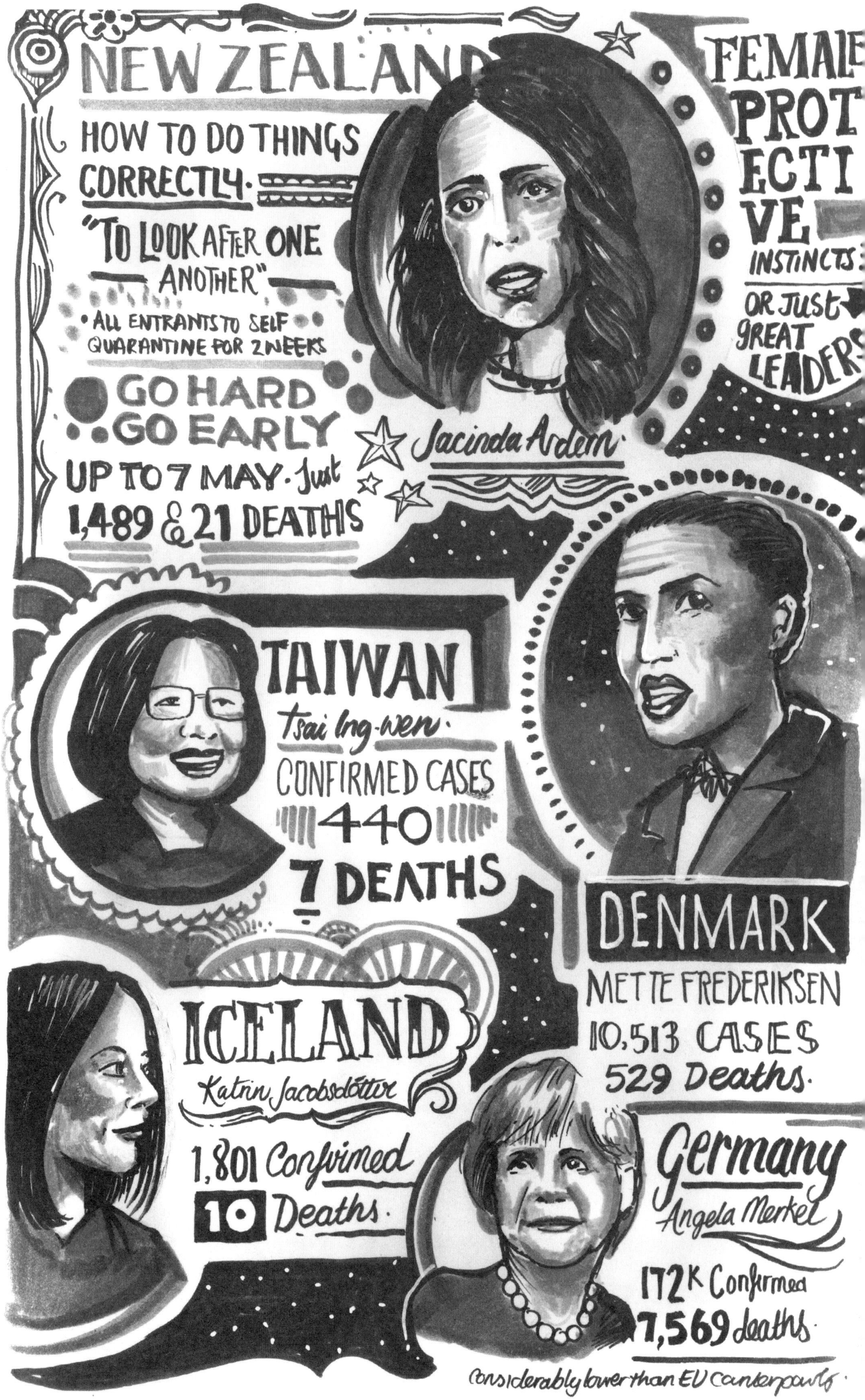

NEW ZEALAND
HOW TO DO THINGS CORRECTLY.
"TO LOOK AFTER ONE ANOTHER"
• ALL ENTRANTS TO SELF QUARANTINE FOR 2 WEEKS
GO HARD GO EARLY
UP TO 7 MAY. Just 1,489 & 21 DEATHS
Jacinda Ardern
FEMALE PROTECTIVE INSTINCTS OR JUST GREAT LEADERS
TAIWAN
Tsai Ing-wen
CONFIRMED CASES 440
7 DEATHS
DENMARK
METTE FREDERIKSEN
10,513 CASES
529 Deaths.
ICELAND
Katrin Jacobsdóttir
1,801 Confirmed
10 Deaths.
Germany
Angela Merkel
172K Confirmed
7,569 deaths.
Considerably lower than EU Counterparts.

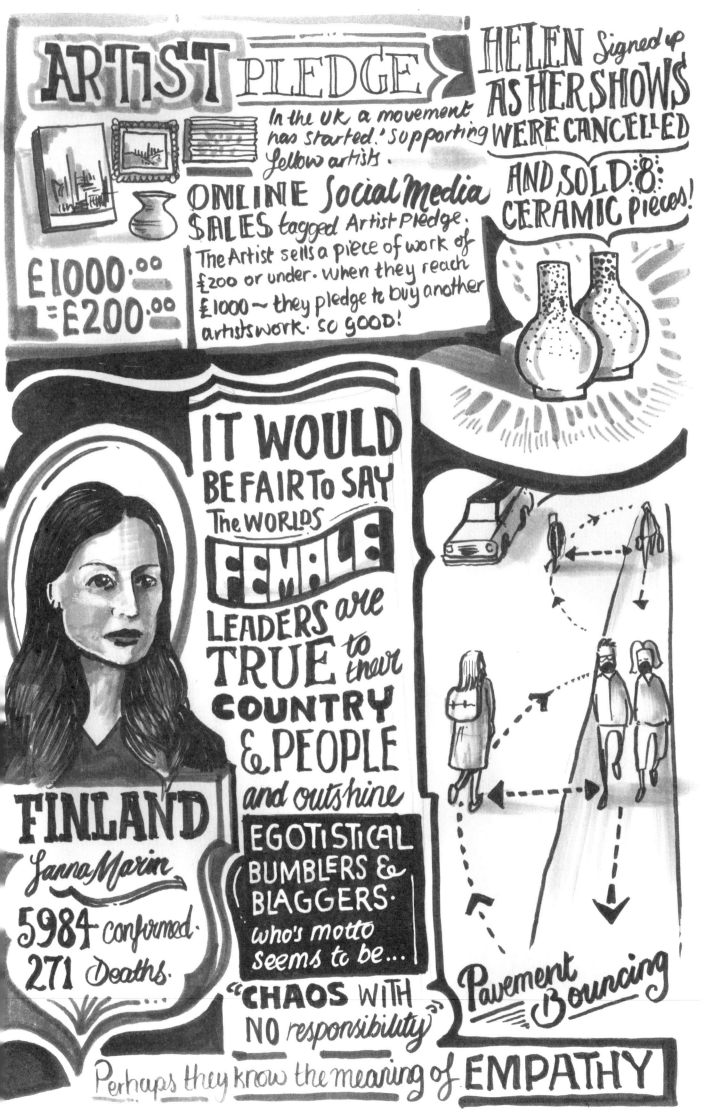

ARTIST PLEDGE

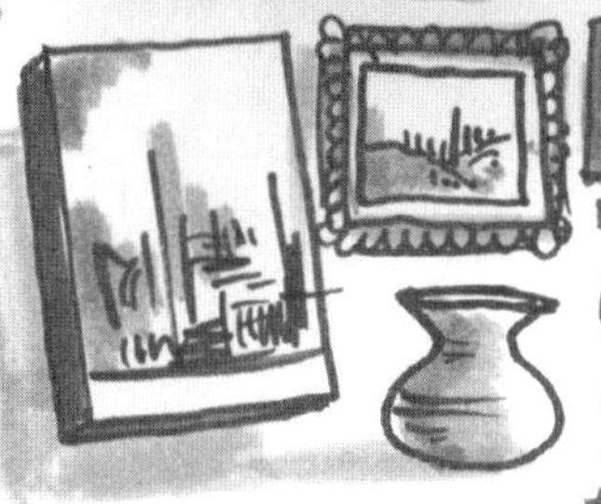

In the UK a movement has started.' supporting fellow artists.

ONLINE Social Media SALES tagged Artist Pledge.

£1000.00 = £200.00

The Artist sells a piece of work of £200 or under. When they reach £1000 – they pledge to buy another artists work. SO GOOD!

HELEN Signed up AS HER SHOWS WERE CANCELLED AND SOLD 8 CERAMIC pieces!

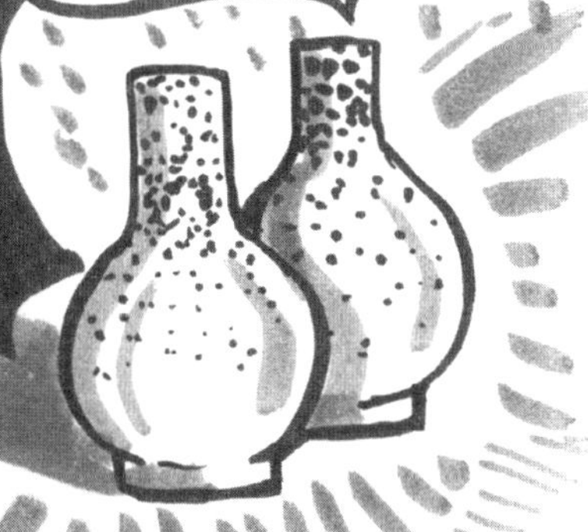

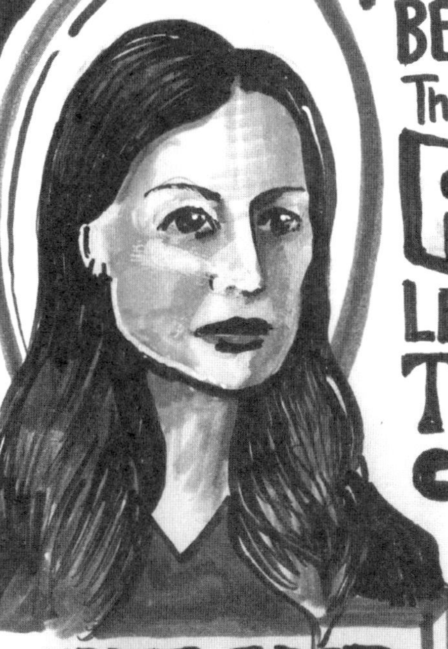

FINLAND

Sanna Marin

5984 confirmed.
271 Deaths.

IT WOULD BE FAIR TO SAY The WORLDS FEMALE LEADERS are TRUE to their COUNTRY & PEOPLE and outshine

EGOTISTICAL BUMBLERS & BLAGGERS. who's motto seems to be...

"CHAOS WITH NO responsibility"

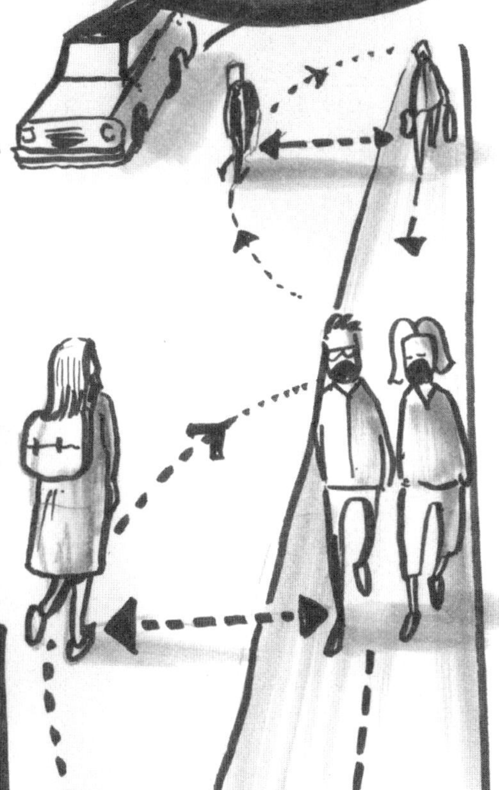

Pavement Bouncing

Perhaps they know the meaning of EMPATHY

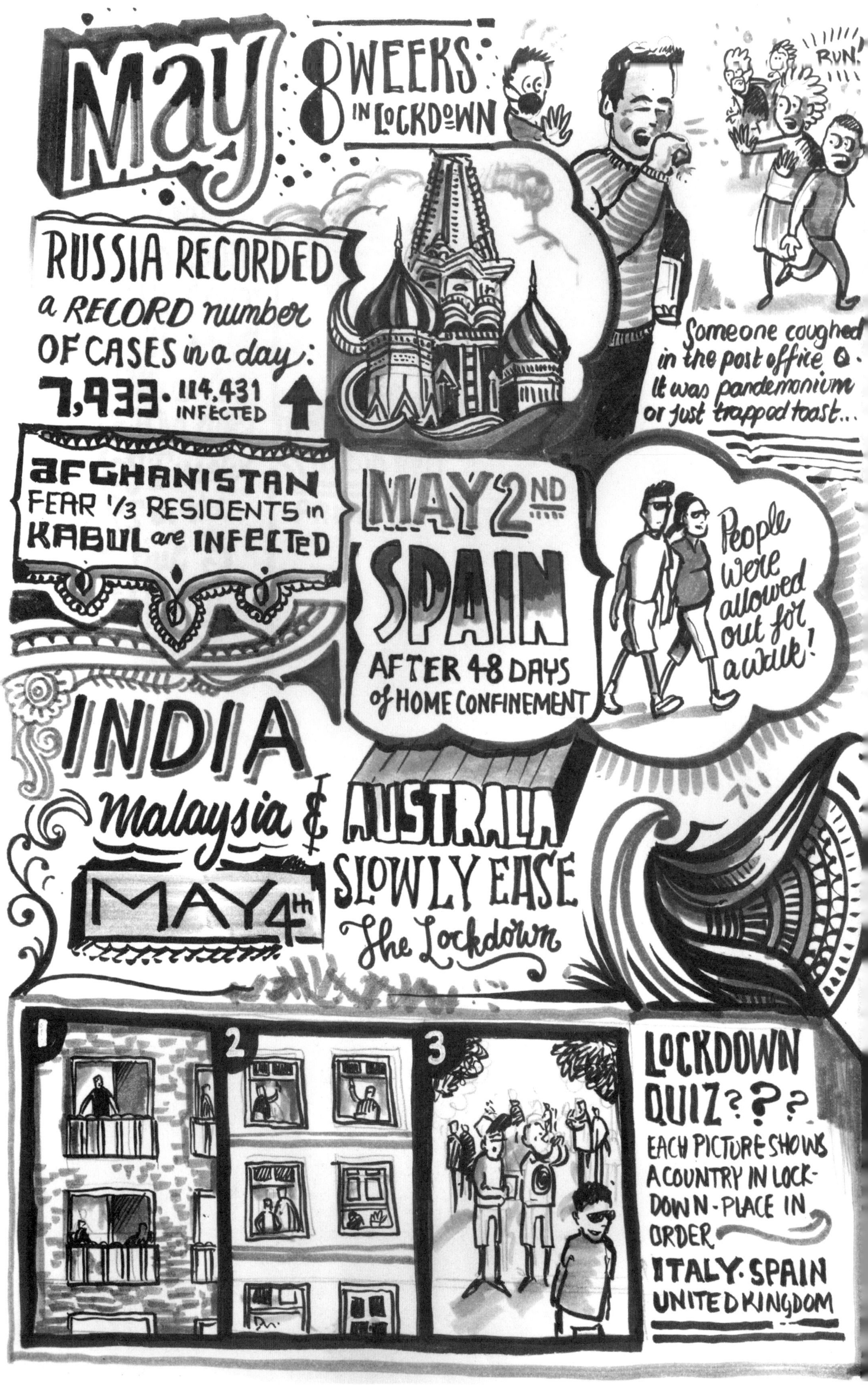
MAY
8 WEEKS IN LOCKDOWN
RUN!
RUSSIA RECORDED a RECORD number OF CASES in a day: 7,933 · 114,431 INFECTED
Someone coughed in the post office Q. It was pandemonium or just trapped toast...
AFGHANISTAN FEAR 1/3 RESIDENTS in KABUL are INFECTED
MAY 2ND
SPAIN AFTER 48 DAYS of HOME CONFINEMENT
People were allowed out for a walk!
INDIA Malaysia & AUSTRALIA SLOWLY EASE The Lockdown
MAY 4th
1
2
3
LOCKDOWN QUIZ ? ? ?
EACH PICTURE SHOWS A COUNTRY IN LOCKDOWN - PLACE IN ORDER
ITALY · SPAIN UNITED KINGDOM

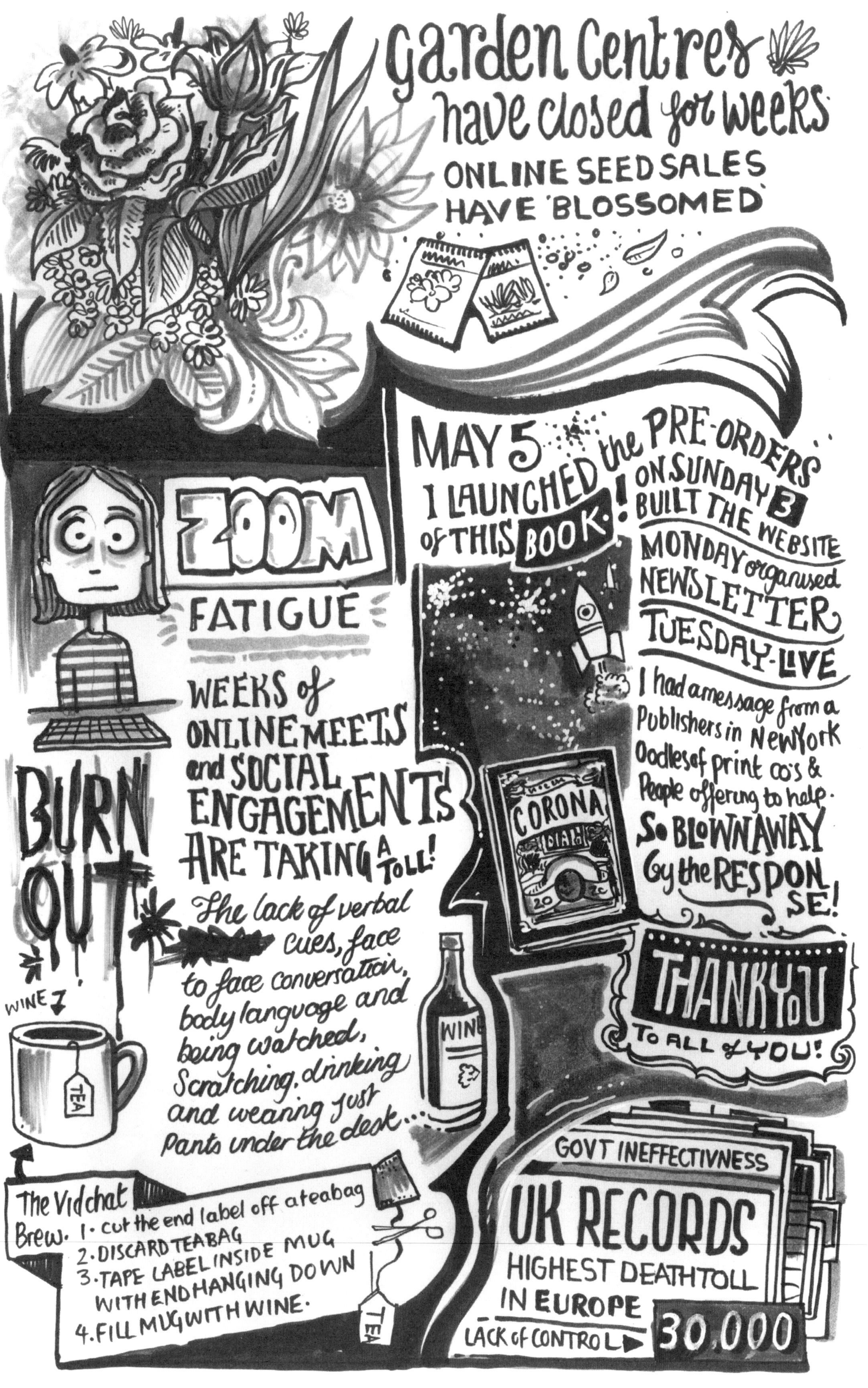

Garden Centres have closed for weeks
ONLINE SEED SALES HAVE 'BLOSSOMED'
MAY 5
I LAUNCHED the PRE-ORDERS of THIS BOOK!
ON SUNDAY 3 BUILT THE WEBSITE
MONDAY organised NEWSLETTER
TUESDAY-LIVE
I had a message from a Publishers in New York
Oodles of print co's & People offering to help.
So BLOWN AWAY by the RESPONSE!
THANK YOU
TO ALL of YOU!
CORONA DIARY
2020
ZOOM
FATIGUE
WEEKS of ONLINE MEETS and SOCIAL ENGAGEMENTS ARE TAKING A TOLL!
BURN OUT
The lack of verbal [redacted] cues, face to face conversation, body language and being watched, Scratching, drinking and wearing just Pants under the desk...
WINE
TEA
WINE
The Vidchat Brew.
1. cut the end label off a teabag
2. DISCARD TEABAG
3. TAPE LABEL INSIDE MUG WITH END HANGING DOWN WITH WINE.
4. FILL MUG WITH WINE.
TEA
GOVT INEFFECTIVNESS
UK RECORDS
HIGHEST DEATHTOLL IN EUROPE
LACK of CONTROL
30,000

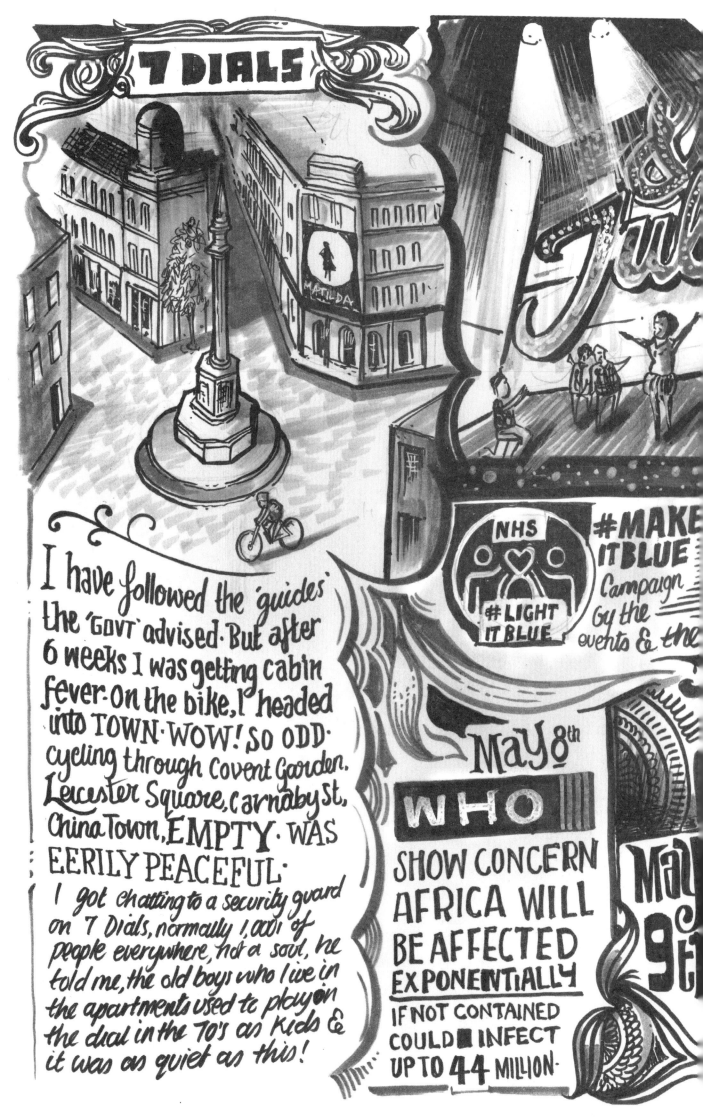

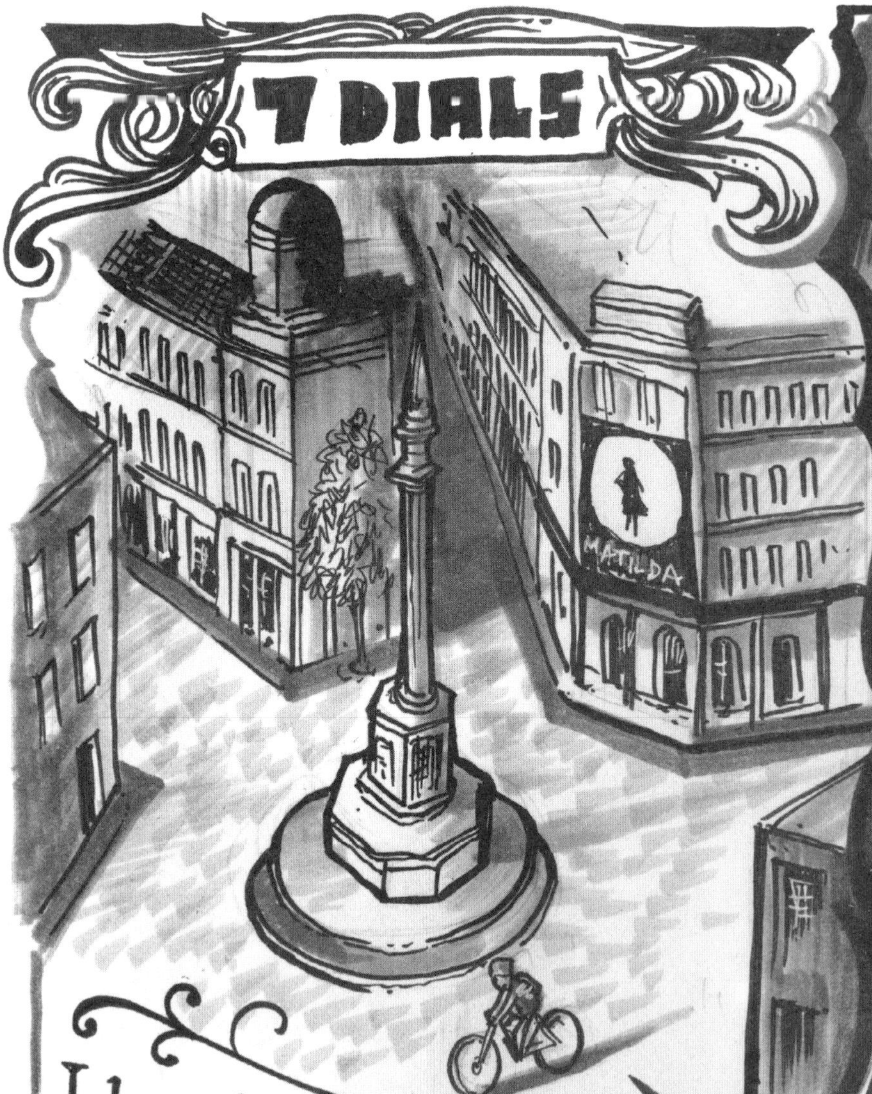
7 DIALS
MATILDA

I have followed the 'guides' the 'GOVT' advised. But after 6 weeks I was getting cabin fever. On the bike, I headed into TOWN. WOW! SO ODD. cycling through Covent Garden. Leicester Square, Carnaby St, China Town, EMPTY. WAS EERILY PEACEFUL.

I got chatting to a security guard on 7 Dials, normally 1,000's of people everywhere, not a soul, he told me, the old boys who live in the apartments used to play on the dial in the 70's as kids & it was as quiet as this!

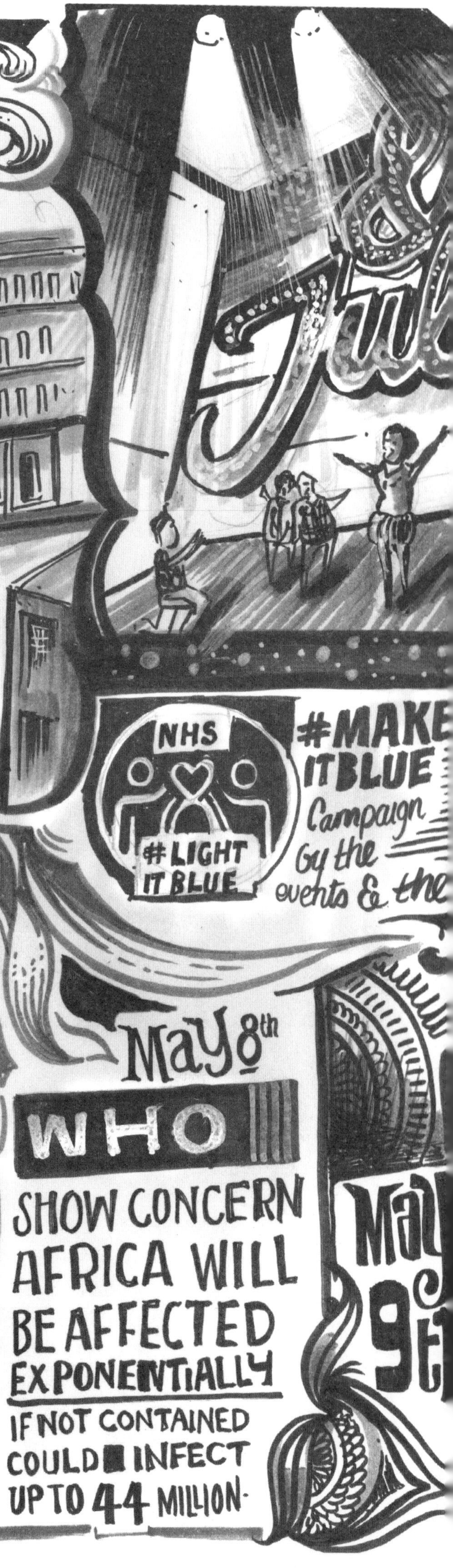
NHS
#LIGHT IT BLUE
#MAKE IT BLUE
Campaign by the events & the
May 8th
WHO
SHOW CONCERN AFRICA WILL BE AFFECTED EXPONENTIALLY
IF NOT CONTAINED COULD INFECT UP TO 44 MILLION.
May
9t

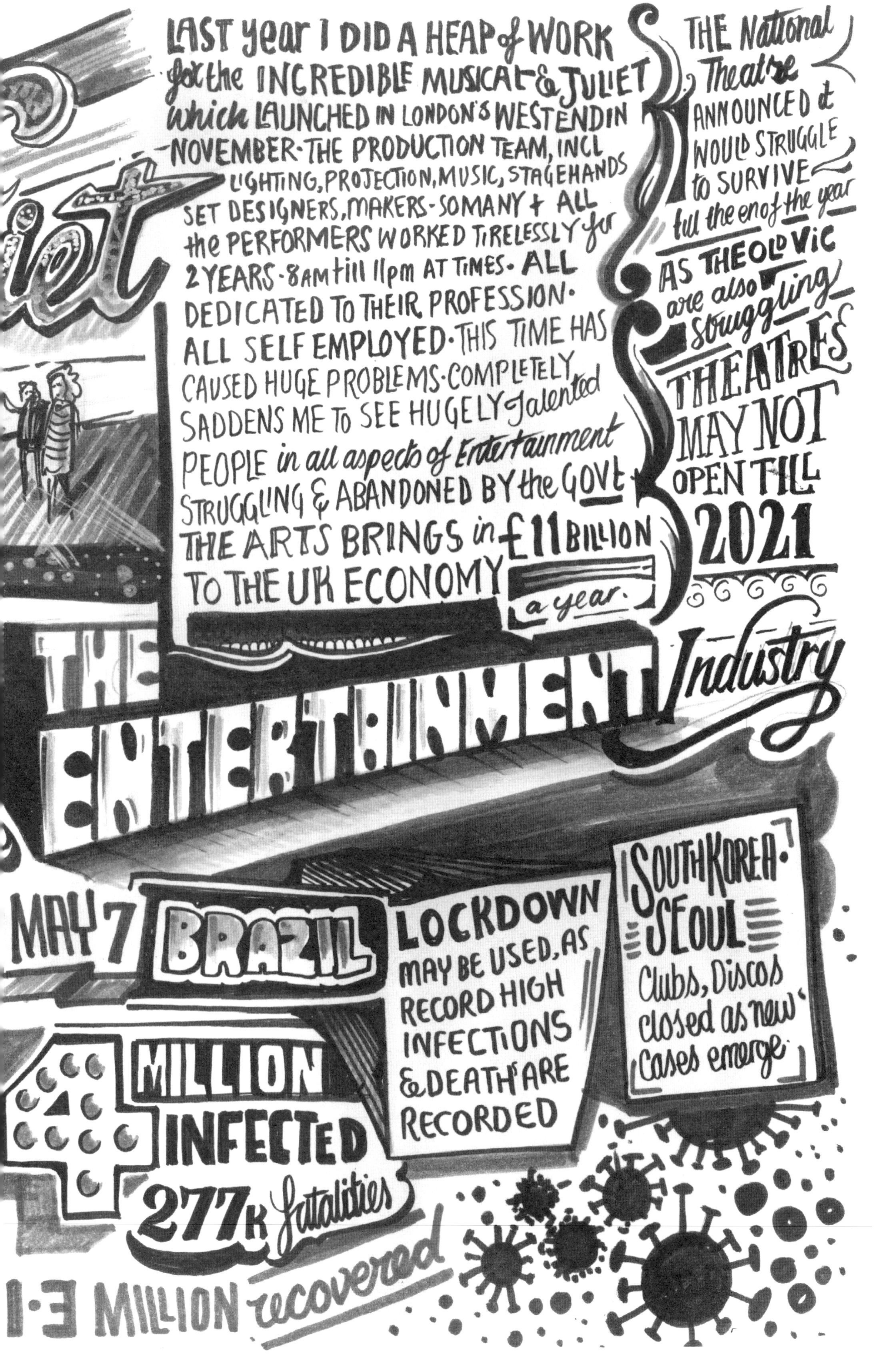
iet
LAST year I DID A HEAP of WORK for the INCREDIBLE MUSICAL & JULIET which LAUNCHED IN LONDON'S WEST END IN NOVEMBER. THE PRODUCTION TEAM, INCL LIGHTING, PROJECTION, MUSIC, STAGEHANDS SET DESIGNERS, MAKERS - SO MANY + ALL the PERFORMERS WORKED TIRELESSLY for 2 YEARS - 8AM till 11pm AT TIMES. ALL DEDICATED TO THEIR PROFESSION. ALL SELF EMPLOYED. THIS TIME HAS CAUSED HUGE PROBLEMS. COMPLETELY SADDENS ME TO SEE HUGELY Talented PEOPLE in all aspects of Entertainment STRUGGLING & ABANDONED BY the GOVt
THE ARTS BRINGS in £11 BILLION TO THE UK ECONOMY a year.
THE National Theatre ANNOUNCED it WOULD STRUGGLE to SURVIVE till the en of the year
AS THE OLD VIC are also struggling
THEATRES MAY NOT OPEN TILL 2021
THE ENTERTAINMENT Industry
MAY 7
BRAZIL
LOCKDOWN MAY BE USED, AS RECORD HIGH INFECTIONS & DEATHS ARE RECORDED
4 MILLION INFECTED
277K fatalities
1·3 MILLION recovered
SOUTH KOREA. SEOUL
Clubs, Discos closed as new cases emerge.

United States of AMERICA

see 80,000 people die

MAY 12

TWITTERBOY 'W'

The R-Naught or R-0 is the virus basic reproductive number Epidemiologic metric the contagiousness of infectious agents

12 MAY

UK 627 DEATHS

TOTAL 32,692

OFFICE for NATIONAL STATISTICS REVEAL FIGURE MAY BE UP TO

40,000

THE R

EVERYONES TALKING 'R'

THE RATE at WHICH THE VIRUS SPREADS

FOOTBALL

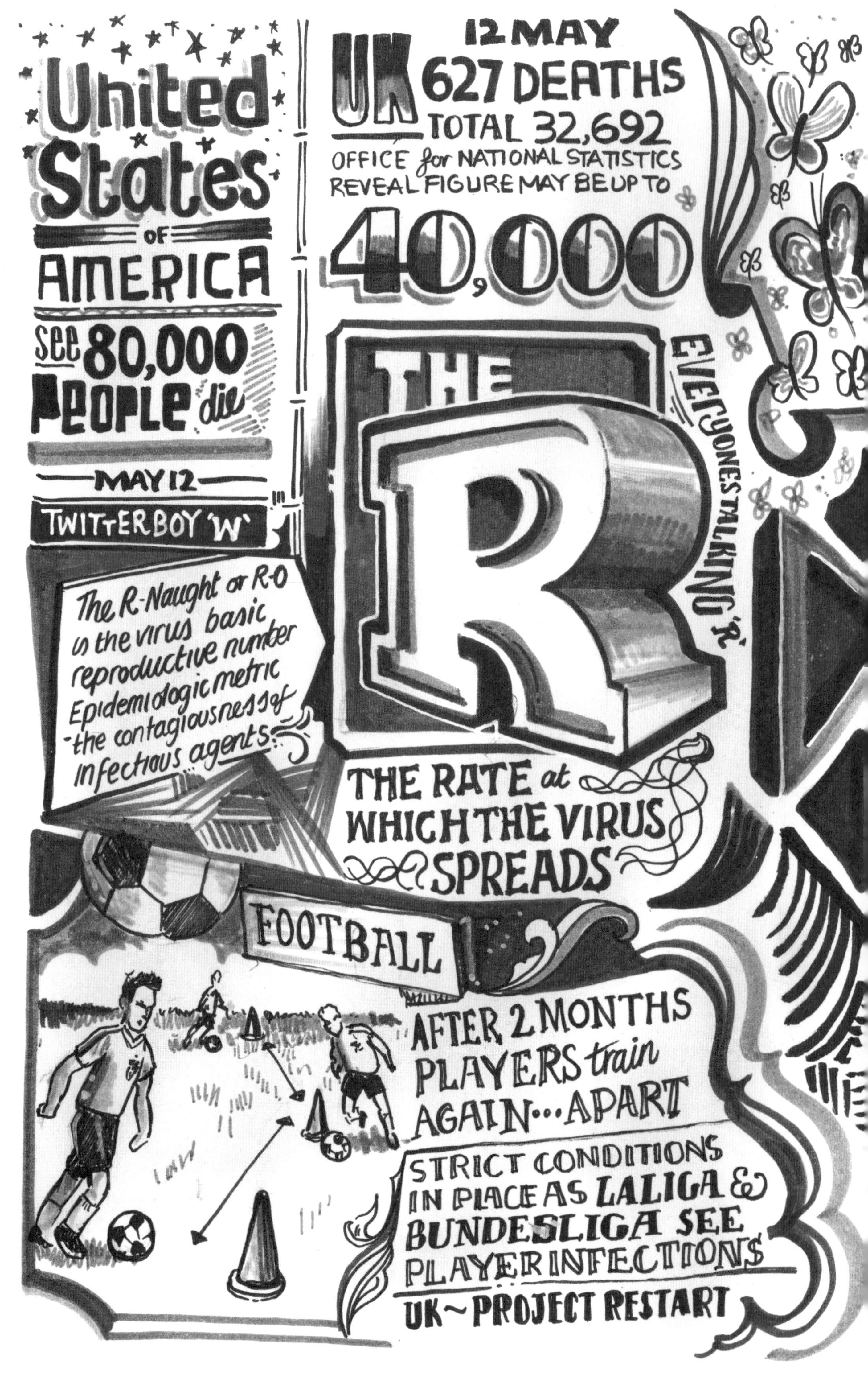

AFTER 2 MONTHS PLAYERS train AGAIN... APART

STRICT CONDITIONS IN PLACE AS LALIGA & BUNDESLIGA SEE PLAYER INFECTIONS

UK ~ PROJECT RESTART

BOJO ENLIGHTENS US WITH SOME of his SHOUTY PEARLS of WISDOM

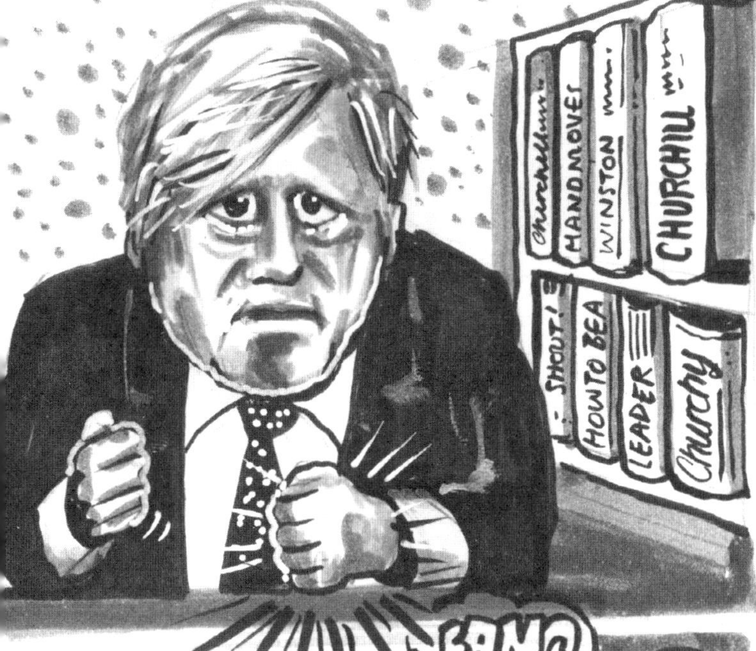
HANDMOVES
WINSTON
CHURCHILL
SHOUT!
HOW TO BE A
LEADER
Churchy
BANG

Stay home, but go to work. Isolate but meet friends Only use public transport if You cant get to work on a magic carpet. Stay awake but go to sleep. Play golf. Run all day, but stay home. Eat but don't eat ~ it was a wee bit confusing until we were told to use our COMMON SENSE ~ Got it!

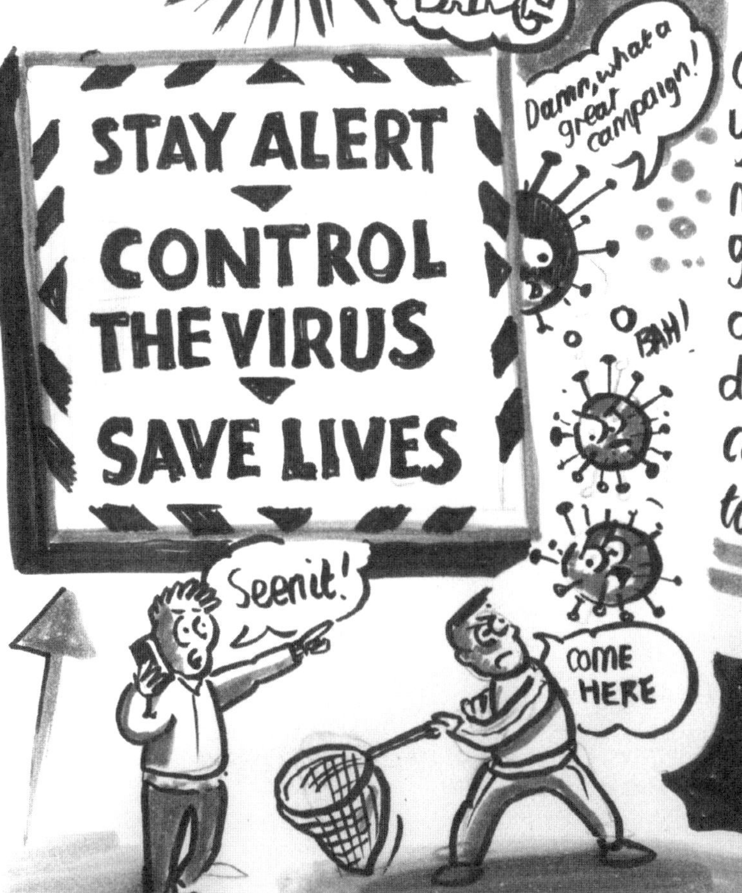
STAY ALERT
CONTROL THE VIRUS
SAVE LIVES
Damn, what a great campaign!
BAH!
Seenit!
COME HERE

CLINICAL TRIALS

are happening all over the world from INDIA to CHINA, Switzerland to ISRAEL.

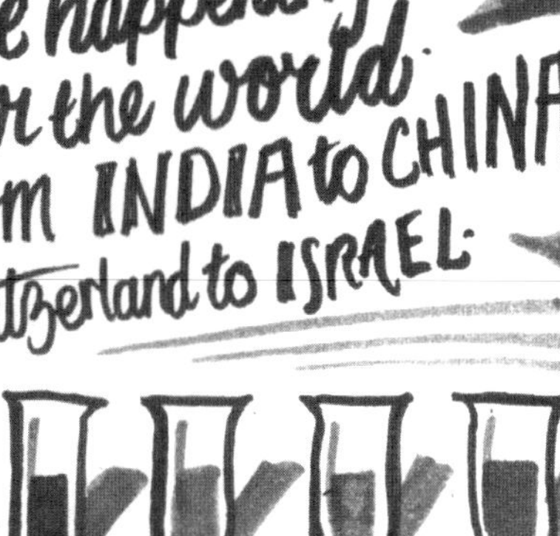

13th

A MAJORITY of the COUNTRIES in the MOST AFFECTED AREAS BEGIN to see A REDUCTION in the NUMBERS of DAILY cases.

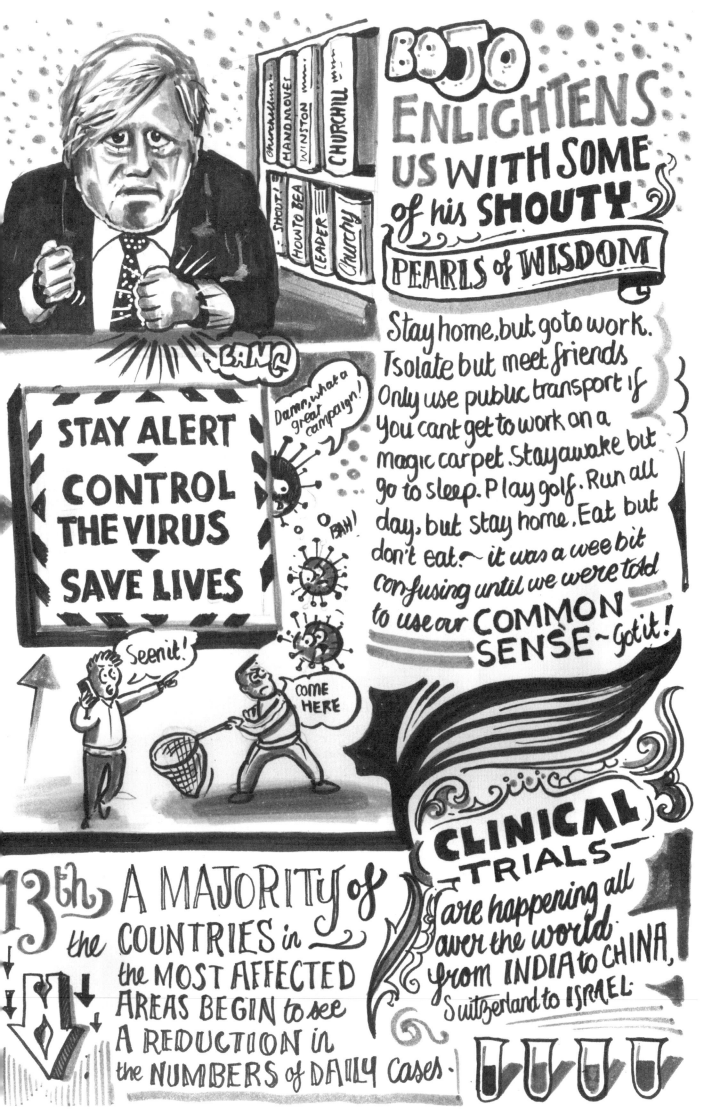

FROM January 1st to March 23rd.

18 MILLION travellers

Arrived in the UK:

LESS THAN 300 WERE QUARANTINED

LETS MOVE ON TO

2 MONTHS

AFTER LOCKDOWN

GOVT announce a 14 day quarantine on all arriving in the UK on the 9th **MAY!**

EASING the LOCKdown Slowly

It all seems a sudden change. As much as I would LOVE things to, is it too soon? I kind of get the economy is kaput in so many places, but complacency at this stage feels... dangerous.

many countries are seeing ↓ **IN NUMBERS**

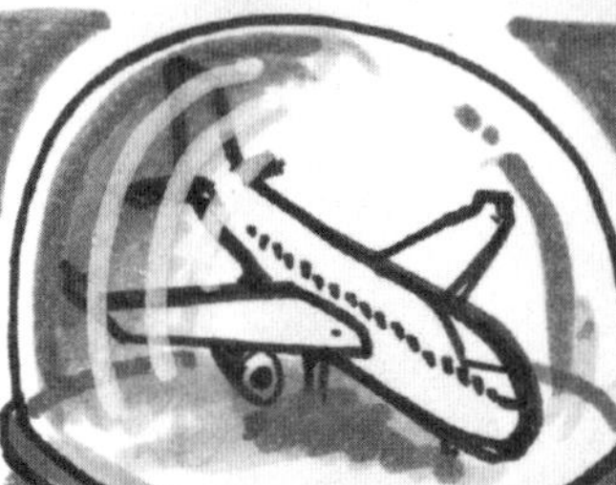

CELEBRITY FREE ZONE

This has been refreshing...
[Vacuous News of nobody doing [redacted] Nothing of any importance!]

New Zealand

TIGHT RESTRICTIONS MEAN MALLS, GYMS CINEMAS, CAFES REOPEN.

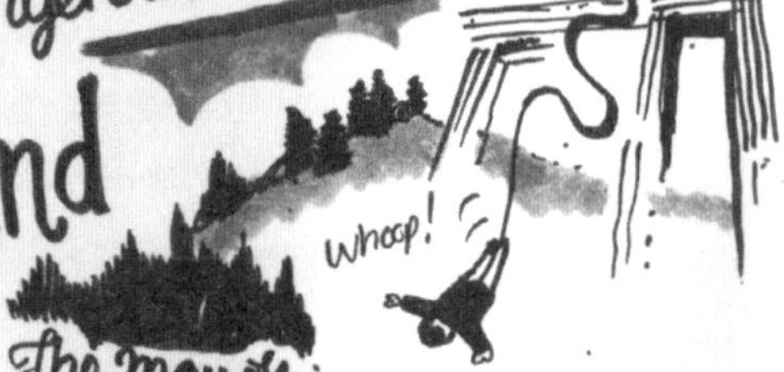
Whoop!

The mayor in Queenstown celebrated easing of lockdown with a BUNGEE JUMP!

AUSTRALIA

Australia have introduced the covidsafe app for tracing

Venues opening for 10 people at a time for 2 hours per person.

TEAM SPORTS & GYMS REOPEN

SPAIN

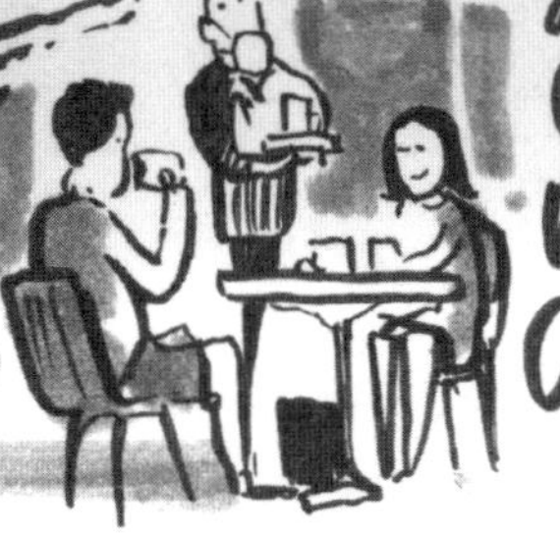

Cafes, restaurants & Hotels, reopen with reduced capacity

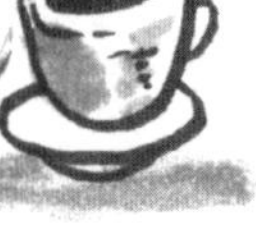

FLATTENING the CURVE

REDUCING CASES of INFECTIONS on a DAILY BASIS

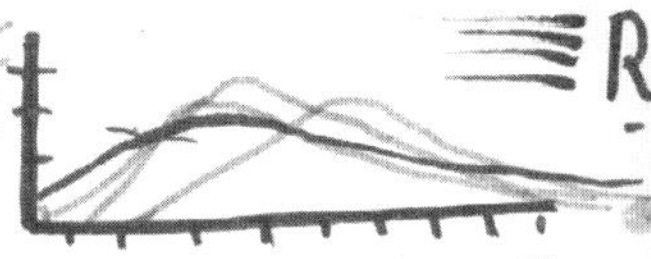

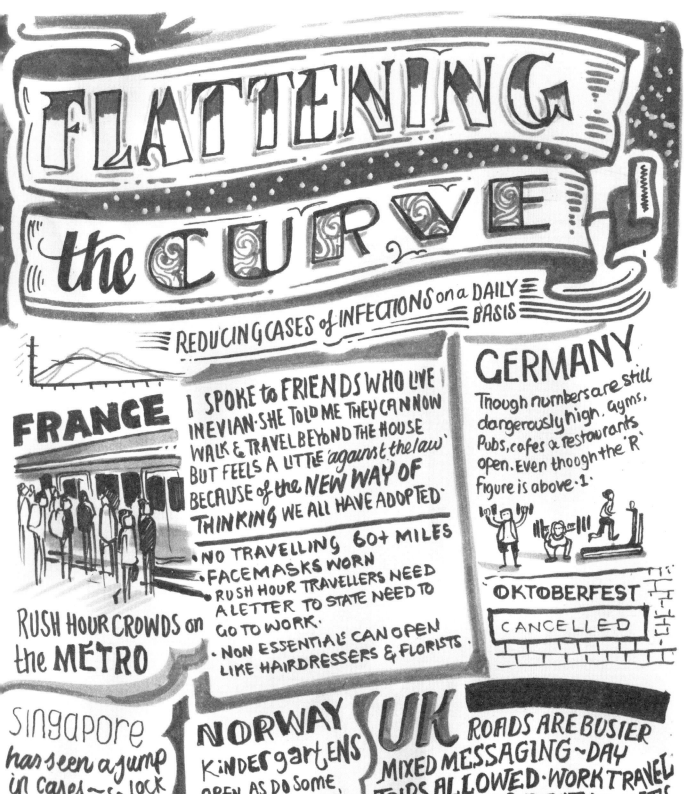

FRANCE

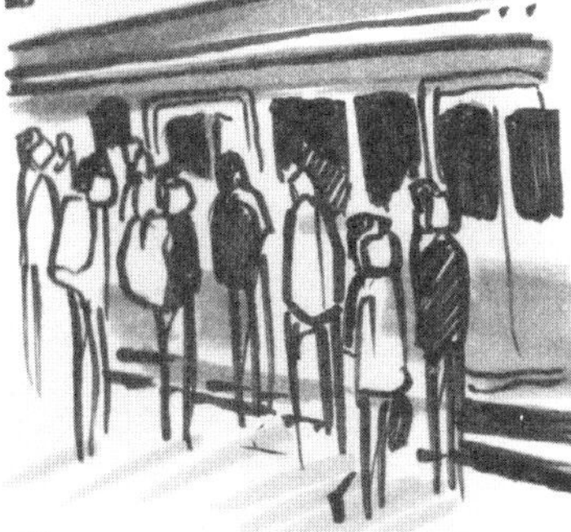

RUSH HOUR CROWDS on the METRO

I SPOKE to FRIENDS WHO LIVE IN EVIAN. SHE TOLD ME THEY CAN NOW WALK & TRAVEL BEYOND THE HOUSE BUT FEELS A LITTLE 'against the law' BECAUSE of the NEW WAY OF THINKING WE ALL HAVE ADOPTED.

- NO TRAVELLING 60+ MILES
- FACEMASKS WORN
- RUSH HOUR TRAVELLERS NEED A LETTER TO STATE NEED TO GO TO WORK.
- NON ESSENTIALS CAN OPEN LIKE HAIRDRESSERS & FLORISTS.

GERMANY

Though numbers are still dangerously high. Gyms, Pubs, cafes & restaurants open. Even though the 'R' figure is above 1.

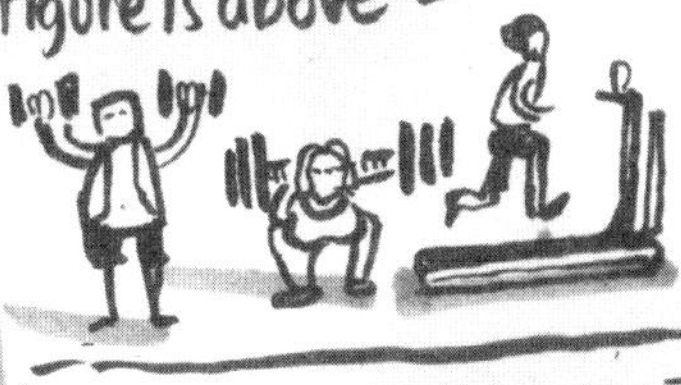

OKTOBERFEST CANCELLED

Singapore

has seen a jump in cases ~ so LOCK DOWN continues

NORWAY

Kindergartens OPEN, AS DO SOME SMALLER BUSINESS.

UK

ROADS ARE BUSIER

MIXED MESSAGING ~ DAY TRIPS ALLOWED. WORK TRAVEL NO BARS OPEN - RESTAURANTS CAN DO TAKE OUTS.

Denmark

Hairdressers, Dentists, Spas, malls and cafes open. OLDER CHILDREN allowed back to school.

GOVt WANT SCHOOLS TO OPEN. PARENTS & UNIONS concerned.

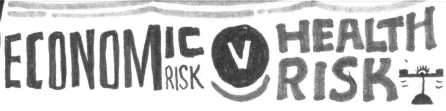

ECONOMIC RISK V HEALTH RISK

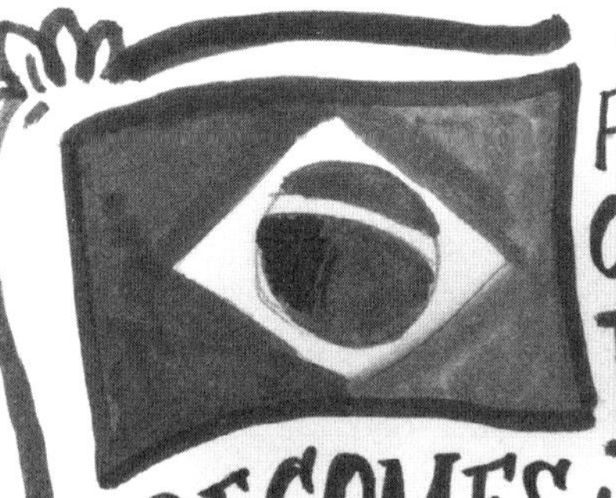

19 MAY

AS EUROPE BEGINS to OPEN its DOORS **BRAZIL** BECOMES the NEW HOTSPOT with 254,220 cases. The President Bolsonaro dismissing covid-19 from the outset.

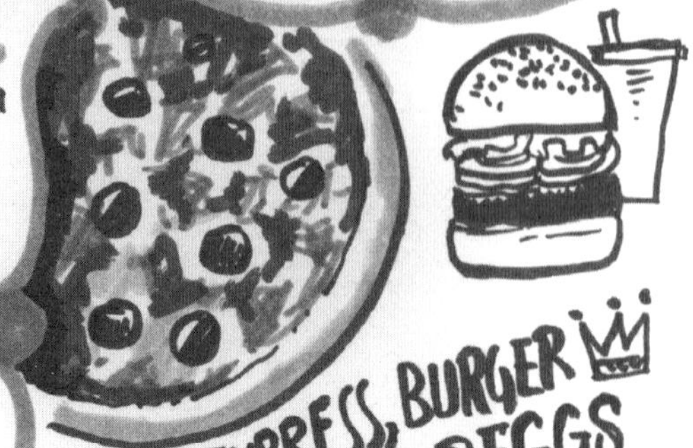

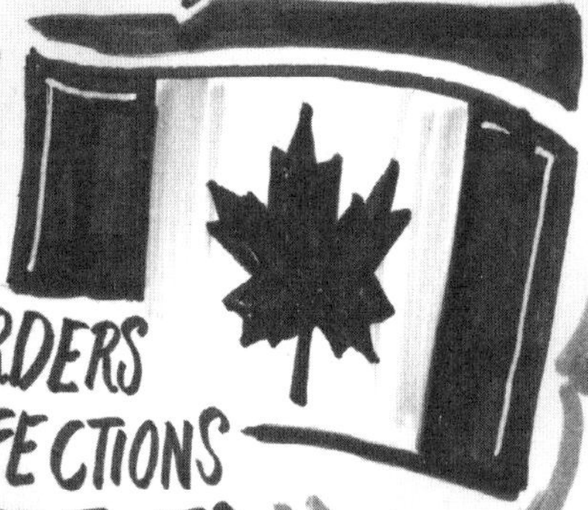

Canada EXTENDS CLOSED BORDERS TO JUNE. LIMITING INFECTIONS TO 78,072 COMPARED TO ITS NEIGHBOUR → THE U.S.A WHICH HAS SEEN OVER **1.5 MILLION** CONFIRMED CASES.

PIZZA EXPRESS, BURGER KING, MACCA'D'S & GREGGS ARE OPENING for TAKE-AWAYS. SO all those in Lockdown who spent 2 months doing **HIIT** sessions and running can start all over again.

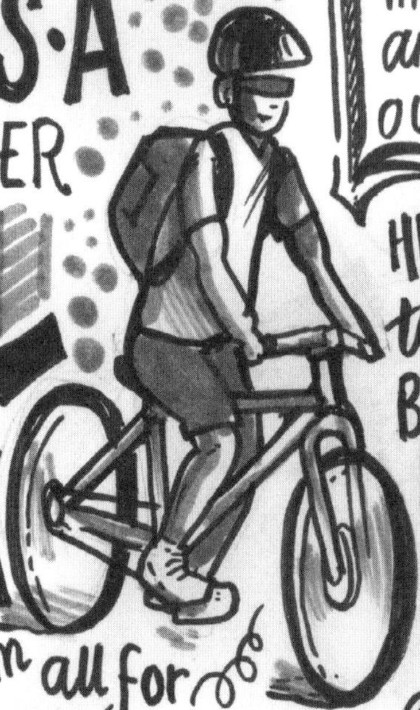

& More countries are promoting cycling, which as a cyclist, I am all for

HERES A THING. I USED to GO FOR COFFEE and BREAKFAST. 1-2 TIMES a WEEK. SPENDING £10-12 A TIME - IN 2 MONTHS I SAVED almost £200! and still had coffee - as much as I wanted and breakfast - BUT at HOME and in my Jimmy Jam's (PJ's)

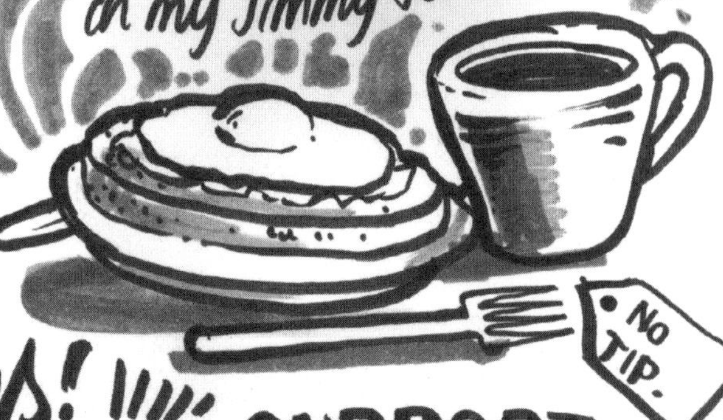
NO TIP.

SO ALL THAT money SAVED WILL BE SPENT ON... my **LOCAL** cafes! BECAUSE WE NEED TO SUPPORT → THE small BUSINESS

'Thanks for your help. Now DO ONE'
-PP-

HOME SECRETARY Priti Patel passes the IMMIGRATION BILL which basically blocks all the, as she says 'UNSKILLED' WORKERS from the UK. You know the ones, all the people who have tirelessly kept the UK going for 2 MONTHS

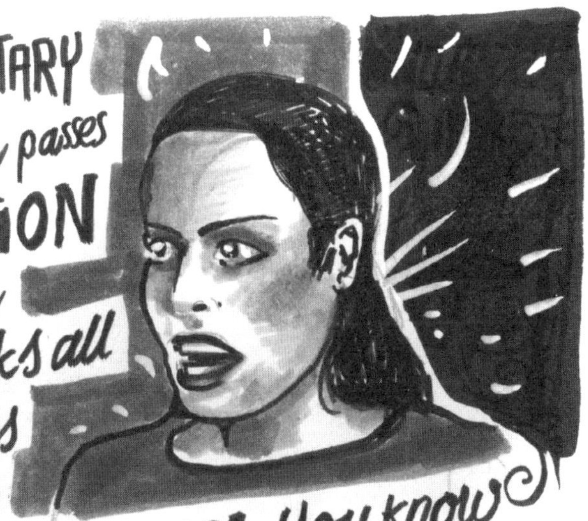

20 MAY

TRUMP says the HIGH number of CASES in the U.S - 1.5 MILLION & 93,000 deaths - is a

BADGE of HONOUR

[for testing! think...]

PRESSURE is growing by international organisations and National Governments to allow an independent investigation into the origins of the virus in

CHINA

BUT NO NEWS... Just yet

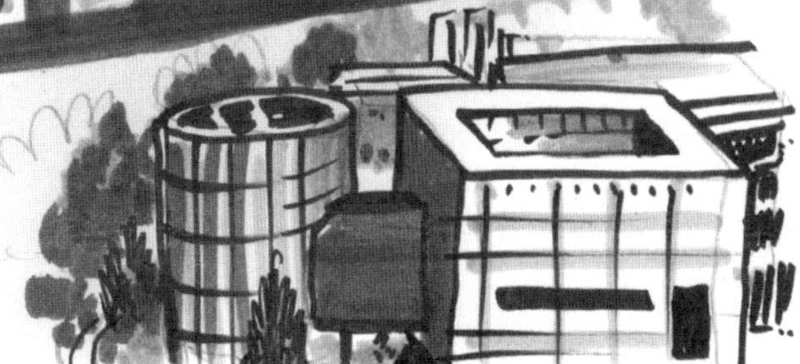

* I didnt realise there was an Institute of Virology in WUHAN. *

WORLD BANK SAYS UP TO 60M PEOPLE COULD BE PUSHED BELOW THE POVERTY LINE

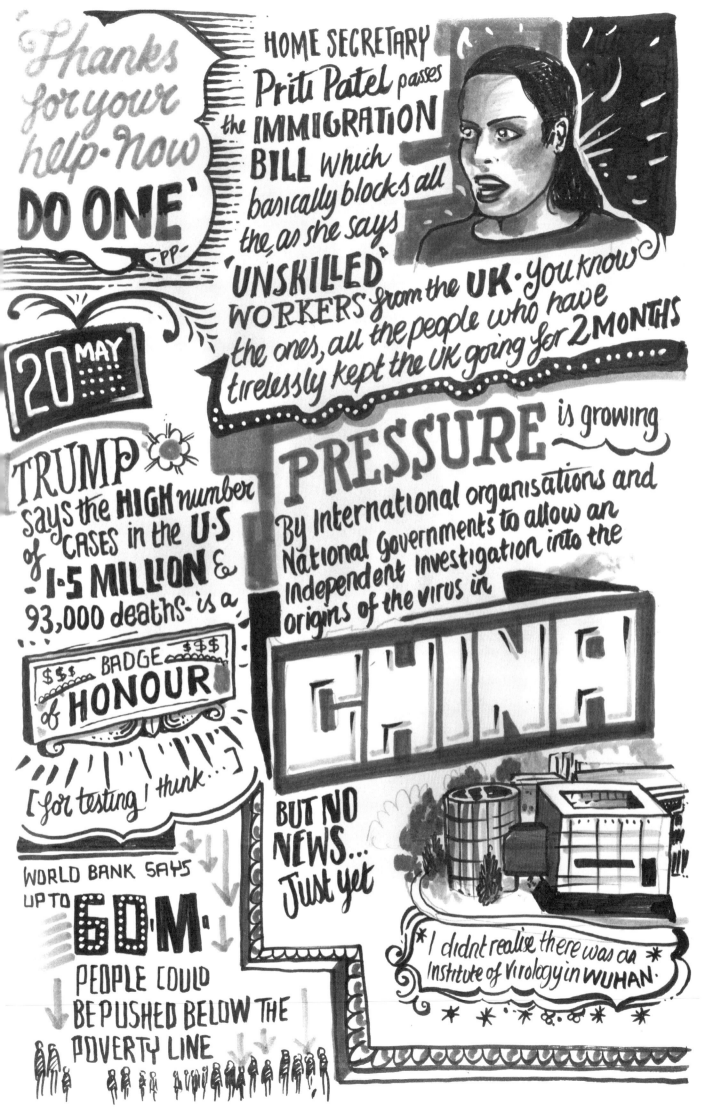

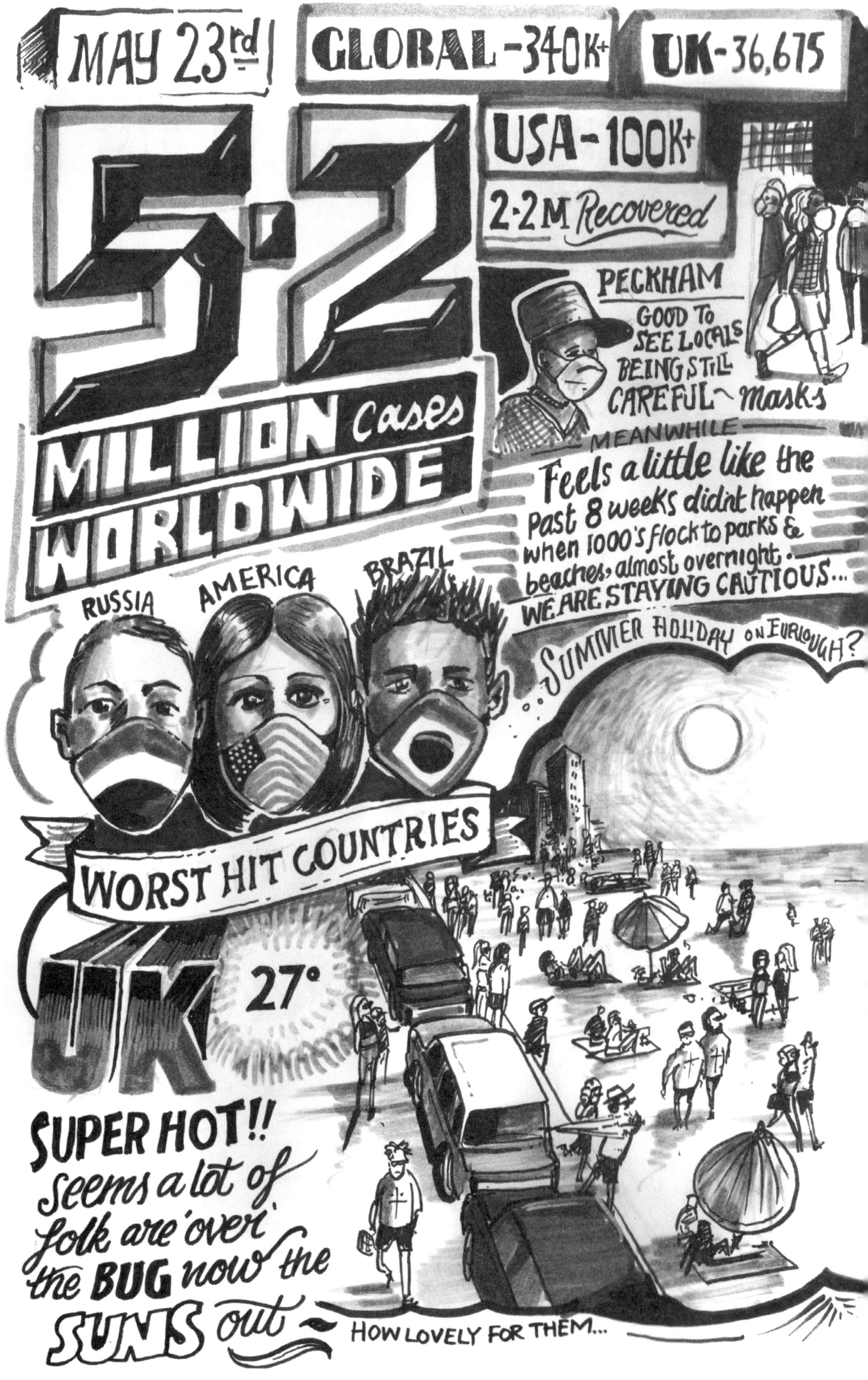

MAY 23rd
GLOBAL -340K+
UK-36,675
5.2
MILLION cases
WORLDWIDE
USA-100K+
2.2M Recovered
PECKHAM
GOOD TO SEE LOCALS BEING STILL CAREFUL ~ masks
MEANWHILE
Feels a little like the Past 8 weeks didnt happen when 1000's flock to parks & beaches, almost overnight.
WE ARE STAYING CAUTIOUS...
RUSSIA
AMERICA
BRAZIL
SUMMER HOLIDAY ON FURLOUGH?
WORST HIT COUNTRIES
UK
27°
SUPER HOT!!
seems a lot of folk are 'over' the BUG now the SUNS out
HOW LOVELY FOR THEM...

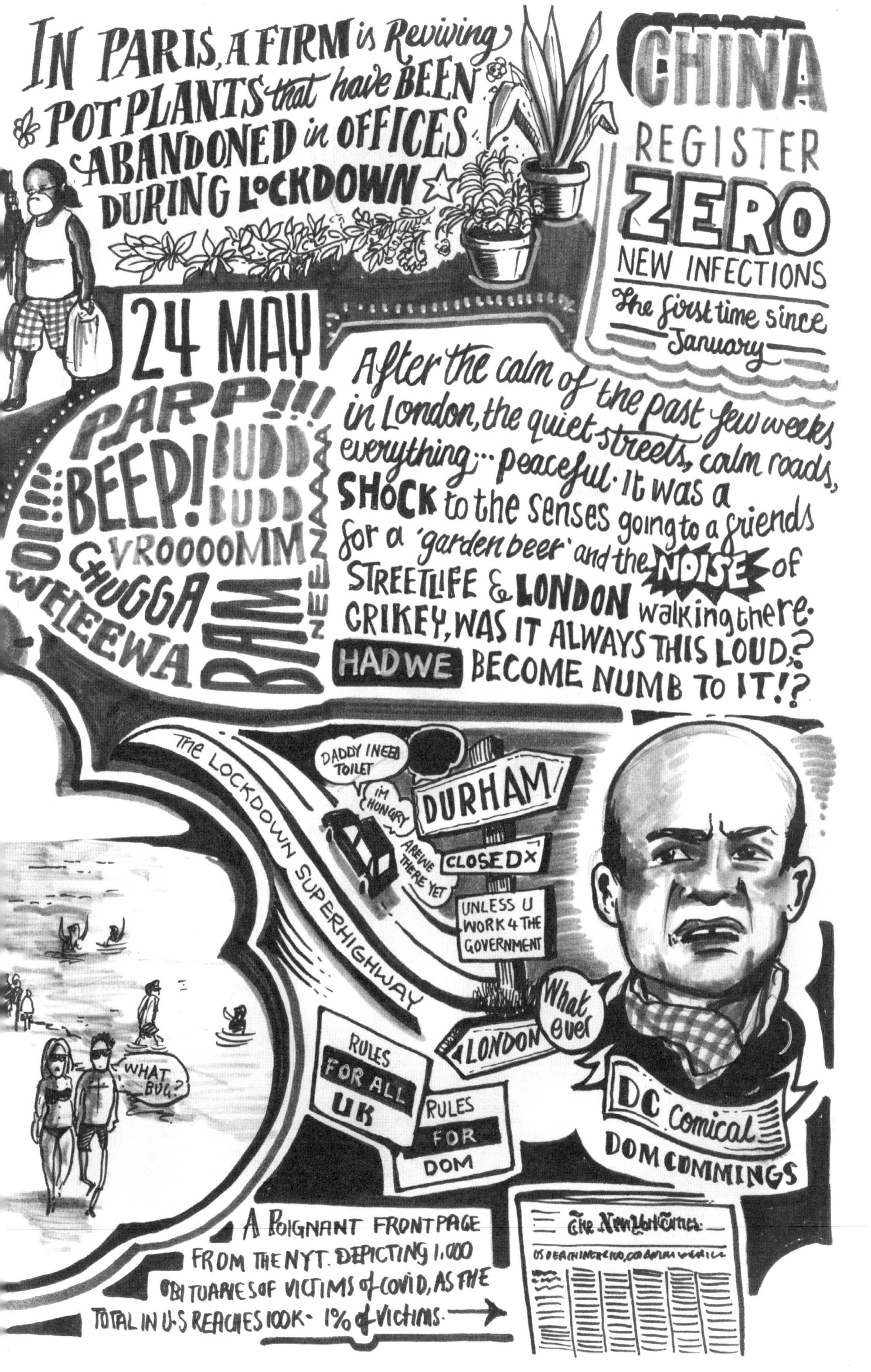
In Paris, a firm is Reviving pot plants that have been abandoned in offices during lockdown
China register zero new infections
The first time since January
24 May
PARP!!!!
BEEP!
BUDD BUDD
VROOOOOMM
OI!!!!
CHUGGA
WHEEWA
BAM
NEENAAAA
After the calm of the past few weeks in London, the quiet streets, calm roads, everything... peaceful. It was a SHOCK to the senses going to a friends for a 'garden beer' and the NOISE of STREETLIFE & LONDON walking there. CRIKEY, WAS IT ALWAYS THIS LOUD? HAD WE BECOME NUMB TO IT!?
THE LOCKDOWN SUPERHIGHWAY
DADDY I NEED TOILET
IM HUNGRY
ARE WE THERE YET
DURHAM
CLOSED ✕
UNLESS U WORK 4 THE GOVERNMENT
What ever
LONDON
RULES FOR ALL UK
RULES FOR DOM
WHAT BUG?
DC Comical
DOM CUMMINGS
A POIGNANT FRONTPAGE FROM THE NYT. DEPICTING 1,000 OBITUARIES OF VICTIMS OF COVID, AS THE TOTAL IN U.S REACHES 100K - 1% of VICTIMS.
The New York Times

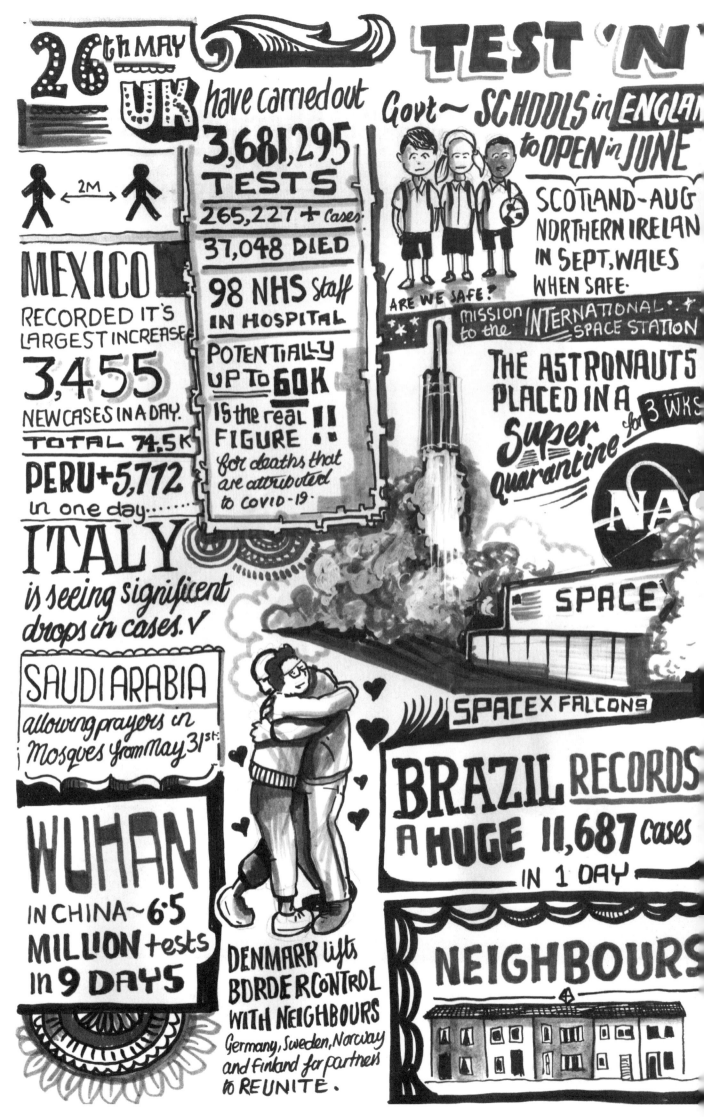

26th MAY

TEST 'N'

UK have carried out 3,681,295 TESTS

265,227 + cases.

37,048 DIED

98 NHS staff IN HOSPITAL

POTENTIALLY UP TO 60K is the real FIGURE !! for deaths that are attributed to COVID-19.

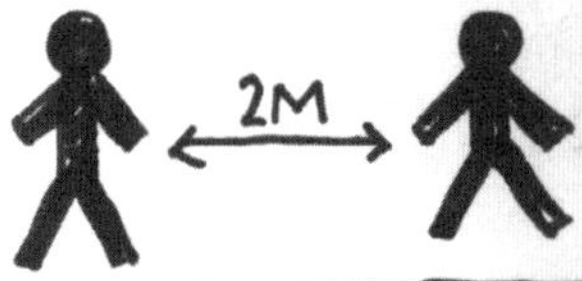

2M

MEXICO RECORDED IT'S LARGEST INCREASE 3,455 NEW CASES IN A DAY. TOTAL 74.5K

PERU + 5,772 in one day.

ITALY is seeing significent drops in cases. √

SAUDI ARABIA allowing prayers in Mosques from May 31st.

WUHAN IN CHINA ~ 6.5 MILLION tests in 9 DAYS

Govt ~ SCHOOLS in ENGLAN[D] to OPEN in JUNE

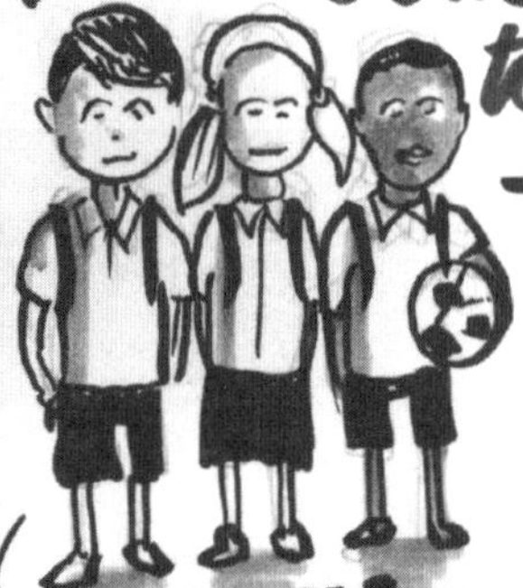

ARE WE SAFE?

SCOTLAND - AUG NORTHERN IRELAN[D] IN SEPT, WALES WHEN SAFE.

mission to the INTERNATIONAL SPACE STATION

THE ASTRONAUTS PLACED IN A Super Quarantine for 3 WKS

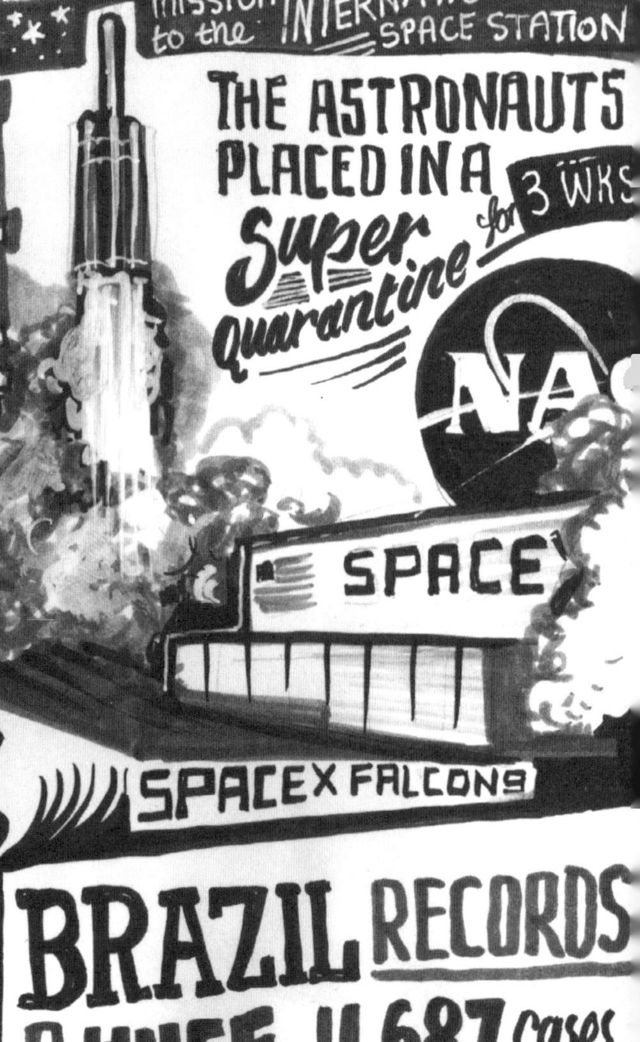

NA
SPACE

SPACEX FALCON 9

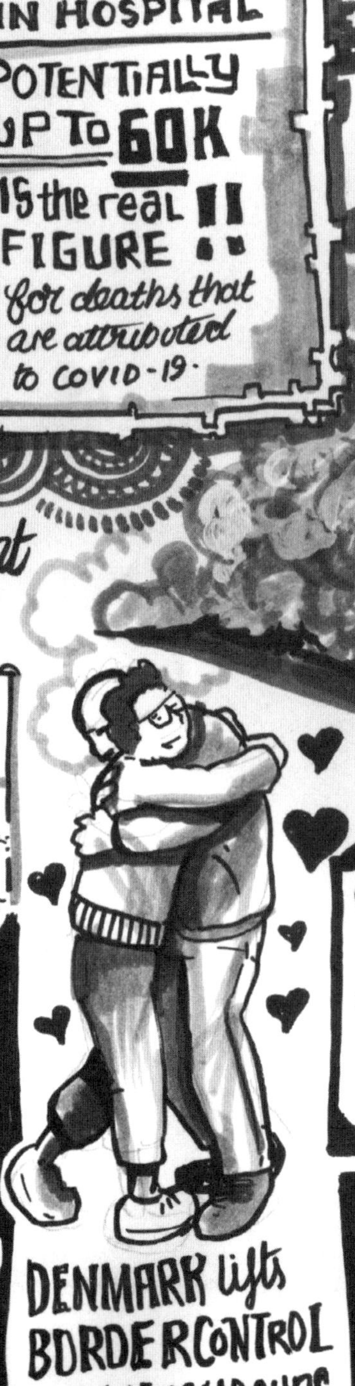

DENMARK lifts BORDER CONTROL WITH NEIGHBOURS Germany, Sweden, Norway and Finland for partners to REUNITE.

BRAZIL RECORDS A HUGE 11,687 cases IN 1 DAY

NEIGHBOURS

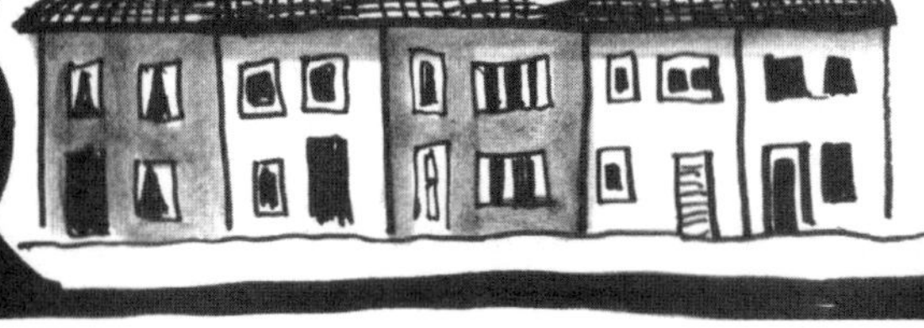

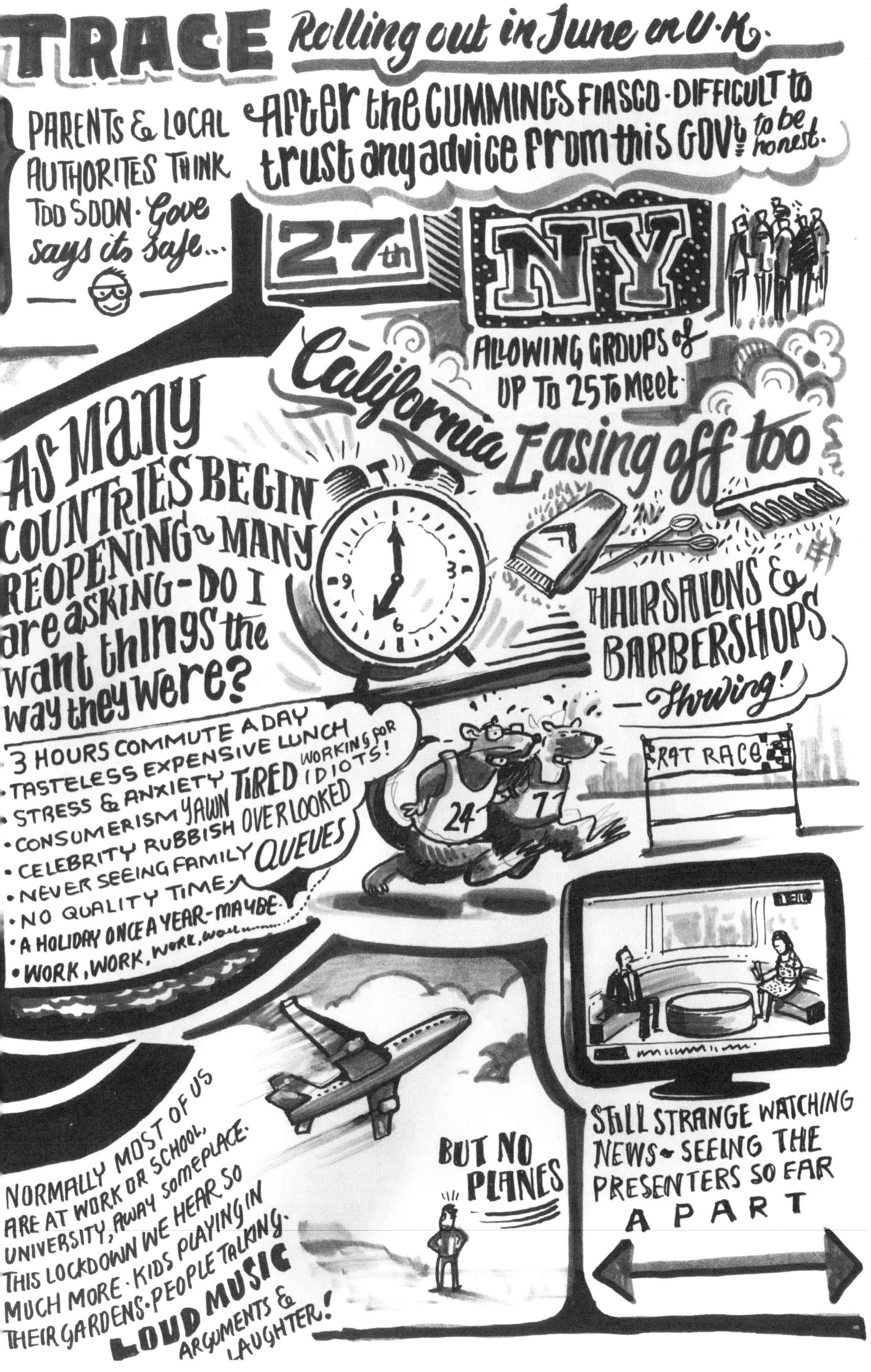
TRACE Rolling out in June in U.K.
PARENTS & LOCAL AUTHORITES THINK TOO SOON · Gove says its safe...
After the CUMMINGS FIASCO · DIFFICULT to trust any advice from this GOVt to be honest.
27th
NY
ALLOWING GROUPS of UP TO 25 To Meet
California Easing off too
As Many COUNTRIES BEGIN REOPENING & MANY are asking - DO I want things the way they were?
HAIRSALONS & BARBERSHOPS - Thriving!
· 3 HOURS COMMUTE A DAY
· TASTELESS EXPENSIVE LUNCH
· STRESS & ANXIETY TIRED WORKING FOR IDIOTS!
· CONSUMERISM YAWN OVERLOOKED
· CELEBRITY RUBBISH QUEUES
· NEVER SEEING FAMILY
· NEVER QUALITY TIME
· NO QUALITY TIME
· A HOLIDAY ONCE A YEAR - MAYBE
· WORK, WORK, WORK, WORK......
RAT RACE
24
71
NORMALLY MOST OF US ARE AT WORK OR SCHOOL, UNIVERSITY, AWAY SOMEPLACE. THIS LOCKDOWN WE HEAR SO MUCH MORE · KIDS PLAYING IN THEIR GARDENS · PEOPLE TALKING · LOUD MUSIC ARGUMENTS & LAUGHTER!
BUT NO PLANES
STILL STRANGE WATCHING NEWS - SEEING THE PRESENTERS SO FAR APART

AS WE HEAD TOWARDS JUNE

The news stories are changing ~ covid-19 is still there - but less. For 8-10 weeks we had news of something invisible that affected us all. We paused the other news, the way humans react to each other. At times it was'nt nice... someones pressed play again. ▶ 😐

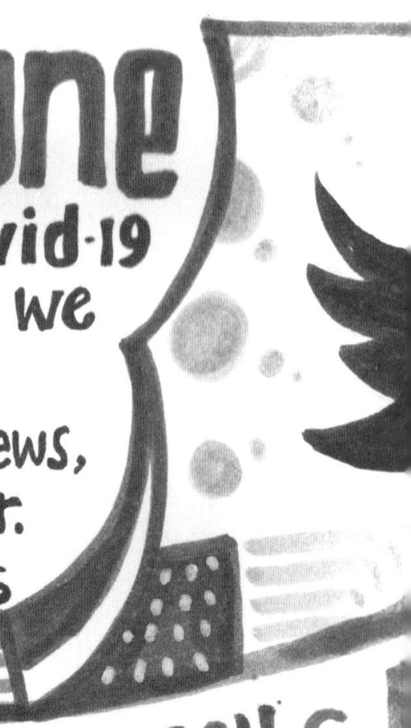

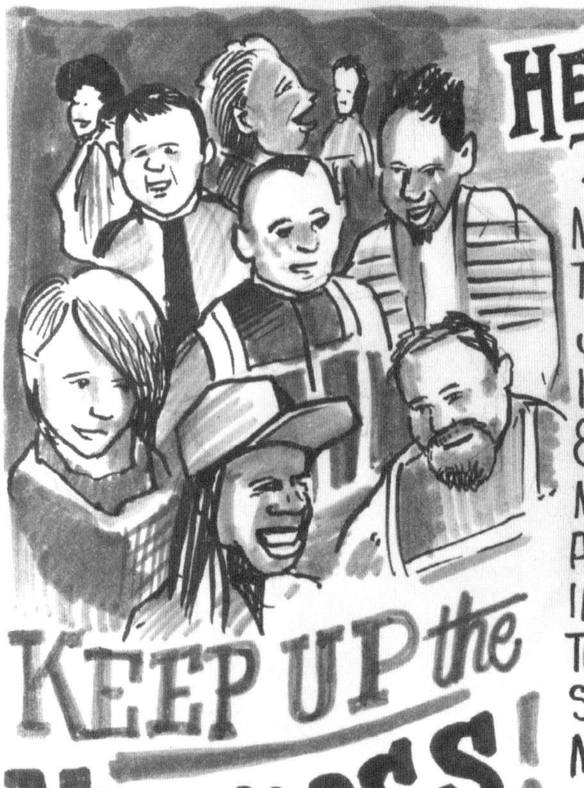

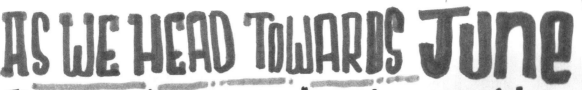

HERES the THING.

MY POPS SPOKE TO EVERYONE. I AM JUST THE SAME. I HAVE MET, SPOKEN & LAUGHED WITH SO MANY PEOPLE THIS PAST FEW WEEKS. IN QUEUES. SHOPS. THE DUMP. IN THE STREET. ☺ MADE ME LIKE HUMANITY SO MUCH MORE.

KEEP UP the NICENESS!

IN MARCH & APRIL

we had news that was scary and sad, but we also had some of the most uplifting ones I have read.

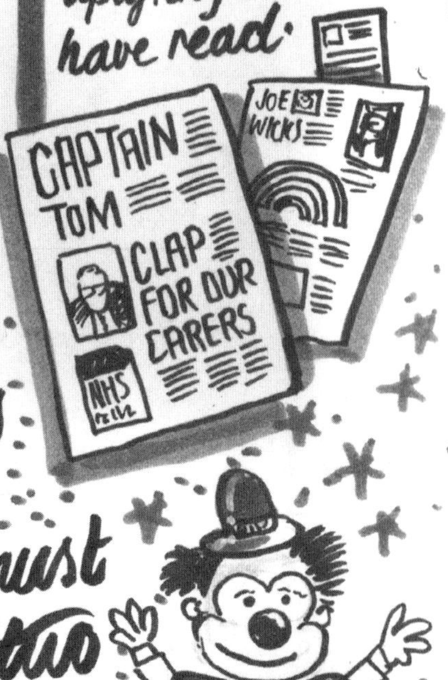
CAPTAIN TOM
CLAP FOR OUR CARERS
NHS
JOE WICKS

The UK GOV have stated all travellers arriving in the UK from 8th June must quarantine for two weeks! About three months too late...

AS EUROPE EASES OUT OF LOCKDOWN. WE FINALLY CATCH UP. JEEZ!

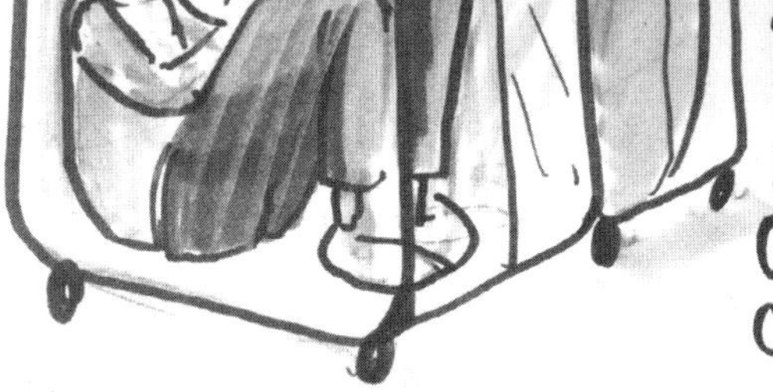

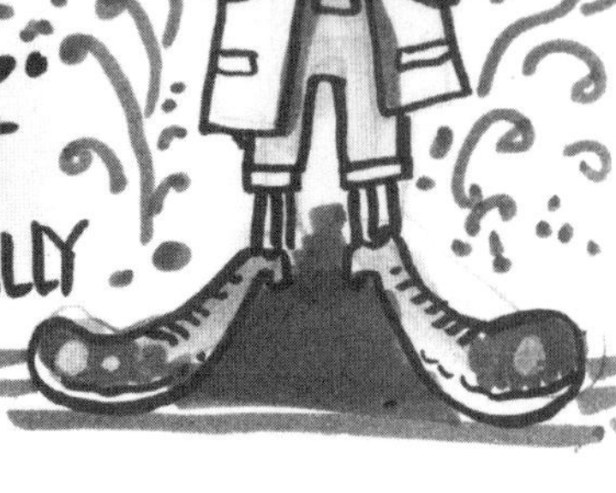

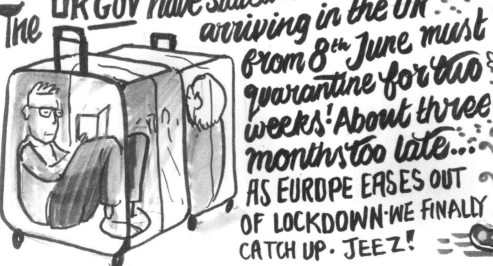

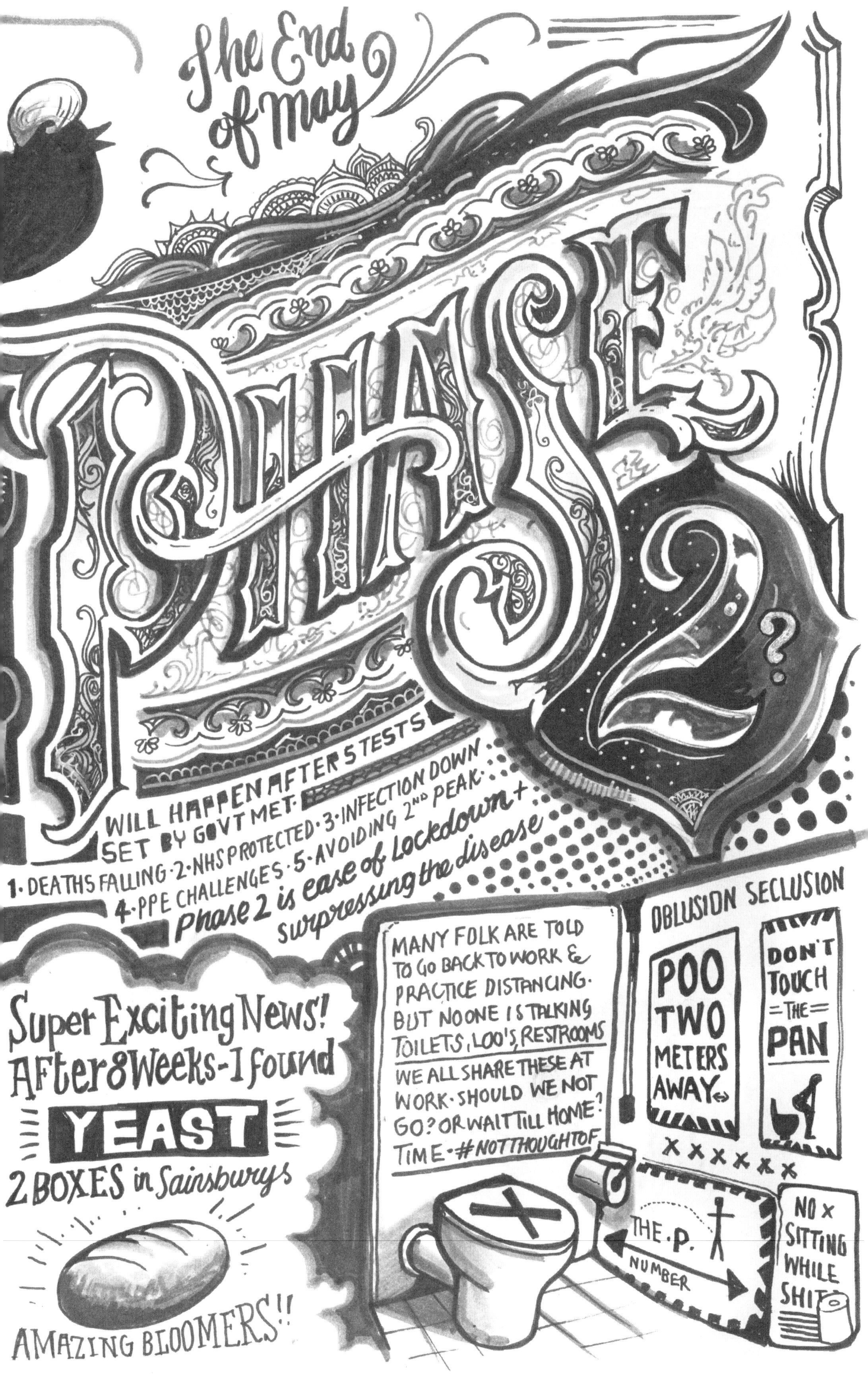
The End of May
PHASE 2?
WILL HAPPEN AFTER 5 TESTS SET BY GOVT MET·
1· DEATHS FALLING· 2· NHS PROTECTED· 3· INFECTION DOWN
4· PPE CHALLENGES· 5· AVOIDING 2ND PEAK·
Phase 2 is ease of Lockdown + surpressing the disease
Super Exciting News! After 8 Weeks - I found
YEAST
2 BOXES in Sainsburys
AMAZING BLOOMERS!!
MANY FOLK ARE TOLD TO GO BACK TO WORK & PRACTICE DISTANCING· BUT NO ONE IS TALKING TOILETS, LOO'S, RESTROOMS
WE ALL SHARE THESE AT WORK· SHOULD WE NOT GO? OR WAIT TILL HOME TIME· #NOTTHOUGHTOF
OBLUSION SECLUSION
POO TWO METERS AWAY
DON'T TOUCH THE PAN
THE ·P· NUMBER
NO SITTING WHILE SHI

May 31st

TRACK & TRACE UK

Not really going too well · Originally ditched in MARCH & hastily re-introduced. many shall we say... GLITCHES

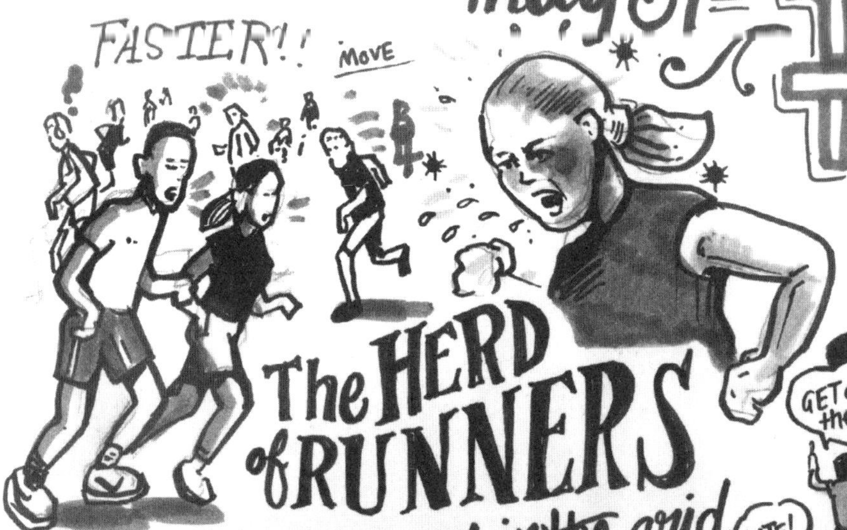

FASTER!!
MOVE

The HERD of RUNNERS

that have appeared, in the arid streets of LONDONS 'BURBS' WAS OK with everyone keeping healthy... till this morning. TAKING A BRISK WALK FOR SOME AIR, AN 'ELITE' RUNNER RAN UP AT US FROM BEHIND · SHOUTED AT US for USING A FOOTPATH(!) FLIPPED the BIRD & RAN OFF: RUNNERS ~ DON'T BE **JERKS**

We as pedestrians have been patient whilst you sweat, wheeze and moisten our air as you run past us on the streets!!

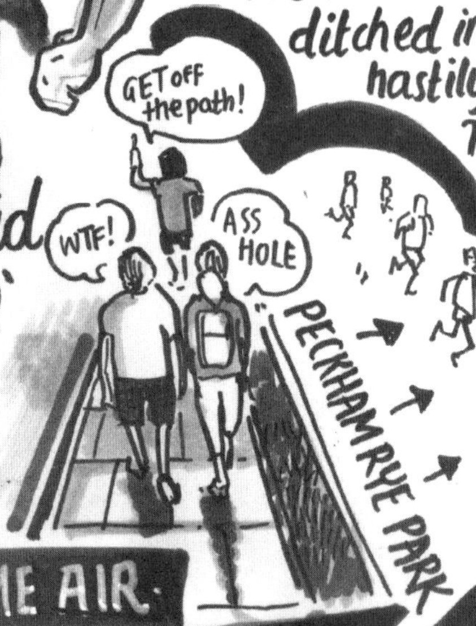

GET OFF the path!
WTF!
ASS HOLE
PECKHAM RYE PARK

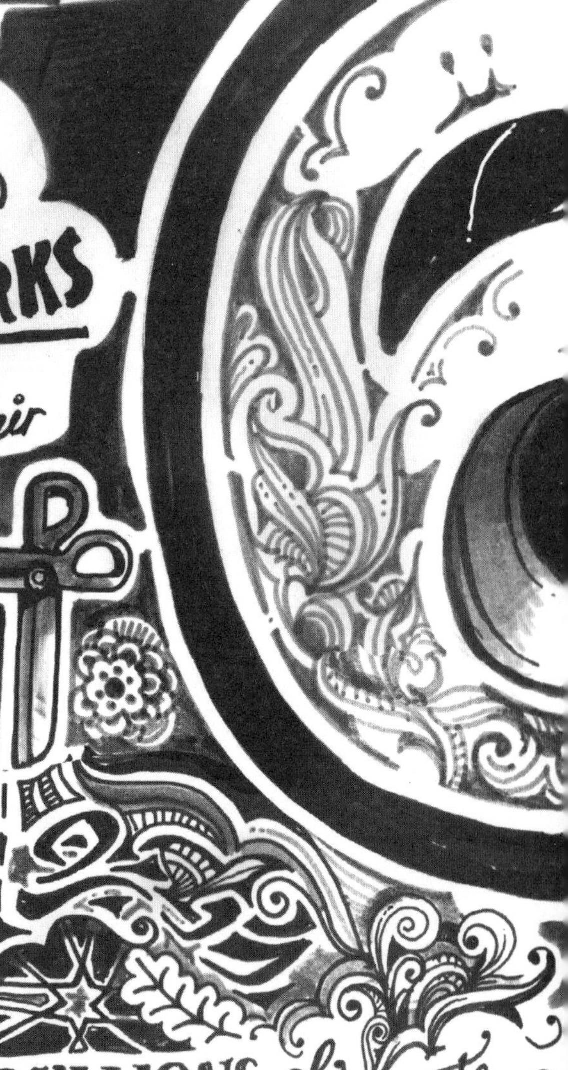

29th MAY

TRUMP terminates USA's relationship with WORLD HEALTH ORGANISATION

24th EID AL FITR

MILLIONS of MUSLIMS celebrate at home

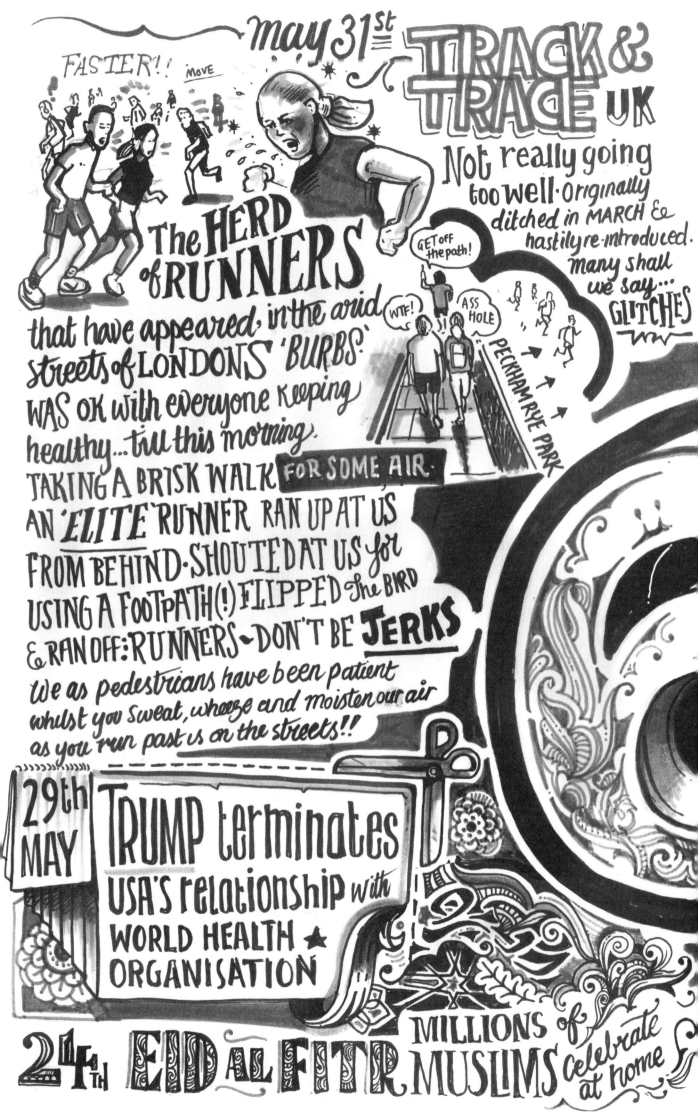

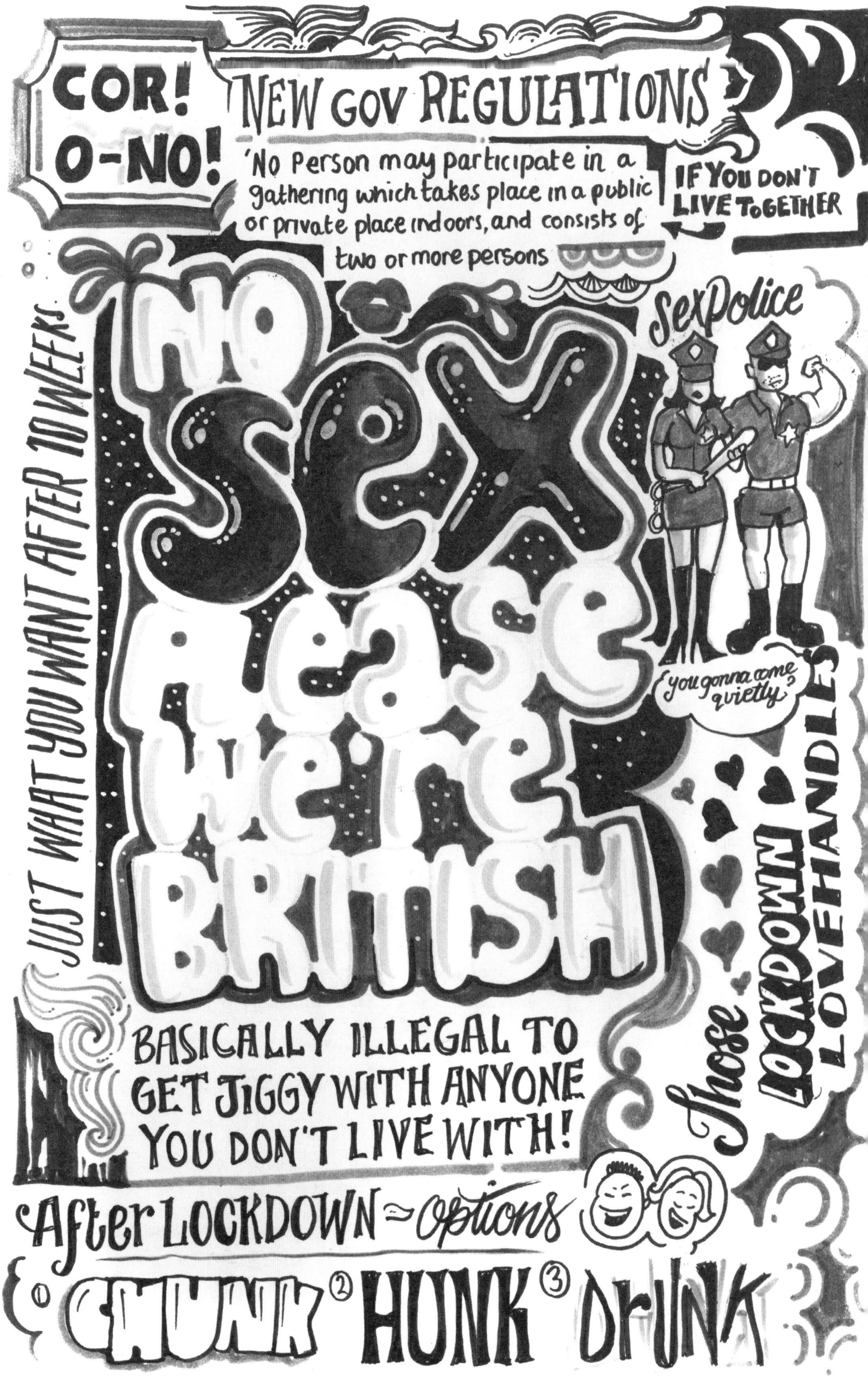
COR! O-NO!
NEW GOV REGULATIONS
'No Person may participate in a gathering which takes place in a public or private place indoors, and consists of two or more persons
IF YOU DON'T LIVE TOGETHER
JUST WHAT YOU WANT AFTER 10 WEEKS
NO SEX PLEASE WE'RE BRITISH
Sex Police
you gonna come quietly?
those LOCKDOWN LOVEHANDLES
BASICALLY ILLEGAL TO GET JIGGY WITH ANYONE YOU DON'T LIVE WITH!
After LOCKDOWN ~ options
1 CHUNK 2 HUNK 3 DrUNK

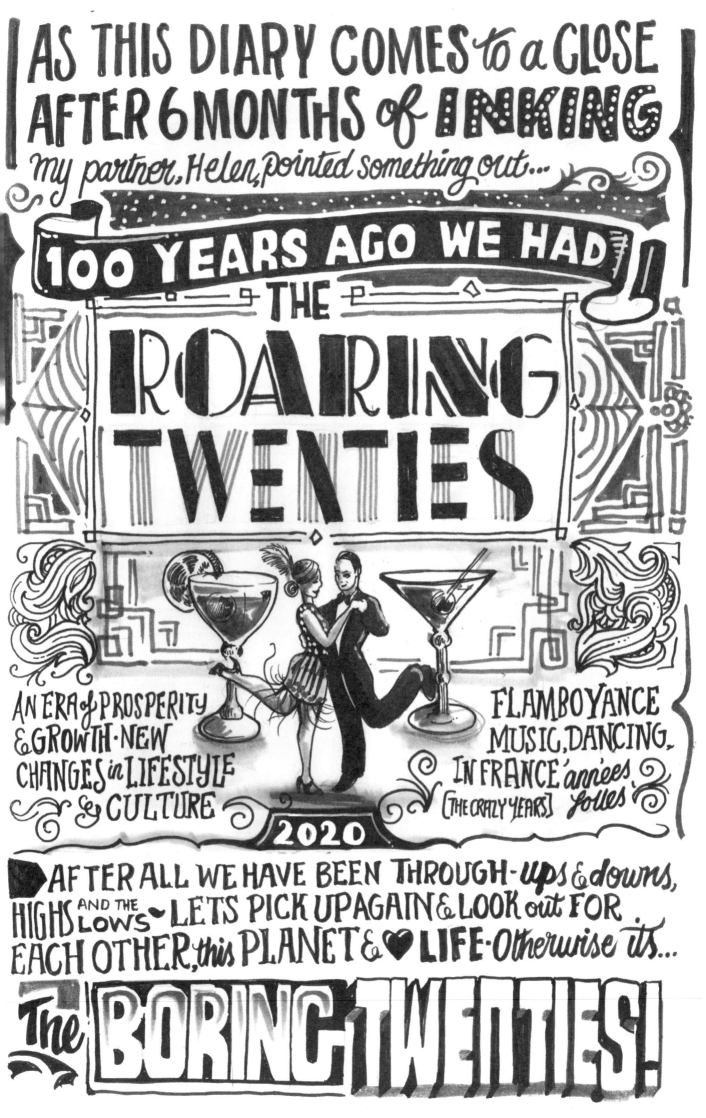

AS THIS DIARY COMES to a CLOSE AFTER 6 MONTHS of INKING my partner, Helen, pointed something out...

100 YEARS AGO WE HAD
THE
ROARING
TWENTIES

AN ERA of PROSPERITY & GROWTH · NEW CHANGES in LIFESTYLE & CULTURE

FLAMBOYANCE MUSIC, DANCING, IN FRANCE 'années folles' (THE CRAZY YEARS)

2020

AFTER ALL WE HAVE BEEN THROUGH · ups & downs, HIGHS AND THE LOWS · LETS PICK UP AGAIN & LOOK out FOR EACH OTHER, this PLANET & ♥ LIFE · Otherwise its...

The BORING TWENTIES!

EPILOGUE

AS the months that followed, we all wanted things to get a little normal... Oh well!

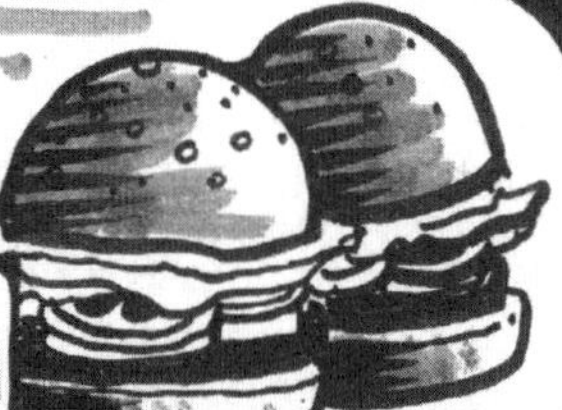

Rishis EAT OUT to HELP OUT JULY

ENCOURAGING FOLK TO USE PUBS & RESTAURANTS to give a well needed boost to th hospitality industry WITH UP TO £10 OFF P.P.

BY AUG 26th OVER 64 MILLION MEALS WERE EATEN (Costing the Treasury £320 million!

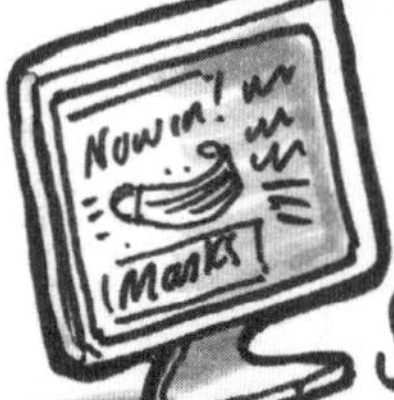

Now in!
Masks

I USED to GET TONS OF EMAIL SPAM for FURNITURE... NOW IT'S PPE!!

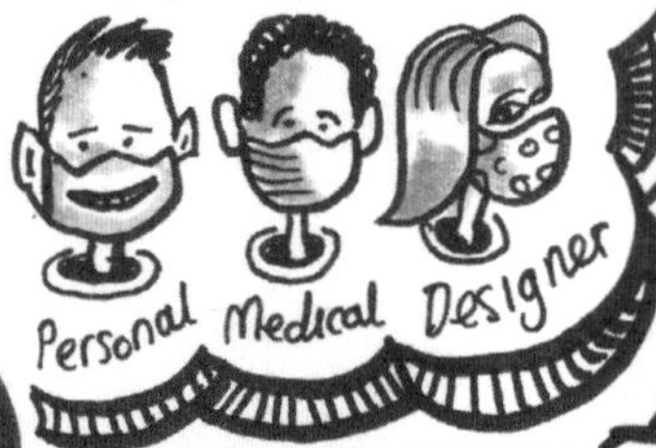

Personal
Medical
Designer

FURLOUGH scheme

LAUNCHED IN APRIL ~ THE SCHEME HAS PAID OUT £35 Billion* AND ENABLED almost 10 MILLION to retain their jobs.

BUT... ALWAYS THE UNSCRUPULOUS & CRIMS EXPLOITING LOOPHOLES WITH SOME WORKING AND GETTING PAID TWICE - BOO!

(* UP TO SEPTEMBER 2020)

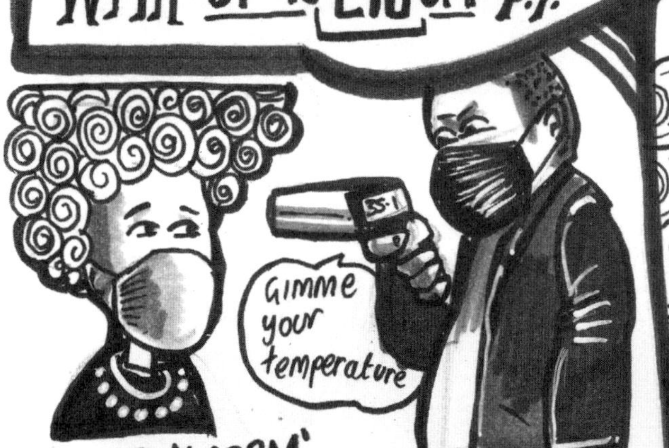

Gimme your temperature

THE NEW 'NORM' BEING SHOT IN THE HEAD by SOMEONE IN A MASK to get A HAIRCUT (well needed) a drink OR EAT IN A RESTAURANT...

SEPT. GOV INTRODUCE THE 'RULE of SIX' - MAXIMUM NUMBER OF PEOPLE ALLOWED TO MEET

BOJO [the INVISIBLE] OPERATION MOONSHOT BY EARLY 2021

To spend £100 Billion TO DO 10 MILLION Tests A DAY. CURRENT SITUATION... DUBIOUS.

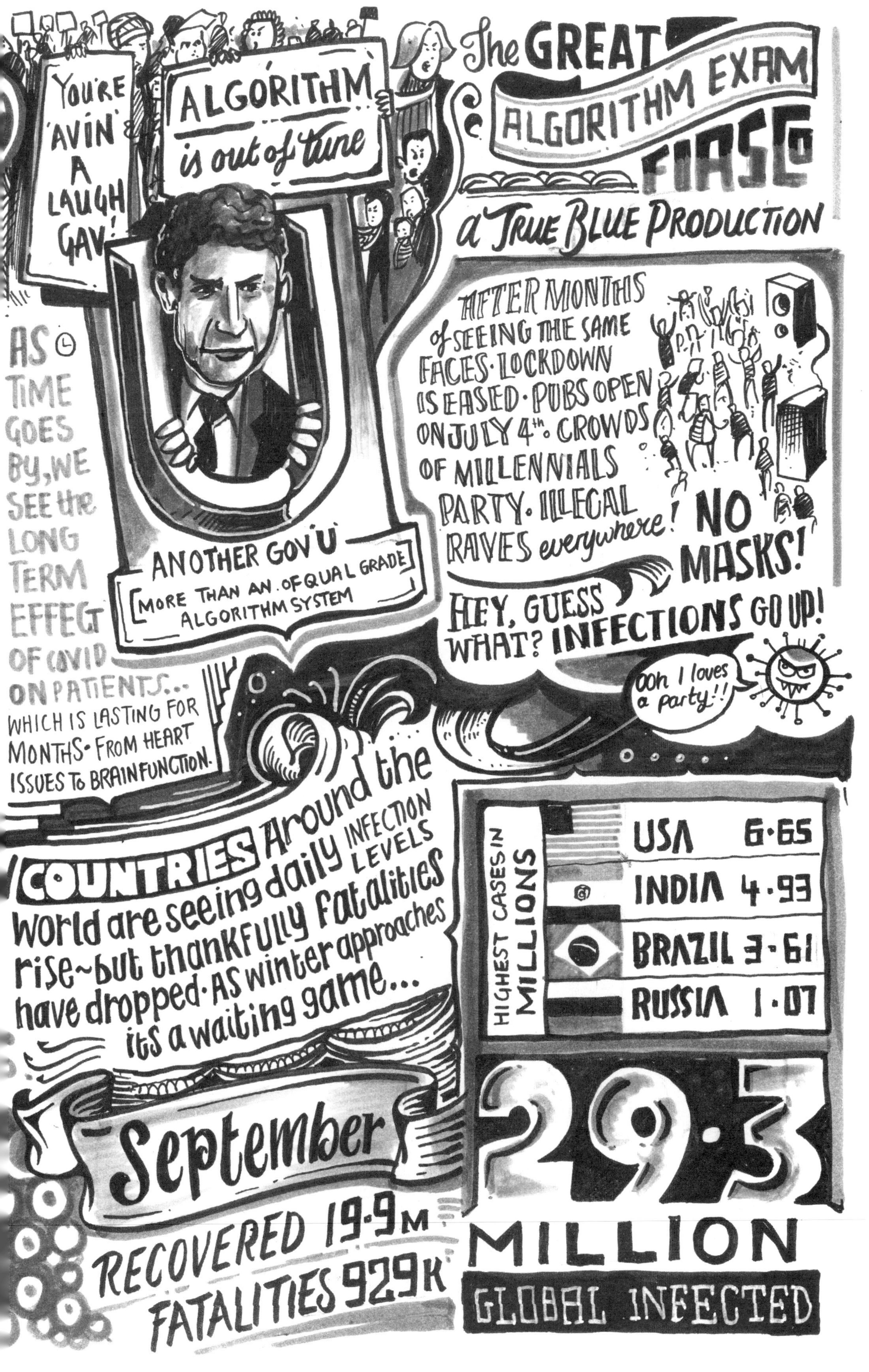

YOU'RE 'AVIN' A LAUGH GAV!
ALGORITHM is out of tune
The GREAT ALGORITHM EXAM FIASCO
a TRUE BLUE PRODUCTION
ANOTHER GOV 'U'
[MORE THAN AN OFQUAL GRADE ALGORITHM SYSTEM
AS TIME GOES BY, WE SEE the LONG TERM EFFECT OF COVID ON PATIENTS... WHICH IS LASTING FOR MONTHS • FROM HEART ISSUES TO BRAIN FUNCTION.
AFTER MONTHS of SEEING THE SAME FACES • LOCKDOWN IS EASED • PUBS OPEN ON JULY 4th • CROWDS OF MILLENNIALS PARTY • ILLEGAL RAVES everywhere!
NO MASKS!
HEY, GUESS WHAT? INFECTIONS GO UP!
Ooh I loves a party!!
COUNTRIES Around the World are seeing daily INFECTION LEVELS rise ~ but thankfully fatalities have dropped • AS winter approaches its a waiting game...
HIGHEST CASES IN MILLIONS
USA 6·65
INDIA 4·93
BRAZIL 3·61
RUSSIA 1·07
September
RECOVERED 19·9M
FATALITIES 929K
29·3 MILLION
GLOBAL INFECTED

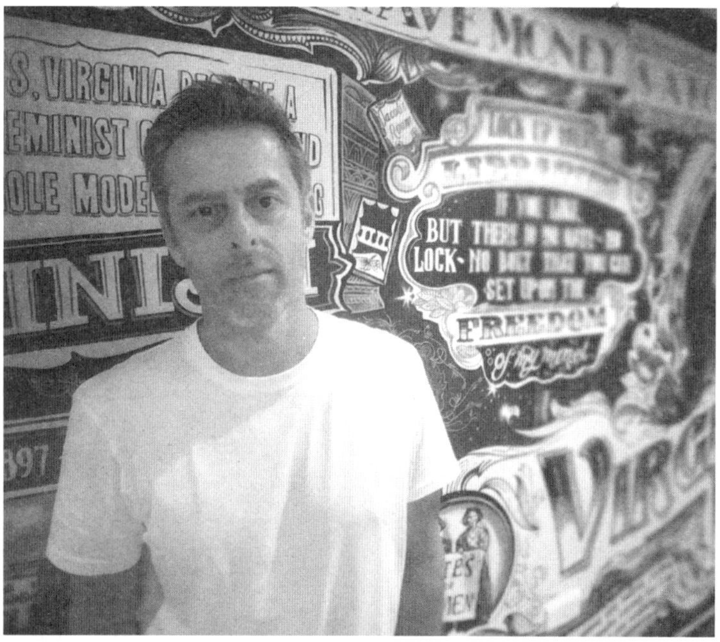
FREEDOM

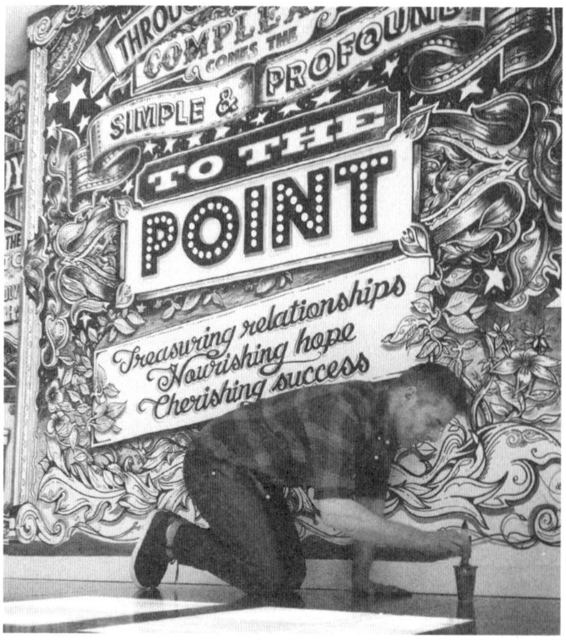
SIMPLE &
TO THE
POINT
Treasuring relationships
Nourishing hope
Cherishing success

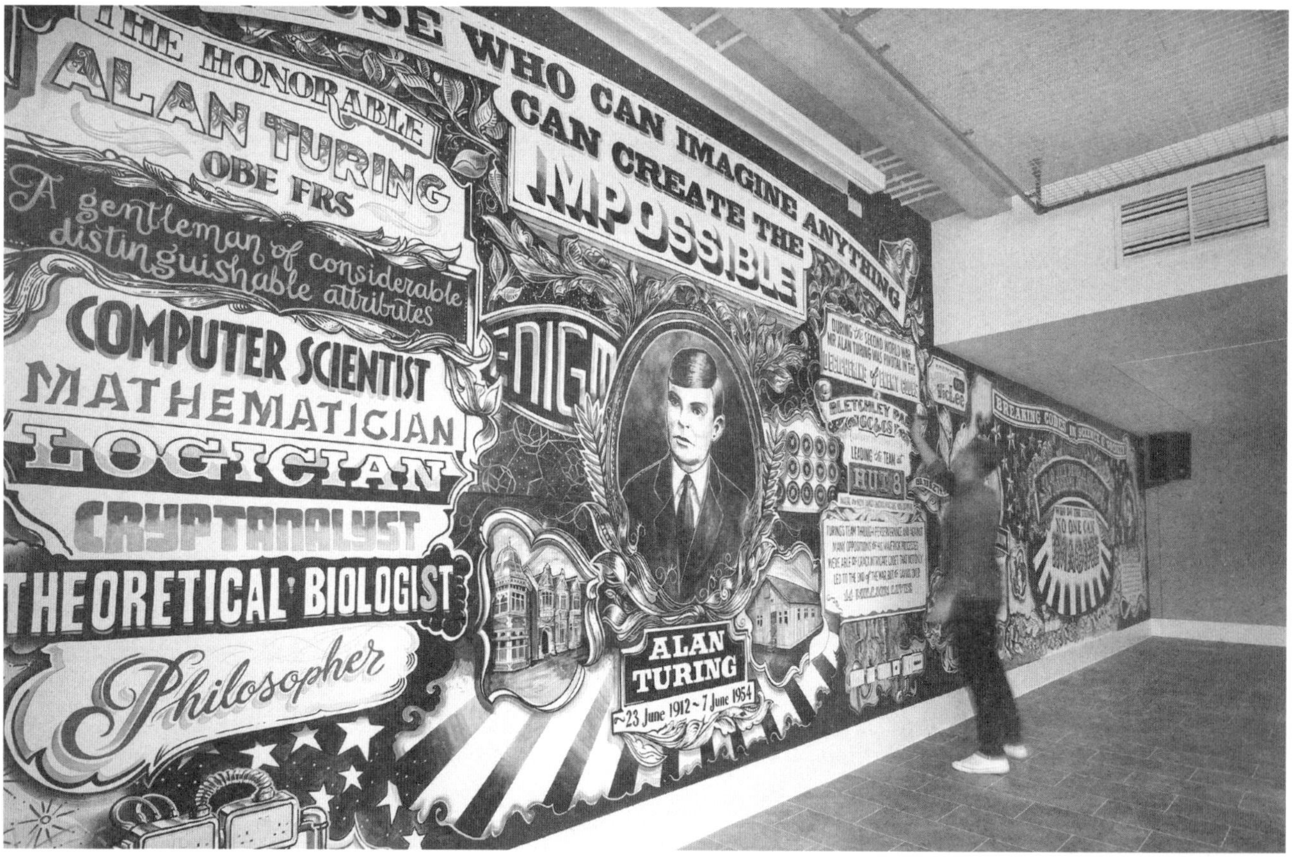
WHO CAN IMAGINE ANYTHING
CAN CREATE THE
IMPOSSIBLE
THE HONORABLE
ALAN TURING
OBE FRS
A gentleman of considerable distinguishable attributes
COMPUTER SCIENTIST
MATHEMATICIAN
LOGICIAN
CRYPTANALYST
THEORETICAL BIOLOGIST
Philosopher
ALAN TURING
~23 June 1912 ~ 7 June 1954

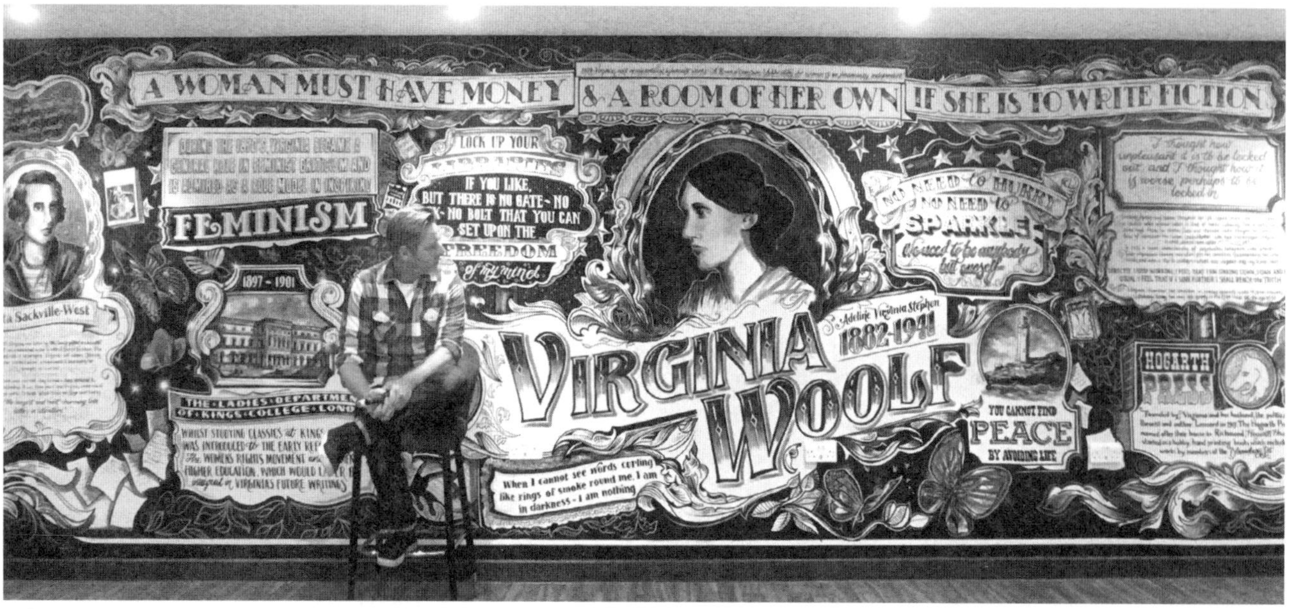
A WOMAN MUST HAVE MONEY
& A ROOM OF HER OWN
IF SHE IS TO WRITE FICTION
FEMINISM
LOCK UP YOUR
IF YOU LIKE, BUT THERE IS NO GATE - NO
NO BOLT THAT YOU CAN SET UPON THE
FREEDOM
of my mind
1897 - 1901
NO NEED TO HURRY NO NEED TO
SPARKLE
Adeline Virginia Stephen
1882-1941
VIRGINIA WOOLF
YOU CANNOT FIND
PEACE
BY AVOIDING LIFE
When I cannot see words curling like rings of smoke round me, I am in darkness - I am nothing
HOGARTH PRESS